D0897748

INTERNATIONAL STUDIES

The Politics of Nuclear Consultation in
NATO 1965–1980

INTERNATIONAL STUDIES

PUBLISHED FOR THE CENTRE FOR
INTERNATIONAL STUDIES, LONDON SCHOOL OF
ECONOMICS AND POLITICAL SCIENCE

The Centre for International Studies at the London School of Economics and Political Science was established in 1967 with the aid of a grant from the Ford Foundation. Its aim is to promote research and advanced training on a multi-disciplinary basis in the general field of international studies.

To this end the Centre sponsors research projects and seminars and endeavours to secure the publication of manuscripts arising out of them.

Whilst the Editorial Board accepts responsibility for recommending the inclusion of a volume in the series, the author is alone responsible for the views and opinions expressed.

ALSO IN THIS SERIES

The Origins of Polish Socialism – Lucjan Blit
The Slovak Dilemma – Eugen Steiner
China's Policy in Africa, 1958–1971 – Alaba Ogunsanwo
Hitler's Strategy 1940–1941: The Balkan Clue – Martin van Creveld
The Totalitarian Party: Party and People in Nazi Germany and Soviet Russia – Aryeh L. Unger
Britain and East Asia, 1933–1937 – Ann Trotter
The Pattern of Sino-American Crisis: Political–Military Interactions in the 1950s – J.H. Kalicki
Britain and the Origins of the New Europe, 1914–1918 – Kenneth J. Calder
The Marxist Conception of Ideology: A Critical Essay – Martin Seliger
The Middle East in China's Foreign Policy, 1949–1977 – Yitzhak Shichor
The Politics of the Soviet Cinema, 1917–1929 – Richard Taylor
The End of the Post-War Era: Documents on Great-Power Relations, 1968–75 – edited by James Mayall and Cornelia Navari
Anglo-Japanese Alienation 1919–1952: Papers of the Anglo-Japanese Conference on the History of the Second World War – edited by Ian Nish
Occupation Diplomacy: Britain, the United States and Japan 1945–1952 – Roger Buckley
The Defence of Malaysia and Singapore: The Transformation of a Security System 1957–1971 – Chin Kin Wah

THE POLITICS OF NUCLEAR CONSULTATION IN NATO 1965–1980

PAUL BUTEUX
Department of Political Studies
University of Manitoba

CAMBRIDGE UNIVERSITY PRESS

Cambridge
London   New York   New Rochelle
Melbourne   Sydney

Published by the Press Syndicate of the University of Cambridge
The Pitt Building, Trumpington Street, Cambridge CB2 1RP
32 East 57th Street, New York, NY 10022, USA
296 Beaconsfield Parade, Middle Park, Melbourne 3206, Australia

First published 1983

Printed in Great Britain at
the University Press, Cambridge

Library of Congress catalogue card number: 82-22016

British Library Cataloguing in Publication Data

Buteux, Paul
The politics of nuclear consultation in NATO
1965–1980.
1. North Atlantic Treaty Organization. *Nuclear
Planning Group*—History
I. Title
355'.031'091821   UA646.3

ISBN 0 521 24798 5

CONTENTS

ACKNOWLEDGEMENTS

In a field as sensitive and as surrounded by secrecy as that of nuclear policy, it will be evident that the sources available are limited and direct documentary evidence will be scarce. Inevitably, inferences must be drawn at times from what is at best indirect evidence; but, nonetheless, the sources seem to me to be adequate for the purpose of this study. Although it is not possible to offer a detailed account of what has gone on in the Nuclear Planning Group, the broad outlines of what has been discussed and the various positions adopted can be made clear, and this is sufficient for the purpose of illustrating a number of general propositions about the character of alliance politics in the field of nuclear weapons as conducted in the Nuclear Planning Group. The bibliography lists the sources used in the study, but a comment is in order on the assistance received from a number of people in official positions who had personal experience of the operations of the NPG. I benefited greatly from personal interviews and discussions with these people who, because of their official positions, would wish to remain anonymous. Information obtained from these sources has been cited as 'personal communication'. However, in addition, a number of these officials read parts of the study and made comments on it. I regarded this as a test of the accuracy of the overall 'feel' of the account of the NPG presented, and as supporting evidence for the relevance of the analysis offered.

An earlier version of the final chapter was originally published as 'Theatre nuclear weapons and European security' in the *Canadian Journal of Political Science*, X, 4, December 1977. I wish to acknowledge the kind permission of the Canadian Political Science Association in allowing me to use material drawn from this article.

I would like to thank Anupam Sharma for his work on the index, and, finally, to acknowledge the support and advice of a particular friend of mine in the arcane field of alliance studies, Philip Windsor. Of course, I offer the usual disclaimer that the responsibility for the opinions and analysis contained in the following pages rests anywhere other than on myself.

ABBREVIATIONS

ABM	anti-ballistic missile
ADM	atomic demolition munition
ANF	Atlantic Nuclear Force
CSCE	Conference on Security and Cooperation in Europe
DPC	Defence Planning Committee
EDIP	European Defence Improvement Programme
FBS	forward-based systems
GLCM	ground-launched cruise missile
GSP	General Strike Plan
HLG	High Level Group
IANF	inter-allied nuclear force
ICBM	intercontinental-range ballistic missile
IRBM	intermediate-range ballistic missile
LRTNF	long-range theatre nuclear force
MBFR	mutual and balanced force reductions
MLF	multilateral nuclear force
MRBM	medium-range ballistic missile
NATO	North Atlantic Treaty Organisation
NDAC	Nuclear Defence Affairs Committee
NPG	Nuclear Planning Group
NPT	Non-Proliferation Treaty
PAL	permissive action link
PGM	precision-guided munition
QRA	quick-reaction alert
SACEUR	Supreme Allied Commander Europe
SACLANT	Supreme Allied Commander Atlantic
SALT	strategic arms limitation talks
SCG	Special Consultative Group
SHAPE	Supreme Headquarters Allied Powers Europe

SIOP	Single Integrated Operations Plan
SLBM	submarine-launched ballistic missile
SRBM	short-range ballistic missile
SSBN	strategic submarine ballistic-nuclear
TNF	theatre nuclear force
TNW	theatre nuclear weapons

PREFACE

The literature on alliances is voluminous; that on nuclear weapons scarcely less so, and yet systematic attempts to examine the impact of nuclear weapons on alliances have been relatively few. Such attempts as have been made have concentrated primarily on NATO, and have tended to concentrate on particular issues of policy concerning nuclear weapons that have arisen in the alliance. Outstanding among these policy issues have been those concerning nuclear strategy and the manner in which a decision to employ nuclear weapons would be made. Thus, a number of studies have appeared examining substantive issues of nuclear doctrine, and assessing the implications of various means by which alliance control over nuclear weapons and over the nuclear strategy serving them might be obtained.[1] Attention has been directed to the analysis of the various policies adopted by members of NATO, and of their compatibility with variously defined alliance objectives. By and large, the literature has been dominated by American authors and, consequently, the definition of alliance objectives has tended to reflect American perspectives. In particular, alliance objectives, and the policies designed to further them, have been measured against their effects on alliance cohesion. In turn, the requirements of cohesion have been established against the broader policy considerations of the United States as world power and alliance leader.

This approach to the analysis of the impact of nuclear issues on NATO has reflected, of course, an important aspect of the political reality of the alliance's functioning, which has consisted in large part of American attempts to persuade more or less reluctant allies to conform to American policy preferences.

However, the examination of the political process within the alliance political system by which a consensus on nuclear policy is sought has been largely neglected. The mechanisms of alliance diplomacy have not received extensive treatment, and little consideration has been given to the analysis of the effects on political outcomes in the alliance of the use of particular kinds of diplomatic technique, and of the impact of various institutional arrangements. The present study is a modest addition to this literature which examines the role of the alliance itself in determining how political issues arising between the allies are resolved.[2] In this case, an attempt is made to examine the way in which a particular political and diplomatic technique, that of consultation, and a particular institution, the Nuclear Planning Group (NPG), have enabled the alliance to deal with problems caused by the presence of nuclear weapons in the security environment in which it operates and, more directly, in the arsenal on which the military planning of the alliance is based.

The published literature on the Nuclear Planning Group is scant.[3] What has been published provides little more than a description of the basic institutional form of the NPG, some account of its activities, and some discussion of the appropriateness of the application to it of certain models of policy-making and consultation. The study presented here represents an attempt to provide an extensive narrative account of the work of the Nuclear Planning Group between the years 1965 and 1980, while at the same time analysing the political context in which consultation on nuclear weapons has occurred. This context can be understood in terms of three major dimensions: the international political environment as it generally affects the alliance; the functioning of NATO as a distinct political system; and the specific context of the NPG itself. The focus of the present study is on the NPG, and the impact of the broader alliance and international dimensions on the politics of nuclear consultation is considered only to the extent that it is necessary to the explanation of developments in the Nuclear Planning Group. Nevertheless, as the study should make clear, the operations of the NPG have been affected continually by links with the broader concerns of the allied participants, and with important international developments. Given the character and salience of nuclear issues, this could hardly be otherwise.

The first two chapters attempt to provide the political and strategic background to which the formation of the Nuclear Planning Group was a response. Chapter 1, apart from describing the broad impact on the alliance of the direct introduction of nuclear weapons into its arsenal, also describes a series of proposals that were designed to mitigate the stress on the alliance caused by the increased emphasis on nuclear weapons in alliance strategy. The examination of these proposals serves to clarify the concepts of nuclear sharing and nuclear control, and to demonstrate the limitations of the various proposals as a means of satisfying allied aspirations with respect to nuclear policy. The second chapter discusses the origins of the Nuclear Planning Group as both a reaction and an alternative to previous proposals for nuclear sharing. The account provided of the work of the 'McNamara Committee' provides the basis for the subsequent discussion of the course of allied nuclear consultation in the NPG itself. The genesis of the institutions which would foster the consultative approach to nuclear sharing in the alliance is considered in association with an analysis of the various allied interests involved.

The following three chapters constitute the basic narrative account of the work of the Nuclear Planning Group up to 1980. The agenda of issues that were dealt with by the NPG is described, and the impact of the processes of consultation on how the role of the Nuclear Planning Group came to be defined is also indicated. Chapter 6 is devoted to an analysis of the limits of consultation as practised between allies, and to a description of the diplomatic functions such consultation can perform. The operation of the NPG as a consultative institution is then evaluated, and its institutional structure described. The final chapter analyses the strategic considerations affecting the deployment of nuclear weapons in the European theatre during the period studied, in order to bring out the kinds of consideration which have affected the work of the NPG in an area which has been of primary political and strategic concern to it.

1. THE IMPACT OF NUCLEAR WEAPONS ON NATO: THE PROBLEM OF NUCLEAR SHARING

The NATO Council meeting of December 1954 can be taken as marking the point at which nuclear sharing emerged as a central military and political issue for the alliance. Although the alliance, since its inception, had been based on the assumption that nuclear weapons were a necessary element in the security of its members, such weapons were not an integral part of the military planning on which the defence of Western Europe was predicated. Rather, nuclear power was committed to European security as the result of a unilateral American guarantee. Now, nuclear weapons were to be deployed directly in a battlefield and tactical role in Europe, thus transforming the strategic posture of NATO and generating a seemingly insoluble series of military and political problems.

The decision to deploy nuclear weapons designed for tactical employment in the European theatre was taken by the Eisenhower administration as part of the series of defence planning decisions characterised in 1953 as the 'New Look' strategy. By the beginning of 1954 the 240mm. atomic cannon was being deployed with the US Seventh Army, and other weapons systems were to follow. It was not until the December 1954 ministerial meeting of the NATO Council, however, that formal approval was given to this development in the alliance's arsenal. Nevertheless, military planners at Supreme Headquarters Allied Powers Europe (SHAPE) had been taking into account the availability of tactical nuclear weapons throughout 1954, and operated on the basis of the widely shared perception that the Lisbon goals of 1952 designating conventional force levels would not be met. Tactical nuclear weapons were seen as compensating for the shortfall in the Lisbon goals and as an essential requirement for meeting the defence objectives of

1

the alliance. The decision that henceforth military planning and preparations would go forward on the basis that tactical nuclear weapons would be available was taken an important step further in December 1957, when it was agreed that stockpiles of nuclear warheads would be built up in Europe to be made available to the allies of the United States in case of need. The forces of those allies willing to participate in the programme would be equipped and trained to use these stockpiled weapons.

This policy of equipping the allies of the United States with nuclear-capable weapons and of stockpiling nuclear warheads for them on the continent of Europe required amendment of the United States Atomic Energy Act in July 1958. This amendment was necessary in order that sufficiently detailed information could be made available to the allies concerning the performance and technical characteristics of the weapons so that the allied forces could be trained to operate them effectively. The amended act enabled the United States to make agreements with her allies that led in effect to the creation of a series of bilateral nuclear forces involving the United States and each participating ally. Command and control of these forces would be secured through the planning and command structure of SHAPE and by the fact that the warheads, prior to a decision by the President of the United States to release them, would be in the hands of units of the American armed forces and subject to their regular command structure. The possible use of these weapons in defence of NATO was to be governed by the doctrine contained in the 'Overall Strategic Concept for the NATO Area' (NATO Document MC 14/2) adopted by the Military Commitee in March 1957.[1]

Under this strategic concept military planning operated on the assumption that nuclear weapons would be used early in any conflict on the Central Front. The deployment of nuclear weapons for tactical use in Europe represented an extension to NATO of the strategic principle being applied to the forces of the United States: that nuclear firepower could compensate for any shortfall in conventional force strength. The role of conventional forces would be to provide a 'shield' behind which the nuclear 'sword' could be readied. Above all but the lowest levels of armed conflict, frequently described in terms of 'border incidents' and 'police actions', the role of conventional forces in the defence posture of the alliance was widely understood as being to act as a 'tripwire' that would initiate a nuclear response to any aggression. The use of conventional forces in this manner would reinforce deterrence by providing an unambiguous threshold beyond which the alliance would use its nuclear weapons. The availability of tactical nuclear weapons was seen as further reinforcing deterrence by providing the alliance with the option of a battlefield nuclear response to any overwhelming conventional attack which, most likely, would have also a catalytic effect on the strategic forces of the United States. In short, the purpose of conventional forces and tactical nuclear weapons was to deter the widest range of contingencies by ensuring that any aggression would be met with massive nuclear retaliation.[2]

From the beginning, the introduction of nuclear weapons into the European theatre aroused debate as to how they might be used and as to what the consequences of such use would be. Having adopted a thoroughgoing nuclear posture, the question arose as to whether the alliance could devise a strategy governing nuclear weapons that would be both militarily and politically credible. A number of concerns with the implications of the tactical deployment of nuclear weapons was expressed; among which may be singled out the contention that their use would be so destructive to the defenders as to be self-deterring, and the feeling that to threaten massive retaliation against a conventional assault when the nuclear capabilities of the Soviet Union were so obviously increasing was of doubtful credibility. Although 'massive retaliation' had considerable political appeal to the Americans and their allies, offering the prospect of deterrence at the lowest possible cost, the increasingly doubtful credibility of this strategic policy in the face of Soviet strategic, tactical nuclear and conventional capabilities gave to the alliance debate on strategy a salience that it had never possessed before. The growth of Soviet nuclear capabilities at the same time as the NATO allies were basing their military planning on the increasing availability of nuclear weapons actually deployed in the European theatre, created tensions between the allies which, in the view of some contemporaries, threatened the minimum degree of cohesion necessary for the alliance to function as a guarantor of the security of its members. Questions of nuclear strategy concerning what that strategy was to be, how it was to be determined, and in what manner it was to be implemented became of major political significance. In particular, these strategic concerns became focussed on the issue of nuclear sharing in the alliance, and on how nuclear weapons deployed in support of the alliance would be commanded and controlled.

The introduction of nuclear weapons into the armoury of NATO forces in Europe had produced the somewhat anomalous situation that control over what had become a central element in the defensive posture of the alliance lay largely outside its institutional framework. Decisions about nuclear weapons with major implications for the security posture of all the allies were primarily within the province of the United States and, to a lesser extent, Britain as the only nuclear powers in the alliance. The demands of the non-nuclear allies for some kind of effective voice in the determination of nuclear policy led to a search for a satisfactory means by which they could be associated with the process of nuclear decision-making. Out of this search there arose a multilevelled set of political relationships within the alliance which linked strategic alternatives with perceptions of status, and questions of political aspiration with issues of nuclear control which, taken together, were a major determinant of inter-allied alignments. The nuclear issue served to structure alliance priorities for the allies, condition their responses to events and define their interests. Until superseded in the late sixties by the broader political concerns associated with détente, issues of nuclear sharing and control provided the dominant theme around which the allies patterned their alliance relationships.

The significance of the nuclear issue arose in part from its relationship to the essential political and institutional character of NATO as an alliance. NATO can be regarded as a well-developed example of the regional mutual security organisation; that is, NATO combines the traditional functions of an alliance with the institutions, procedures and operations of an international organisation. When coalition is wedded to organisation, an alliance becomes institutionalised and it imposes constraints on the conduct of policy beyond those determined by the special character of any issues that may arise and in addition to the normal pressures of diplomacy. Generally, these constraints may be seen as contained in the appreciation by the allies of the costs of any action that might weaken the cohesion of the alliance or in any way contradict its purposes, and in the diplomatic procedures entailed by alliance membership. The procedures are laid down by the necessity to communicate and, from time to time, make agreements within the context of an ongoing international organisation equipped with a secretariat, specialist committees, representative councils and an international legal personality. Membership in effect creates an extra dimension to foreign policy related to, but distinct from, the overt functions and purposes of the alliance. This aspect of policy is concerned with the attempt to gain weight, influence and prestige within the alliance and weight and influence over its decision-making processes. Thus, within NATO are created subsidiary functions and purposes: purposes of mutual influence and functions concerned with the means by which this influence may be attained and expressed. With changing circumstances and changing objectives, the allies may vary in the intensity of their concern with this aspect of alliance politics; but, nevertheless, within the alliance as a whole, there is a constant involvement with this subsidiary 'politics of influence'. After 1954, issues of nuclear strategy became inextricably involved with the search for influence in the alliance which, in turn, affected the substantive debate on nuclear policy and complicated the task of securing an allied consensus in this area.

The problems created for NATO by the incorporation of nuclear weapons into alliance defence planning can be seen as having had a number of different dimensions. First, there was the impact on the security positions of the various allies. Clearly, some allies were more immediately affected by the deployment of nuclear weapons than others. For them, questions of nuclear strategy had an urgency manifested by their relationship to essential national objectives. Secondly, there was the effect on allied political relationships and on the agenda of issues of concern to them. Finally, there was the possibility of exploiting nuclear issues as part of the constant search for position and influence within the alliance. (Of course, the various allies, although affected by each of these dimensions, were nonetheless more sensitive to some of them than others.) Thus, for Germany, the introduction of nuclear weapons into SHAPE military planning meant confronting the stark possibility of a nuclear battle being fought on her territory. For Britain, on the other hand, her own nuclear status provided an essential underpinning to the 'special relationship' with the United States and this very much affected her approach to the nuclear problems of the alliance. France, perhaps of all the allies, sought to exploit the nuclear issue most for its potential impact on broader policy objectives, with respect both to the alliance, and to France's international status generally, whereas, for the United States, decisions concerning nuclear weapons were fundamental to her international role and to the character of her nuclear commitment to NATO. Indeed, for all the allies, nuclear weapons have had important political, military and security implications.

Naturally, the allies have sought to use alliance mechanisms as a means of dealing with the implications for them of membership in a nuclear alliance. A major consequence of the introduction of nuclear weapons into NATO was to raise questions concerning the extent to which nuclear weapons actually fell within the scope of the decision-making processes of the alliance. In other words, how far decisions with respect to nuclear policy were to be made within the alliance political system and what the scope of these decisions would be. In a sense, the whole debate on nuclear control and nuclear sharing can be construed as a means of determining what the role of the various allies, nuclear and non-nuclear, would be with respect to decisions regarding the planning, deployment and use of nuclear weapons. These weapons had been introduced into the alliance with few changes in the arrangements by which military planning was undertaken, policy determined and command and control of the military forces assigned to the alliance exercised. This meant that, in addition to the strategic deterrent possessed by the United States, allied military planning was based on the deployment and possible use of theatre nuclear weapons over which the United States not only retained full control, but also exercised the predominant influence on the strategy that would govern them.[3] In effect, the operational control of the military posture of the alliance had passed into American hands and the non-nuclear allies had lost the control over the issues of peace and war that the complex institutional structure of the alliance had been designed, in part, to give them. Dissatisfaction with this state of affairs generated a great deal of stress on the alliance and ensured that nuclear issues would engage the major interests of the allies in NATO.

This dissatisfaction greatly increased after 1961 when the United States sought to revise alliance strategy away from 'massive retaliation' in the direction of 'flexible response' with far greater emphasis on the role of conventional forces. Under the new doctrine the relationship of conventional and nuclear forces was in effect reversed. The role of conventional forces was now to become that of the 'non-nuclear sword' behind the 'nuclear shield'. The new American strategic policies, which became identified by the label of the 'McNamara strategy', not only proposed substantial changes in the role of nuclear weapons in overall alliance military planning, but had major implications for the individual defence policies of the various NATO allies as well. The American strategic initiatives affected both allied perceptions of their security and, perhaps more importantly, areas of domestic politics to which several allied governments were extremely sensitive. No government felt more vulnerable to the security and domestic implications of the changed American policy than the German but, in their different ways, all the other allies were affected too. The result was to give even greater urgency to the search for an acceptable arrangement for nuclear sharing in the alliance.

By the early 1960s a number of proposals for the wider sharing of allied control over nuclear weapons had emerged. At its simplest, control over nuclear weapons can be understood as the possession of authority over military operations involving the potential or actual use of nuclear forces and, by extension, the idea of control can also be applied to the preparation of military plans and to decisions affecting the acquisition and deployment of nuclear weapons. In practice, a threefold set of distinctions could be applied to the objectives of the allies with respect to the issue of nuclear control in the alliance. On the one hand there was the question of allied participation in the process by which the strategy governing the deployment and possible use of nuclear weapons was decided. Secondly, there was the question of who should possess the authority to decide on their deployment and use. Finally, there was the problem of maintaining adequate contact between political and military authorities so that the implementation of a properly authorised decision concerning nuclear weapons could be monitored: in other words, the problem of 'command, control and communication' (C^3).[4]

Two broad approaches to the problem of securing these objectives were possible. One way was to ensure some form of physical control or possession of nuclear weapons, with the corollary that such possession would ensure authority over decisions concerning their operational use. Ultimately, this approach led to the consideration of various forms of allied ownership of nuclear weapons: the so-called 'hardware approach'. Of course, the most direct way of securing the benefits of ownership was for the allies to develop their own national nuclear forces. This had been the route taken by the British who, in turn, were emulated by the French.

American concern with the possibility of further proliferation, which in the case of the prospect of increased German access to nuclear weapons was shared by the other allies, very much affected the response of the United States to European aspirations concerning nuclear weapons. American opposition to national nuclear forces was clearly stated by Robert McNamara in his widely reported speech at Ann Arbor in June 1962. In this speech, which it has been said was a public version of an address given at the Athens meeting of the NATO Council in May, McNamara characterised small national nuclear forces, in a famous phrase, as 'dangerous, expensive, prone to obsolescence and lacking in credibility as a deterrent'.

In addition such forces would derogate from the unity of planning, concentration of executive authority and central direction of nuclear weapons which were at the heart of the new American strategic policies.[5]

On the other hand, it was necessary for the Americans to respond positively to allied calls for a more direct influence over nuclear decision-making. In particular, the Americans were sensitive to the claims of the Germans not to be discriminated against, and for a status within the alliance commensurate with their increasing military and economic weight. By 1961, these German claims had become an important political variable that was independently affecting the course of the debate on alliance nuclear sharing. The reactions of the other allies to these German claims, especially those of Britain and France, helped to ensure that nuclear issues would be linked directly to the whole question of the balance of power and influence within the alliance.[6] This meant in turn that any proposal concerning allied access to nuclear weapons would be appraised not only on its technical merits, but also in terms of its impact on inter-allied relationships. The United States, then, sought some kind of arrangement that would meet both allied demands and her own desire to maintain ultimate control over the possible employment of nuclear weapons in any conflict and, at the same time, keep the stress on the alliance caused by nuclear weapons to a minimum. Of the various hardware arrangements suggested, the proposal that the alliance establish a multilateral nuclear force (MLF) was politically the most important, and exercised the alliance in the politics of nuclear weapons until the mid-sixties.

A second approach to the problem of securing allied access to the control of nuclear weapons in a way that would be acceptable to all concerned was to avoid questions of ownership and physical possession of these weapons. Instead, attention was directed to the ways in which the non-nuclear allies might be associated with the procedures by which those actually owning and possessing nuclear weapons reached decisions concerning them. This involved various proposals for the elaboration, modification and reorganisation of existing

NATO institutional structures in order to provide for at least more effective alliance consultation on matters of nuclear planning and policy. In other words, the problem of nuclear sharing was to be dealt with by the creation of an appropriate institutional form which would provide not for the physical control of nuclear weapons, but for allied influence over their deployment and over plans for their potential use. McNamara, again at Athens in May 1962, advocated such an approach with his suggestion that a Nuclear Committee be established in order that the non-nuclear allies might be better informed as to the disposition of nuclear weapons in Europe, and of the rationale behind American strategic policies. In addition, guidelines were presented governing commitments by the United States and Britain to consult if possible with their allies before using nuclear weapons.[7] These arrangements were largely stillborn, in major part because of the attitude of the French, but they did reflect a proposed solution to the problem of nuclear sharing which proved to be more viable later when it was revived in the 'McNamara Committee' and took permanent form in the Nuclear Planning Group. What was emphasised in the American suggestions at Athens was the consultative approach to nuclear sharing: the idea that allied aspirations and American nuclear policies could be reconciled best by extending the range of allied consultations on these matters, and by creating institutional arrangements in which these consultations could take place.[8]

Of course, as the history of the alliance debate on nuclear sharing has borne out, the possession and consultative approaches to nuclear sharing are not necessarily imcompatible. For different approaches to the problem of control can be taken with respect to different types and categories of nuclear weapons. In effect, this has always been the case in NATO, and the recognition of this fact in the politics of the alliance was clearly demonstrated by General Norstad in 1960 when, in a speech at SACEUR outlining the nuclear requirements of his command, he distinguished between four types of nuclear force: intermediate-range missiles which were already being deployed (Jupiter); medium-range missiles which he desired to see deployed in Europe; strategic forces having a retaliatory role; and tactical nuclear weapons supporting the conventional capabilities of the alliance. He accepted that the forces already deployed were subject to different control arrangements, and attempted to use what he hoped would be the deployment of new systems as an opportunity to further his own scheme for dealing with the problem of nuclear sharing. This was the creation of a multilateral authority in the alliance which would turn NATO into the 'fourth nuclear power'.[9] Thus, it was early recognised in the alliance that there could exist a mix of nuclear sharing arrangements corresponding to the mix of weapon systems available. However, the mix of weapons available in terms of yield and in terms of the range, type and vulnerability of the means of delivery, would have substantive impact on how the allies perceived their political and security interests in the alliance. The control accepted by the allies as appropriate for any given weapon mix would not necessarily survive changes in it, nor would they necessarily survive changes in the strategy governing nuclear weapons since both could affect the political and security interests of the allies. One other variable is pertinent here, and that of course is the impact on the allies of the policies adopted by the potential enemy. What all this amounts to is the observation that issues of nuclear sharing have been linked with decisions concerning nuclear strategy and with policies determining weapons acquisition and deployment.

The issue of the sharing of nuclear control in NATO became particularly salient for the alliance at a time when new weapons were being deployed and when major revisions in strategy were being proposed. Two major weapons developments were taking place. First, there was the increasing availability in the European theatre of large numbers of nuclear weapons designed for tactical use and, secondly, there was the appearance in the armouries of both the United States and Soviet Union of inter-continental range ballistic missiles. Both these developments had an effect on the strategy of the alliance and on the character of the central strategic balance between East and West. Inevitably, therefore, there were consequences for the politics of nuclear control. Arguments about nuclear control were linked to arguments about strategy and with arguments about the need to deploy certain types of weapons which, in turn, were linked to arguments about where nuclear weapons were to be deployed and how they were to be commanded.

The politics of nuclear sharing were particularly sensitive to developments in American strategic thinking and to American proposals for the revision of the strategic posture of the alliance. Since the United States was the source for the overwhelming majority of the nuclear weapons available to NATO she was in a position to effect *de facto* changes in alliance strategy through her own unilateral actions. It was the uncomfortable necessity for the allies to accommodate themselves to this fact that made the absence of an acceptable arrangement for the sharing of nuclear control so potentially damaging to alliance cohesion. What the allies of the United States sought, non-nuclear and nuclear powers alike, was a means of mitigating the influence that American decisions about nuclear strategy could have on their own political situations. Strategic decisions being concerned essentially with the principles and reasoning by which military capabilities are related to the ends they are desired to serve, they were thus significant not only with respect to their influence on military posture, but also for their impact on the relationship between armed forces and foreign policy. In other words, strategy and foreign policy were interdependent. The character of the strategic doctrine underlying the military posture of NATO influenced the political options available to the various allies and, consequently, this helped to account for the tensions that the debate over alliance strategy generated. An ally's commitment to NATO extended only so far as membership in the alliance advanced its foreign policy interests, and only to the extent that the interests pursued through alliance were sought at a cost that was not too burdensome in terms of other desirable national objectives. By 1966, France, for example, had decided that the costs of participation in the military arrangements of the alliance were too burdensome: a decision that reflected France's dissatisfaction with the direction that alliance strategy was taking, and with her inability adequately to influence that strategy within the alliance framework.

NATO has provided the institutional link by which the nuclear guarantee of the United States to Western Europe has been maintained. The credibility of this guarantee has been much affected by American strategic policies, and since the credibility of those policies has been crucial to the value that the allies derive from alliance membership, the cohesion of NATO has depended in large degree on the level of satisfaction that the allies have had with American strategic policy. Reflecting this state of affairs, it can be noted that a common denominator of all proposals for nuclear sharing in NATO has been the desire to influence the impact of American policies on alliance strategy. There have been three interrelated aspects to this: access to the process by which alliance strategy is brought into line with that of the United States; the opportunity to counteract American decisions which allies feel are inimical to their interests; and, finally, the possibility of exercising some influence on American strategic decisions themselves. Beyond this common denominator, however, there has been from time to time wide diversity in allied approaches to the problem of nuclear sharing.

This diversity has stemmed from differences as to what various allies have wanted from nuclear sharing. Some have aspired to the kind of influence offered by the direct ownership of nuclear weapons. Others have sought to increase their influence over nuclear policy, and be assured that they would be consulted before decisions were taken that affected their interests, but without aspiring to the actual ownership of weapons.

The French and the British both used their national nuclear programmes as a means of dealing with the issue of nuclear control in the alliance, although French and British decisions concerning nuclear weapons stemmed from different strategic and political circumstances and were intended to procure different political and strategic ends, nevertheless both countries saw their nuclear forces as a powerful means of influencing the way in which the United States might exercise its nuclear options in the event of a war in Europe. The British believed, and the French agreed with this perception, that national nuclear forces brought generalised influence in the alliance and specific input into the planning process. And, anyway, national forces gave those that possessed them a nuclear option outside the alliance framework. It was unfortunate for the French that they began to achieve a nuclear capability at a time when American policy was moving strongly against national nuclear forces. Certainly a major French objective in any system of nuclear sharing, access to American nuclear technology, was unavailable to them. The British already benefited from the information made available by the preferential amendments in their favour of the US Atomic Energy Act, consequently their approach to nuclear sharing was conditioned by their special relationship with the United States, and by their concern with the implications of greater German access to nuclear weapons. The increasing weight of the German desire to achieve at least equality of status in the alliance with Britain and France came directly into conflict with French nuclear aspirations, for the sensitivity of the problem of how the Germans were to be associated with nuclear weapons increased the difficulty of accommodating the French. An essential political precondition for any successful scheme for nuclear sharing was that it provide a broad alliance framework within which the problem of Germany and nuclear weapons could be made less acute. As it happened, none of the schemes proposed was capable of satisfying the French.[10]

For all the American concern with national nuclear forces in the alliance, realistically this was an option available only to the British and French. None of the other allies, including Germany, was in a position to develop and deploy its own nuclear capability. In the case of Germany, quite apart from the legal constraints on German manufacture of nuclear weapons imposed by the Paris agreements of 1954, any formula which enabled the Germans to exercise direct control over nuclear weapons would have evoked vigorous opposition from most NATO allies, and also would have provoked a strongly negative reaction from the Soviet Union as well. It subsequently became clear that, as a result of Russian concerns about Germany and nuclear weapons, there was a linkage between the satisfactory resolution of the issue of nuclear sharing in NATO and the pursuit of arms control agreements with the Soviet Union. Thus the settlement of what essentially was an internal alliance issue became a precondition for the development of détente. Germany's own response to this alliance issue was in turn much affected by the fact that the nature of her access to nuclear weapons was a highly salient question not only in the broad context of alliance politics and East–West relations, but also within the context of German domestic politics. For none of the other non-nuclear allies was the issue of nuclear sharing as sensitive and important as it was for Germany. Nonetheless, they were all affected by a mixture of political, military and security considerations which affected their response to the issue of nuclear sharing and which made it relevant to them. For all that there was a certain amount of political posturing, there was a shared appreciation that national nuclear forces would not be an appropriate way of meeting their objectives with respect to the nuclear posture of the alliance. How these objectives were to be met, however, was something about which there was considerable debate.

In a press conference held just prior to the first meeting of the Nuclear Planning Group in 1967, Robert McNamara listed eight suggestions that had been made over the previous ten years as to how 'the non-nuclear allies might have a greater voice in assessing the nature of the nuclear threat to the alliance, in determining what forces were required to meet that threat, and in working out how and under what conditions these forces would be employed'.[11] All of these were 'hardware' suggestions in that allied access to nuclear decision-making was linked to agreement as to how the command and control of these forces could be shared. Agreement on how and to what extent the allies should participate in the nuclear policy process was thus linked to agreement about the ownership and composition of nuclear forces and to agreement on decision-making formulae. This aggregation of issues, each potentially divisive, reinforced the intractability of the whole problem of nuclear sharing.

Two suggestions for allied nuclear sharing were sponsored by General Norstad as Supreme Allied Commander in 1960. First, there was the proposal that a European consortium be created which would produce medium-range ballistic missiles in order to meet the SHAPE requirement for a NATO force of MRBMs. This requirement had been formally generated by the Council decision of December 1957 which had led to the deployment of Thor missiles in Britain and Jupiter missiles in Italy and Turkey, and the proposed MRBM force was intended to serve in the 1960s as a more flexible and up-to-date replacement for these missiles. Behind the suggestion that the MRBMs be produced by a European consortium from technical data provided by the United States was the hope that this would serve as a step towards giving the European allies a nuclear capability under some form of joint alliance control. Apparently, one suggested form of control arrangement which emerged from inter-allied discussions during 1960 was that the MRBM force should be operated under the command of SACEUR, be targeted as an integral element of SHAPE planning, and the decision to fire be given by the Supreme Commander under the authority of the President of the United States.[12] This latter arrangement would have conformed to a previously expressed desire on the part of the Germans that the powers of SACEUR be expanded.[13]

A second, related proposal associated with Norstad was that NATO should become the 'fourth nuclear power'. In effect, the above proposal, if implemented, would have resulted in NATO acquiring such a status. However, Norstad had been careful to distinguish between his military requirement for MRBMs as an effective delivery system given the military problems facing his Command, and for the shared production of which the European consortium had been proposed, and the shared control of nuclear warheads. In theory, under the consortium proposal, European allies would be able to exercise direct control of the means of delivery so produced, but the warheads for them would have remained in American custody. Norstad's suggestion was that NATO might establish a multilateral authority to exercise control over the warheads for the planned missiles, and over the developing stockpiles of warheads designed for tactical use which currently were virtually under exclusive American control.[14] Actually, Norstad never publicly committed himself to specifying the details of any arrangement by which NATO as an alliance could exercise control over nuclear weapons. What he sought from the 'fourth nuclear power' proposal (and in this he had been supported by the Secretary General, Paul-Henri Spaak) was a political alternative to the development of nuclear forces in Europe outside alliance control. The NATO force was to fill a political rather than a military need. It was designed to head off further pressures for national nuclear forces and, more particularly, limit the disruptive effects on alliance cohesion of French nuclear policies which increasingly presented the French nuclear programme as the basis for a potentially autonomous European defence system.[15]

The feeling on the part of the Americans that it was politically necessary to respond to European nuclear aspirations led, in 1960, to a third 'hardware' proposal. This was presented to the December NATO Ministerial Council by the outgoing Secretary of State, Christian Herter. The American Secretary of State put forward the tentative concept of a collective alliance force to be built around a commitment by the United States to the alliance of five Polaris submarines armed with eighty missiles. This offer would be conditional on the allies purchasing an additional one hundred missiles which would be multilaterally manned, owned and controlled. It seems that, as originally formulated, Herter's proposal envisaged the multilaterally owned missiles being deployed at sea, either in submarines or in surface vessels, alongside the American Polaris submarines. Subsequently, however, by the time Herter addressed the Council meeting on the topic the possibility of the missiles being deployed on land was also held out. This was in response to representations from SACEUR who was concerned that the Herter initiative might compromise his stated military requirement for land-based MRBMs to be deployed in Europe.[16] If an additional condition were also met, that the allies agree on an effective system by which the force might be commanded and controlled, then the future possibility was held out that the United States would combine its Polaris force with the allied missiles and so create a NATO strategic deterrent.

The genesis of Herter's proposal can be found in a report prepared by Robert Bowie which had been commissioned by the United States Assistant Secretary of State for Policy Planning, Gerard Smith.[17] The prospect that the manufacture of missiles in Europe in order to meet the SHAPE MRBM requirement might lead to arrangements by which weapons capable of striking directly at the Soviet Union might come under German command was viewed with some alarm in the State Department. Bowie's report produced an alternative to the Norstad proposals as to how the allies could be collectively associated with nuclear weapons.[18] Out of the Bowie report and the use made of it by Herter in the NATO Council were to come eventually the more specific multilateral force (MLF) proposals of 1963. Although Bowie did not specify precisely how his proposed collective force would be controlled, his suggestion that it be mix-manned in order to prevent elements of the force from being seized for national use in a crisis by the forces of a single power was a distinctly original contribution to the control debate. The question of control, however, would have to be settled within the context of allied agreement on strategy. It is noteworthy that Bowie associated his collective force with a recommendation that the conventional forces of the alliance be strengthened in order to provide the possibility of an effective conventional response to something below an all-out conventional attack.[19] In addition, Bowie was of the opinion that any solution to the problem of nuclear control should meet three criteria. These were first, that it should add to alliance cohesion. Presumably what Bowie meant here was that any system of control should be supported by a positive alliance consensus: one that had not been forced on reluctant allies. Second, any scheme should assure responsible control over the nuclear weapons included in it and 'unify the deterrent'. The assumption underlying this was that the security of the North Atlantic area was indivisible. In Bowie's view it would be foolhardy to suppose that a separate defence of either the United States or Europe was feasible, but this did not mean that control should be monopolised by a single country. Finally, whatever solution was adopted, it would have to take into account change and evolution occurring in the relations of the North Atlantic countries. What was needed was something which would lay the basis for a constructive solution which could be worked toward over a period of time.[20]

Bowie's views represented something of a transitional phase in the development of American policy towards nuclear sharing between the approach exemplified by Norstad on the one hand, which stressed the need for direct European participation in the operation of nuclear forces, and that subsequently associated with McNamara, which stressed allied consultations on the revision of alliance strategy, revisions which in the American view would reduce the salience of the control issue by giving the allies greater confidence in the deterrent and military effectiveness of the strategic posture of the alliance. There is a degree of irony in the fact that the revisions proposed under the 'McNamara strategy' were to give even greater urgency to the question of nuclear sharing in the alliance. A major reason for this was the fact that changes in American strategic policy having major impact on the alliance were taken unilaterally, without any consultation other than an *ex post facto* attempt to persuade the allies to endorse American actions. The allies found themselves in the position of responding to unilateral American initiatives and seeking to protect their own interests at the level of policy implementation. Indeed, what the various hardware proposals mostly amounted to was a means by which the non-nuclear allies, through their physical access to the means of delivery and through their potential ability to 'veto' the use of the accompanying nuclear warheads, could have some effect on the implementation of American strategic decisions.

In the early sixties, discussion of two further variations on existing hardware proposals, if adopted, would have given the allies greater control over nuclear weapons by means of an increased ability to determine when and if they would be used. These were first, the idea that a mobile MRBM force might be deployed under NATO command and in 1961, following on from the Herter proposal, there was secondly, continued discussion in the alliance of the idea of some kind of NATO seaborne force. The new Kennedy administration was by and large lukewarm to the Herter proposal. The administration initiated a review of strategic policy which led to the conclusion that the strategy of the alliance should place much greater emphasis on conventional forces and that operationally nuclear forces should be subject to overall centralised control. The strategic review was undertaken by a committee meeting under the chairmanship of Dean Acheson, and the work of the committee led to an analysis which significantly departed from existing NATO policy. In the first place it was argued that it would be undesirable for any major part of American nuclear forces to be subject to a European veto, although it was accepted that some of those deployed in Europe might have to be. Secondly, in the interests of being able to conduct a nuclear war in such a manner that deterrence might continue even after fighting had broken out, the United States should endeavour to secure a veto over nuclear weapons deployed by her European allies. This was in order that the United States could maintain tight central control over any nuclear battle which might be fought in what could be conceived of as a single theatre of operations. Thirdly, there should be a much higher conventional threshold before the use of nuclear weapons.[21] Such conclusions not only reinforced American opposition to her allies' possessing national nuclear forces, but also ruled out any degree of autonomy for SACEUR, or for any devolution of operational control in connection with the Herter suggestion that Polaris submarines might be assigned to the alliance. Nevertheless, given that there had been positive allied responses to what Herter had said, the new administration was unable to abandon entirely the idea of a NATO seaborne force. Thus, in a speech given in Ottawa in May 1961, President Kennedy held out the possibility of establishing such a force which would be truly multilateral in ownership and control, but, reflecting the work of the Acheson committee, this in his view could go forward only after NATO had met its non-nuclear goals. As in the original Herter proposal, the establishment of the force would depend upon the allies agreeing on an adequate control arrangement.[22]

The idea that some form of land-mobile MRBM force might be deployed in Europe had been discussed in NATO circles from the time that SHAPE had originally formulated an MRBM requirement following the 1957 decisions on the nuclearisation of the alliance. In 1960, as already noted, a fairly specific proposal had emerged in connection with the suggestion that a European consortium might build a land-mobile version of the Polaris missile which could be deployed by road or rail in the European theatre.[23] This proposal, which was linked with the desire of SACEUR to increase generally the nuclear responsibilities of his command, had not been received sympathetically in the United States and action on it had been stalled. Still, the idea of a mobile NATO land force of MRBMs continued to have currency even after the Kennedy administration came into office, and did not finally drop out of sight until negotiations on the MLF were underway. Neither in the case of the seaborne force, nor in the case of continued discussion of the land-mobile MRBM suggestion, did any clear conception emerge as to how such forces would be controlled. The relationship between the ownership and control of the means of delivery and the warheads which would make them operational also remained unsettled and obscure.

Despite the fact that discussion continued (mostly informally) in the alliance about the possibility of NATO land-based or seaborne nuclear forces as a solution to the problem of nuclear sharing, most of the nuclear diplomacy of the alliance in 1961 and 1962 was concerned with the allies' response to the new administration's strategic policies. In the absence of American initiatives concerning schemes by which the allies could share in nuclear policy-making, the nuclear debate was channelled into a largely hostile response to the implications of the new direction in American strategic thinking. It was in part in order to deflect this hostility and make what came to be called 'flexible response' more acceptable, that McNamara proposed new consultative arrangements for nuclear weapons at Athens in May of 1962. As already indicated, in large part due to the attitude of the French, these arrangements were largely ineffective. Nevertheless, another factor was also operative which had broad implications for the prospects for nuclear sharing in the alliance. This was the factor of secrecy.

Those in the American administration closely associated with the strategic innovations sought to persuade the European allies to accept the new line by encouraging them to undertake the kinds of strategic analysis that had led the members of the Acheson committee to their conclusions. In order to do this, it was felt necessary to provide the allies with far more detailed information about nuclear weapons, their technical characteristics, their deployment and the operational exigencies governing their use, than had ever been done before. As part of a process of strategic education, the reasoning ran, the United States should relax somewhat its approach to nuclear secrecy. In strategic briefings given towards the end of 1961, and at Athens in 1962, the Americans went much further than ever before in briefing their NATO allies on relative force levels and on the strategic concepts underlying American policy. However, the momentum gathered by this approach was largely dissipated during 1962 owing to the absence of any machinery through which nuclear information could be routinely disbursed and a 'seminar' on nuclear strategy conducted. In addition, there was opposition to this whole approach, which had been sponsored mainly in the Defence Department, from other sectors of the administration. In particular, opposition had been expressed in the State Department and in the Joint Chiefs of Staff.[24] An important consequence of all this was that the Americans were both unwilling and unable to provide enough detailed information about nuclear weapons to satisfy the European allies and fuel the Athens machinery. Nevertheless, in effect, the framework of nuclear consultation that was later to be embodied in the Nuclear Planning Group had been anticipated.

Despite the failure of the Kennedy administration to follow up the Herter proposal, increasing tensions in the alliance over questions of nuclear strategy and nuclear sharing, tensions which had been exacerbated by the new American policies, led the United States to undertake new initiatives in 1963 towards the problem of nuclear sharing. A 'hardware' solution was again sought: this time through the reformulation of the Herter proposals in the form of a specific proposition that the alliance establish a multilaterally owned and manned nuclear force (the MLF). Two events in particular stimulated the new initiative. These were the crisis in Anglo-American relations brought about by the decision of the American administration to cancel the Skybolt missile on which the British were relying to prolong the life of their independent deterrent, and the French veto of Britain's application to join the European Community which was closely followed by the signature of the Franco-German Cooperation Treaty on 22 January 1963. The Skybolt crisis dominated the meeting of Kennedy and Macmillan at Nassau in December 1962 at which the British were offered Polaris missiles as a way of ensuring their continued possession of a strategic deterrent in return for an undertaking that the resulting British submarine force 'would be made available for inclusion in a NATO multilateral nuclear force'.[25] The French actions, which were not unrelated to these developments in Anglo-American nuclear relations, reinforced the views of those in the United States who felt that a renewed gesture towards German nuclear aspirations was necessary in order to counteract the diplomatic leverage that strategic issues were giving the French. In particular, the French veto and the Franco-German treaty were seen as compromising American policy towards 'Atlantic partnership' and so strengthened the position of those mainly in the State Department who argued that a collective, multi-lateral nuclear force could provide a major vehicle for the Atlantic Community policies of the United States.

During 1962, proponents of the collective force idea in the State Department had been elaborating the concept of a multilateral force. By the fall, European governments were being briefed on the MLF idea as it had been developed under the State Department initiative. The force would consist of 200 Polaris missiles deployed on 25 surface ships which would be jointly owned and operated by the participants. Each ship would be mixed-manned (following the Bowie proposal) in order to reinforce the multilateral character of the force. Multilateralism was an essential feature of the scheme so that no national contingent could control any particular ship, nor any individual government be able to withdraw any particular component of the force for national purposes.[26] The need to provide some kind of governing body for the force would have the advantage, according to the MLF advocates, of encouraging

European integration in conformity with the 'two-pillar' concept of the Atlantic Community being presented by the Kennedy administration. The events of December and January led to the MLF proposal being taken up by the administration as a matter of priority. A major effort was to be made to persuade the allies to accept the MLF idea and Livingstone Merchant was appointed as a special ambassador to coordinate negotiations with NATO. The two preconditions for the establishment of a multilateral force outlined by President Kennedy in his May 1961 speech in Ottawa: that of a conventional build-up by the allies, and of prior agreement on control arrangements, were dropped. For the next two years the MLF proposal provided the centrepiece of allied diplomacy on nuclear sharing.

Although the advocates of the MLF had seized upon the references to 'multilateral' in the Nassau communiqué as justification for pushing ahead with their initiative and, somewhat disingenuously, as evidence for British approval in principle of the multilateral force, in fact there was no agreement at all. What was implied in the joint statement of Kennedy and Macmillan by the references to a multilateral nuclear force was not clear, and the resulting ambiguity covered major differences between the British and Americans as to what was involved in the idea of an MLF and what relationship British nuclear forces would have to it.

It was possible to interpret the Nassau communiqué as having made reference to two different types of collective alliance nuclear force. The first, which subsequently became known as the inter-allied nuclear force (IANF), stemmed from paragraph 6 of the 'Statement on Nuclear Defence Systems' attached to the communiqué. This involved the assignment of elements of the British V-bomber force to NATO together with allocations from American strategic forces. These strategic forces, when added to tactical nuclear forces already in Europe, would form the basis of a NATO nuclear force and be targeted in accordance with NATO plans. The second type of collective force was outlined in paragraph 8 of the same statement. Here it was indicated that the British Polaris submarines that were to be built as a result of the Nassau agreement would be made available for inclusion in a NATO *multilateral* nuclear force. At least equal American forces would be made available as well. However, the paragraph also included the statement that the British Polaris forces would be 'assigned and targeted in the same way as the forces described in paragraph 6', and that 'except where Her Majesty's Government may decide that supreme national interests are at stake' these forces would be used in all circumstances for the defence of the Western alliance. Clearly, there was ample scope for different interpretations of what was intended by the statement in paragraph 7 that the two governments were agreed that with respect to the provision of Polaris their purpose must be the development of a multilateral nuclear force in closest consultation with other NATO allies.[27]

Certainly, the British felt that with respect to Polaris they had committed themselves to nothing more than their allocation to NATO in accordance with the inter-allied force idea. They did not believe that they had accepted that the Polaris forces should be part of the MLF as presented by the State Department. Such a commitment would have been entirely contrary to the primary British objective at Nassau: the maintenance of an independent British deterrent.[28] Thus the British prepared a proposal for an IANF which they planned to present to the meeting of the NATO Council scheduled for Ottawa in May 1963. Under the British scheme, strategic forces under national command would be assigned to SACEUR under the same kind of terms as other forces were assigned to the alliance. (That is, the forces would only come under the operational command of SACEUR as a result of specific national authorisation and, while assigned, would anyway be available for national tasks outside the NATO area.) The British were prepared to assign their V-bombers and their Polaris submarines, when built, to such a force and envisaged that the nuclear-capable strike aircraft of Germany and the other allies would be assigned to the force also. Those countries participating in the force would form a committee to deal with policy questions arising in connection with the IANF.[29]

Under such an arrangement as was proposed in the inter-allied force it would always be possible for national units to be pulled out. The national command structure governing the assigned forces would be intact and an explicit right to employ the forces in accordance with a unilaterally determined national interest would be recognised. This, of course, was in complete contrast to the arrangement suggested in the MLF where the multilateral feature, when coupled with mixed-manning, was designed to ensure that there could be no unilateral, national use of the force. The command arrangements in themselves proposed for the IANF would have been enough to have aroused concern and opposition among the proponents of the MLF, but there was an additional factor to be considered, too. This was that the inter-allied force could be interpreted as continuing to discriminate against the non-nuclear allies in general and the Germans in particular. Although under the British proposal the German nuclear-capable strike aircraft would be included, the nuclear weapons for the aircraft would remain under exclusive American control. A major objective of those in the American administration advocating the MLF had been to head off any pressure in Germany for national nuclear forces arising from a sense of discrimination, and to encourage European integration. The MLF would help achieve this by providing for German participation on the same basis as all the other allies of the United States, and provide a means by which British (and possibly French) nuclear forces could be 'dissolved' into the new arrangement. In addition, the prospect was held out that as European integration increased, then control of the force might be devolved upon a purely European grouping.[30]

The Americans, pushing the MLF proposal together with those elsewhere in the alliance who for one reason or another were opposed to the British initiative, managed to restrict the British presentation to the NATO Council in Ottawa to the formal assignment by the United Kingdom to SACEUR of her V-bomber force, it being understood that the British Polaris submarines would be assigned later as they became operational. The United States matched the British commitment by assigning three of her own Polaris submarines to SACEUR too.[31] This arrangement, involving only Britain and the United States, was compatible with the inter-allied force that the

British felt themselves committed to as a result of Nassau, while at the same time preserving the multilateral option. The Ottawa communiqué linked the announcement of other steps modifying the organisation of the nuclear forces available to him. These were the appointment of a Nuclear Deputy to SACEUR who would be a European and would be responsible for such matters as training and the provision of information on operations; the appointment of allied officers to the Strategic Air Command Headquarters at Omaha; and the fuller supply by the United States of political and military information concerning nuclear weapons.[32] These latter steps were in line with the approach to nuclear sharing that had been taken by McNamara at Athens, and indicated that despite the attention being given to hardware proposals like the MLF, the prospect of a consultative alternative had not receded.

The MLF option still being open after the Ottawa meeting, steps were taken to seek allied agreement on its specific form. To this end two committees were announced in the summer of 1963. The first was a working group of NATO permanent representatives from the countries interested in the project, who met in Paris and concerned themselves with the legal and political problems associated with the force. It was understood that it would be the task of the working group to draft a treaty. The second committee, which was considered a sub-group of the other, met in Washington and considered the military implications of the establishment of the MLF.[33]

The proposal that was under consideration was essentially that which had been presented to the European capitals in the fall of 1962; that is, for a surface fleet of 25 ships. Had the Americans been able to include the offer of Polaris submarines in their proposal, more European governments might have responded more positively and favourably to the idea of a NATO multilateral force. As it was, politically it was impossible for the American administration to include submarines in the package (which helps explain the desire of the MLF advocates to get the British submarines that were being laid down included in the force), and only the German government had unequivocally committed itself to participation. The other governments participating in the working group, Italy, Greece,

Turkey, Belgium, the Netherlands and Britain, did so with varying degrees of reluctance. In effect, the allies were responding to American pressure because they perceived that the Americans thought it important, but they all had doubts as to whether the force was worthwhile in terms of cost, military effectiveness and strategic relevance.[34] The actions of the British were crucial. If the British participated, then so would several of the smaller allies because they would think it politically prudent to do so, and not because they thought the MLF would be a militarily effective solution to the problem of nuclear sharing.

Of all the technical questions raised concerning the structure, ownership and operation of the MLF, the most significant in terms of resolving how the allies were to participate jointly in nuclear decision-making were those concerning how the force was to be commanded and controlled. From the early stages of the development of the proposal it was clear that the United States would insist on retaining a veto over any use of the force, although, as has already been pointed out, the incentive was to be offered to the allies that, in the event that they could develop unified political arrangements and that they felt it to be desirable, the United States might in the future relinquish its veto. Control over the force was to be shared, however, by extending the right of veto to other participants in the MLF. Thus the inevitable question was raised of 'how many fingers on the trigger' would have what effect on the military effectiveness and deterrent credibility of the force? This was never satisfactorily answered, and by its nature probably could not be. As discussions in the working group proceeded, various suggestions for majority voting were canvassed as a means of reaching decisions on force policy, and for limiting decisions on use to the major participants who would act on the basis of agreed guidelines. Nevertheless, agreement was never reached. The American negotiators, conscious that the implementation of any MLF agreement would have to obtain enabling legislation from Congress, were unable to offer any real concessions on the American veto.[35]

It did emerge that operational control of the force would devolve upon SACEUR. There had been some suggestion that

SACLANT might be a more appropriate authority, or that an entirely separate command arrangement might be established, but the effect of any such arrangement would have been to create in effect a separate nuclear alliance within NATO. Strong opposition to any development of this kind could be expected not only from the French, but from other European allies also. As for some of the operational problems that could be expected to arise from the mixed-manning feature, these were subject to investigation in the mixed-manned cruise of the *USS Biddle* (renamed *Claude Ricketts*).

In the summer of 1964, the British proposed in the working group that land-based missiles and aircraft be the basis of a collective, multilateral NATO interdiction force. The force would consist of aircraft and missiles already assigned and deployed in support of NATO in an interdiction role, and to which would be added projected tactical strike systems then under development. Like the MLF, the force would be jointly financed and controlled under the operational command of SACEUR, and the units making up the force could be mixed-manned in some way. The British idea was that a NATO force should be based on what was already available rather than investing in entirely new weapons systems.[36] In putting up the idea for study the British were seemingly attempting to delay negotiations on the specific American MLF proposal, but it can also be seen as representing the genesis of a subsequent proposal from the new Labour government in December for an Atlantic Nuclear Force (ANF).

As announced in the House of Commons on 16 December, the Wilson government proposed that the Atlantic Nuclear Force should consist of the British V-bombers, the Polaris submarines that were being built (significantly, these were omitted from the previous British proposals to the working group in the summer), a matching number of American Polaris submarines, any forces that France might be persuaded to contribute, and a mixed-manned jointly owned component in which the non-nuclear allies could participate. This multi-lateral component should consist of land-based missiles and aircraft rather than the surface Polaris fleet envisioned in the MLF. An elaborate control arrangement was also suggested.

The countries participating in the force would constitute the governing authority for it. The United States would have a veto over the release of weapons to the force, as would any other member country that so desired it. Possibly, however, the European members could exercise their veto as a single group. The United States and Britain, and France if she participated, would have a veto over the use of all elements in the force and over any changes that might be proposed for the control system. Nevertheless, it was made clear with respect to the Polaris submarines that they would remain nationally owned and would be nationally manned. Wilson informed the House of Commons that nothing would interfere with the right of the British government to withdraw the submarines, but the government was prepared to commit its forces 'for as long as the alliance lasts'.[37] Unlike the MLF arrangement, the proposed ANF would be subject to a separate command structure, and although closely aligned with NATO would not be placed under the operational command of SACEUR.

The British proposal had been designed more to serve the political needs of the Wilson government at home than to attract allied support. Still, it did have a diplomatic purpose primarily related to the bolstering of British objections to the MLF and to the reinforcement of the British bargaining position with the Americans on the issue of nuclear sharing. As it happened, by the time Wilson was describing the ANF to the House of Commons it was already redundant. Earlier in the month, Wilson had met with President Johnson in Washington and from that meeting it had emerged that the Americans had lost interest in pushing for the MLF. The Americans would now wait for a proposal from their allies that would have substantial European support. In effect, though it was not finally interred until the Johnson–Erhard meeting of December 1965, the MLF was dead. The British government kept the ANF suggestion in circulation for a while, partly to satisfy certain domestic political needs and partly to try it out on the Germans, but the ANF, too, was destined for oblivion, the Germans making it clear to the British that they did not consider the ANF an acceptable nuclear sharing arrangement. In the hiatus that ensued, proposals for the greater sharing of nuclear information and increased alliance consultation on nuclear policy re-emerged.

The Atlantic Nuclear Force was the last of the series of hardware suggestions as to how nuclear sharing among the allies might be brought about that had followed from the direct incorporation of nuclear weapons into alliance military planning. They each represented a particular approach to the problem of how nuclear sharing might be achieved and, by inference, particular definitions of what the problem was about. Although in many ways a surrogate for other political differences, nevertheless the politics of nuclear sharing in NATO were affected by the different definitions of nuclear sharing offered, both in terms of their content and in terms of their consequences. Each of the various proposals offered may have been designed to fit a particular set of circumstances and to secure particular political objectives; but each if adopted would have had much broader institutional and political implications for the alliance than were initially circumscribed by the proposals themselves. In other words, the solution to the problem of nuclear sharing adopted was likely to be of greater long-term significance than the satisfaction and resolution through alliance mechanisms of immediate political demands.

The history outlined above of the various hardware suggestions as to how the non-nuclear allies could be associated with decisions concerning nuclear weapons, reveals three basic elements in the concept of nuclear sharing. First, there is the possibility of sharing the ownership of nuclear weapons through some kind of joint or collective force. Second, there is the attempt to share control of nuclear weapons by sharing in some way the decision as to whether or not to fire them. Third, there is the sharing of policy determination concerning nuclear weapons and, in particular, the sharing of participation in the process by which the strategy governing nuclear weapons is developed and implemented.

In certain respects the sharing of ownership of weapons entails sharing of control over their use and participation in the determination of the strategic policies that are to apply to them. Ownership of something is usually understood to confer rights as to when and how it will be used, and so there was an obvious plausibility in the collective ownership approach to nuclear sharing. A share in ownership would seem to ensure a share in the substantive benefits of the possession of nuclear weapons; that is, if, when and how to use them on behalf of national interests. Thus a number of proposals were made by which the NATO allies could jointly own components of a nuclear force. First, there were the proposals that a European consortium should build missiles to meet SACEUR's MRBM requirement, then there was the Herter suggestion that the allies purchase 100 Polaris missiles from the United States to be multilaterally owned and controlled, and finally there were the central elements of multilateral ownership in the MLF and ANF proposals. However, in terms of gaining control over nuclear weapons, these suggestions for shared ownership were of limited value to the allies.

The extent to which shared ownership of nuclear weapons would gain access to nuclear policy-making and decisions over use would be in part a function of what was actually owned and in part a function of what kinds of rights ownership would confer. An important point of distinction between the various collective ownership suggestions existed between those that offered ownership of the means of delivery and those that also offered collective ownership of nuclear warheads. Of all the several hardware proposals, only the various mutations of the MLF and the multilateral component of the ANF offered the possibility of shared ownership of warheads. Possession of the means of delivery could ensure that the delivery vehicles would not be used without the owners' consent, but of course there could be no assurance that those controlling stockpiles of nuclear warheads for such delivery vehicles would release them at the owners' request. Essentially, this is the situation with respect to the stockpiles of nuclear warheads for tactical use in the European theatre maintained by the United States for the nuclear-capable forces of its allies. Those possessing nuclear-capable forces are dependent on a decision by the United States to release warheads to its allies for use. Conversely, although the United States may accede to a request stemming from alliance authorities that weapons be released from the stockpiles, there is no guarantee that particular national authorities will authorise their nuclear-capable units to employ them.

Another distinctive feature of the multilateral force proposals which served to distinguish them from the arrangements governing the tactical weapons being deployed in Europe was that the means of delivery would be multilaterally owned. Thus, rather than individual countries determining whether national units would employ any nuclear warheads made available, the responsibility would rest with the joint owners of the force. This feature, among others, differentiated the multilateral suggestions from those collective force proposals like the inter-allied nuclear force which would have been made up of national units. For any elements in a multilaterally owned force to be fired, all presumably would have to agree; some governments could not decide to authorise their units to employ nuclear weapons while others did not. The force would have to be used as a whole, under a single chain of command, although it would not be necessary to assume that all the nuclear weapons available to the force would have to be fired simultaneously. In the case of the MLF, the feature of mixed-manning, in addition to safeguarding against the possibility that in a crisis elements of the force might be seized for national purposes, also reinforced the requirement that there be joint agreement on its use. More accurately, perhaps, with multilateral ownership, mixed-manning generated a necessity to agree on how a decision to employ the force would be reached. With respect to the implications of multilateral ownership for determining whether elements in the force would be employed, the MLF was particularly sensitive because the warheads would be *in situ*, and not, as in the case of those stockpiled for possible tactical use by the allies, in the separate custody of American forces.[38] Mixed-manning, then, was also an additional control mechanism to ensure that the force could not be used (or withheld) for purely national purposes. This dilution of the element of national control over the force very much reduced the political attractiveness of the MLF to the allies of the United States. Rather than making the issue of command and control over alliance nuclear forces easier to resolve, the MLF proposal highlighted the need to develop an agreed formula by which the participants in the MLF could reach decisions regarding its use. It is significant that the way in which the force was to be controlled and commanded was never resolved although, as already noted, a number of suggestions for majority voting and multiple vetos were canvassed.

The problem of how to control a collectively owned force, however, was more extensive than the question of determining what fingers would be on the trigger. The resolution of that problem was in turn dependent on agreement as to the strategy that would govern force planning. The period under consideration here, 1957–65, was marked by considerable differences concerning the strategy of the alliance, and it was inevitably difficult to reach agreement on how nuclear hardware was to be shared while there was no strategic agreement. And even if it were possible to deal satisfactorily with the question of alliance strategy, there would nevertheless remain the further question of the relationship of a collectively owned force to the allied nuclear forces which remained outside the circle of collective ownership. In terms of military and strategic significance, the nuclear forces of the United States were far away the most important, but in terms of their impact on the politics of nuclear sharing in the alliance, the national forces of Britain and France were of considerable significance too.

The collective ownership proposals were designed not simply to give the non-nuclear allies access to nuclear weapons. In one way a number of allies already had this through the bilateral agreements some of them had entered into with the United States governing the training and equipping of nuclear-capable tactical forces.[39] However, it was envisioned that any collective alliance force would include strategic weapons; that is, weapons capable of reaching major counterforce or counter-value targets in the Soviet Union. The original hardware proposals associated with General Norstad arose from his desire to have missiles under his command capable of being targeted against the missiles that were being deployed in the western part of the Soviet Union and which in turn were targeted against Western Europe. Apart from the military and strategic implications of the allies acquiring ownership of such a force there was the major political consequence that the Germans would have some title to nuclear weapons capable of being launched against major Soviet targets and, from the American point of view, it was better that any German aspirations in this area be accommodated within the framework of a collective arrangement in which the United States could have a decisive voice, rather than the Germans seeking a more independent solution.

Such a perspective on the part of the Americans was reinforced after 1960 when the new Kennedy administration emphasised the need for centralised and unified control over nuclear strategy and over the conduct of any war that might occur involving the forces of NATO and the Warsaw Pact. Indeed, the general hostility to national nuclear forces generated by such an approach to alliance strategy led certain elements in the American administration into favouring a collective alliance force as a way of bringing the British and possibly the French nuclear forces under shared control. The incorporation of allied strategic forces in a collective arrangement, particularly a multilateral one, would extend to the United States a power of veto over them and thus ensure that allied forces would not be used in ways incompatible with American strategic preferences. Since the United States would retain exclusive control of the great bulk of her own strategic capabilities, she would be able to exercise centralised command over the conduct of any nuclear battle. For the Americans then, one function of a collective ownership solution to the problem of nuclear sharing was to circumscribe the possibility of the independent use of allied strategic forces. In effect, participation in a collective force would have given the Americans greater freedom of action to implement their preferred strategic policies.

The irony of a situation in which the allies of the United States were being offered access to strategic forces in order that the Americans would be able to implement a strategy about which those same allies had serious reservations, served to reinforce allied doubts about any collective force proposal that failed to give them any effective influence over American strategic decisions or, alternatively, did not ensure that the force would be targeted and operated in accordance with allied strategic preferences. However, although the allies had reservations about the course of American strategic policies, there was no substantial agreement among them on what alliance strategy should be. In fact there were major differences of view between, for example, the British, the French and the Germans, differences which tended to be reflected also in the responses of the smaller allies to issues of nuclear sharing. In these circumstances the ability of any control formula for a collective force to satisfy the varying strategic needs and aspirations of the several participants had at best to be considered highly problematic. Collective ownership would not confer sufficient rights on the individual owners to ensure that the force would be used *positively* in accordance with their own perceptions of alliance interest.

The strategic value of a collective force (as distinguished from any political purposes it might serve) would also be assessed in terms of whether it could serve any viable strategic purpose. None of the collective ownership proposals would have allowed access to the nuclear weapons allocated to it except under some system of dual or multiple veto. Given the circumstances in which a decision on the possible use of the force would be called for, and given the different strategic perspectives of the allies, it was natural that there should be considerable doubts about the deterrent credibility of such a force. If the only assured right conferred by collective ownership would be the right to veto the use of a force of doubtful credibility, and if the security of the alliance would continue to rest effectively on the strategic forces of the United States, then most allies would see little value in incurring the political, military and economic costs of participation. Essentially this was the situation with respect to the MLF. The establishment of a multilateral force would not have altered the situation that the non-nuclear allies would continue to be entirely dependent on the nuclear commitment of the United States, and that the security of all the allies, both nuclear and non-nuclear, would continue to be highly sensitive to American strategic decisions.

The history of the various proposals made in NATO for the collective ownership of nuclear weapons demonstrates that by itself joint ownership was not a satisfactory means of resolving the political problems generated by allied demands for improved nuclear sharing arrangements. Shared ownership was seen to be largely irrelevant if the second element in the concept of nuclear sharing, the sharing of the decision as to whether or not to employ nuclear weapons in combat, was not provided for in an acceptable way. Shared control over nuclear weapons could take a number of forms and could be concerned with different components of nuclear policy. Most obviously control could be exercised in connection with a decision to fire nuclear weapons. Any system of shared control over this decision would inevitably involve according to the participants the right to veto, that is, the right to deny to others the employment of the weapons involved. During the MLF discussions suggestions were made, as they were in connection with the ANF, that the right to decide on use be delegated to selected members of the force. Unless the delegation were made to a single power, however, there would still be shared control over the decision to fire and the necessity for all involved in the decision to concur before nuclear weapons could be used. Shared control of the decision to fire had political appeal to those allies that wished to restrict the independent action of others but could have little appeal to those who sought greater influence over nuclear decisions.

Any system of shared control in order to be credible and to hold out the prospect of operating effectively in a crisis would have to be premised on some agreement as to when, how and under what circumstances the force might be used. The generation of such an agreement would require allied consultation on strategy and, if possible, the development of guidelines indicating the circumstances and manner in which the allies felt nuclear weapons might be used. The various hardware proposals suggested in the late fifties and early sixties did little to advance allied participation in the determination of strategic policy beyond what had been offered at Athens in 1962. Little was done to resolve such questions as the actual role of the allies in the determination of the nuclear strategy of the alliance; what the relationship was between the nuclear forces directly assigned to NATO and American strategic forces; and to what extent the allies should be consulted about American strategic decisions. In practice, the allies had little power but to resist at the stage of implementation the application to them of American strategic policies which were felt to be incompatible with their interests: hence the European resistance to the substantially unilateral American attempt to apply the doctrine of flexible response to NATO defence planning. Again, what the debate on nuclear sharing had revealed was that joint ownership and collective control of nuclear forces did not necessarily provide access to the arena in which strategic decisions vitally affecting the security of the allies were made.

The proposals on nuclear consultation and the suggested guidelines on nuclear use that McNamara had made at Athens, together with the innovations concerning existing nuclear arrangements announced at Ottawa in 1963, indicated that the sharing of information about nuclear weapons and the sharing of inputs into the process of strategic policy determination was possible without necessarily requiring agreement on a collective force arrangement. Throughout the phase of allied diplomacy on nuclear sharing that accompanied the multilateral force proposal, the possibility remained in the background of bringing about a greater allied share in the determination of NATO nuclear strategy by extending allied consultation on the subject. Given appropriate political circumstances, the possibility of seeking to satisfy allied aspirations with respect to nuclear weapons through the consultative approach could emerge as a major alliance initiative. By the summer of 1965 such an initiative seemed plausible in terms of the likelihood of evoking a positive alliance response, and the initiative came in the form of a McNamara suggestion that a new nuclear committee be established to examine ways in which allied participation in the making of nuclear policy might be increased.

2. THE ORIGINS OF THE NUCLEAR PLANNING GROUP

The proposal which was to prove to be the genesis of the Nuclear Planning Group was made by Robert McNamara to a meeting of NATO defence ministers held in Paris in the early summer of 1965. McNamara proposed a 'select committee' of four or five allied defence ministers who would look for ways in which allied consultation on the possible use of nuclear weapons might be improved and the role of interested allies in the process of nuclear planning might be extended.[1]

It seems that, as originally put forward, the McNamara proposal was for a committee made up of the defence ministers of the United States, Britain, Germany and, if she were willing to join, France. In addition Italy or perhaps some of the smaller allies in rotation might also serve. However, McNamara was open to suggestions as to the precise composition and size of the committee. The American delegation emphasised that it should be small and yet representative enough to study effectively ways of increasing allied participation in the determination of alliance nuclear policy.[2] If the committee were established it was intended that the defence ministers would meet as frequently as possible in order to discuss proposals concerning the whole process of alliance nuclear consultation. According to the thinking of the US Department of Defense, the committee might deal initially with methods to improve communications in the event of an emergency. This would enable the United States to implement better the commitment made in Athens in 1962 to consult with its allies if at all possible in the event that the use of nuclear weapons was contemplated. Subsequently, the ministers might attempt to develop guidelines as to the circumstances in which allied consultation on the use of nuclear weapons would take place. Finally, if this should go well, then the committee might move on to discuss contingency plans concerning the use of nuclear weapons in the European context. Thus the intention was to improve and extend through the new committee allied participation in the use of US nuclear forces including her strategic weapons.[3]

There were a number of precedents in the NATO experience for the kind of *ad hoc* committee that had been proposed by the American Secretary of Defense. In particular, there were the examples of the Four-Power Berlin Contingency Planning Group and the MLF Working Group. The Berlin Group had provided a method by which the joint consideration of a concrete problem had helped overcome major allied differences on a subject of great importance. In turn, the experience of the MLF Working Group had shown that such a salient issue as nuclear sharing, if not resolved, at least could be dealt with outside established alliance procedures.[4] A more specific proposal for a committee of the kind proposed by McNamara had been made as early as 1961 by Henry Kissinger. Reflecting discussions that were then taking place as to how political command of a NATO nuclear force might be achieved, the suggestion had been made that a NATO steering committee be established. This would be composed of four permanent members (US, Britain, France and Germany), and three rotating members chosen by election. The steering committee would have broad responsibility for defence, strategic and disarmament policies.[5] The McNamara proposal by its flexible and *ad hoc* character conformed to these precedents and sought to provide a new political framework for the discussion of nuclear policy.

In December 1964 the Americans had decided not to continue pressing for allied acceptance of the MLF. And in making his initiative the Secretary of Defense was conscious of the need to establish some alternative basis for securing acceptable alliance nuclear arrangements. Officially the MLF and ANF proposals remained on the alliance agenda and McNamara carefully pointed out that his proposal was made independently of the possibility of continued consideration being given to plans for some kind of alliance nuclear force.

Much to the embarrassment of the Erhard government, after the American decision in December the Germans had been left out on a limb as the only firm supporters of the MLF. If for no other reason than not to disturb German sensibilities further, McNamara was careful not to present his proposed nuclear committee as an alternative to 'hardware' solutions to the problem of nuclear sharing.[6] Nevertheless, the McNamara proposal was an alternative to the MLF and was seen as such. Still, as it turned out, McNamara's proposal amounted to more than a conciliatory gesture to the Germans.

The initial reactions of the allies to McNamara's proposal were by no means enthusiastic. The smaller allies were concerned that they might be excluded from this new exercise in nuclear policy-making while each of the larger allies also had some reservations. Of the larger allies the British were perhaps most immediately receptive to the idea of a nuclear committee. By June 1965 it was clear that their suggested ANF had just about exhausted its political usefulness both domestically and within the context of inter-allied relations. At home, the ANF proposal had successfully obfuscated the whole question of the status of the British independent deterrent, while in the context of alliance politics the meeting between Wilson and Erhard in March had removed any lingering doubts that the Germans considered the ANF proposal as it stood an acceptable alternative to the MLF.[7] Now, the British were anxious to see a non-proliferation treaty (NPT) successfully negotiated and were willing to meet the Russians in their objections to the various 'hardware' approaches to nuclear sharing in NATO. In so far as the British had doubts about the McNamara Committee (as the American proposal became dubbed by the Press), these concerned their anxieties that the special nuclear relationship with the United States might be buried in the new NATO committee. In fact the British together with the Americans, through their advocacy of the NPT, had rather isolated themselves from the other allies who saw this as a way of downplaying what many of them saw as the main issue of nuclear sharing. In part, this accounted for the initial suspicion with which the McNamara proposal was greeted.[8]

The Italians were hesitant initially in their response to the McNamara Committee since they were unsure of their status with respect to it and were not clear as to whether they would qualify for membership of the inner circle.[9] The Italian reaction was one indication that the question of membership on the new committee would prove to be contentious. However, in terms of immediate political impact the two countries most affected by the McNamara proposal were Germany and France.

The position of the Federal Republic had been crucial to the form and substance of the nuclear sharing issue as it had developed in the alliance from 1957 onwards and in many ways the development of the various 'hardware' proposals was a direct response to the need to accommodate German aspirations for a greater influence in the determination of alliance nuclear policy. The difficulty was, however, in securing this in a way that was acceptable to the other allies (and for that matter to the Russians as well).

The German Foreign Minister, Gerhard Schröder, and the Minister of Defence, Kai-Uwe von Hassel, had both evinced strong interest in the MLF and their initial reaction to the McNamara Committee was coloured by the American virtual abandonment of any interest in a multilateral ownership and control approach to the nuclear problems of the alliance. For the Germans a major attraction of the MLF had been that it was seen as a way of strengthening the nuclear link between the Germans and the Americans in particular, and between Western Europe and the United States in general. The changes in American strategic policy that had occurred since the inauguration of the Kennedy administration, together with the strategic changes that were being urged on the alliance by the Americans, had served to lessen German confidence in the credibility of the American commitment. These German doubts concerned the credibility of the American commitment not so much to the security of the Federal Republic as such, as to the *status quo* in Central Europe, and to the likelihood of continued American support for German policy on the whole question of reunification and a European settlement.

Thus, despite the loss of American interest in the MLF that

had taken place at the end of 1964, the desire of the German government for some form of direct access to nuclear weapons was not finally put aside as a policy objective until after the elections in the fall, and after Erhard's visit to the United States in December. Prior to that visit Erhard had still maintained that he wished to discuss with the Americans some form of direct access to nuclear weapons.[10] Additionally, one other consideration affected the German response to the McNamara proposal and this was a desire to avoid if possible the raising of issues which would further divorce France from the rest of the alliance.

In fact in some circles the McNamara proposal was interpreted as being a device further to isolate the French. The American initiative was seen as manoeuvring the French into a position in which they would have to accept membership on the new committee or abandon any attempt to influence American strategic policy through alliance institutions. According to this interpretation, the intention would be to offset de Gaulle's campaign against American strategic policy by confronting the French with the choice of either cooperating with the alliance or relying entirely on their own efforts for access to nuclear weapons.[11] In the event of the expected French refusal to participate, the French could be shown as unwilling to accept any form of alliance nuclear cooperation except on her own terms: terms that were unacceptable not only to the United States, but to the other allies also. McNamara denied that his proposal was intended to 'smoke out' the French, and maintained that the door had been left open for French participation, but inevitably his initiative challenged the French to put up their own specific suggestions as to the nuclear policy of the alliance and for an appropriate institutional structure to deal with it. Clearly, given the course of French policy towards the strategic policy of NATO, it was impossible for the French to respond with proposals standing any chance of broad allied acceptance without seriously compromising Gaullist policy generally. However, by the time the McNamara Committee was suggested, the French were already isolated with respect to NATO policy and their further withdrawal from the military structures of the alliance considered likely. For the French, the outcome of the McNamara proposal simply provided an additional reason for the subsequent French withdrawal from the integrated command system.[12]

It was agreed at the Paris meeting of defence ministers that further considerations of the McNamara proposal would be undertaken by the permanent representatives. The French, whose initial reaction to the proposal, as expected, had been unsympathetic, soon announced their decision. On 7 July at a regular ambassadorial meeting of the NATO Council the French announced their rejection of the McNamara Committee. In their view the American proposal was not broad enough to merit the attention of defence ministers but was merely a 'technical' proposal which could be handled at a much lower level. As if to underline the point the prepared statement was read to the Council by the number-two man in the French delegation.[13] Discussion continued, however, among the representatives of the remaining allies interested in the American initiative and this led to the establishment of a Special Committee of Defence Ministers. Consequently, the defence ministers of Belgium, Canada, Denmark, Germany, Greece, Italy, the Netherlands, Turkey, the United Kingdom and the United States met under the chairmanship of Manlio Brosio in Paris on 27 November 1965. Until almost the last moment there was uncertainty as to who would be represented. This was due to the vacillation of the Danes and the Norwegians; the Danes eventually deciding to participate, but the Norwegians finally deciding not to attend.[14]

The creation of the Special Committee represented something of a modification of the original McNamara suggestion. The Americans were anxious that alliance nuclear policy be discussed at the highest level among a limited number of informed participants; those whose views on nuclear weapons would in fact carry weight in determining the overall strategic posture of the alliance. Such an approach of course ran counter to the alliance principle of equality of representation and discussion in the NATO Council had revealed that broad alliance acceptance of a 'select committee' of four or five ministers would be difficult to achieve. The November meeting of interested defence ministers was again the result of an American initiative. In this case the more broadly representative format produced an interim report for presentation to the December ministerial meeting of the NATO Council on how allied consultation on nuclear policy might be improved.[15]

After reviewing existing nuclear capabilities and arrangements within the alliance, three working groups were set up by the defence ministers at their November meeting. These would be concerned with communications, data exchange and nuclear planning. They would operate under the guidance of a steering committee made up of the permanent representatives of the participating countries.[16] The working group on communications would concern itself with various alternative schemes to enhance the ability of the allies to keep one another informed and to consult in an emergency. Consideration of the kinds of data and other intelligence that would be required by member governments engaged in consultation on the possible use of nuclear weapons was the task of the group on data exchange. Finally, the working group on nuclear planning would examine and discuss the strategic and tactical nuclear resources available to the alliance, the possible circumstances in which they might be used and the likely consequences of such use. The group on nuclear planning would also consider ways in which the alliance might organise to carry on future discussion of these subjects.[17]

Despite the expansion to ten members of the original proposal for a committee of four or five defence ministers, the adoption of the working group formula meant that discussion could still take place within small, intimate groups. This was felt by the Americans to be particularly important in the case of the group considering nuclear planning which all members of the Special Committee recognised as being the most significant of the three working groups. Agreement on the composition of the three groups was difficult to secure, particularly in the case of the one on nuclear planning. It was readily agreed that the United States, Britain and Germany should be members, and that Italy as the remaining larger power in the alliance should be represented also. What was contentious was the representation of the smaller allies.

Canada and the Netherlands made strong representations on the rights of the smaller allies and on the principle of sovereign equality, and it was settled that one seat on the nuclear planning working group would be provided for the smaller members of the alliance. Agreement, however, could not be reached on who would occupy the final seat. The matter was finally resolved by the drawing of lots, and Turkey was thus chosen.[18]

The composition of the other two groups was eventually established as follows. The working group on communications consisted of the United States, Britain, Canada and the Netherlands; that on data exchange was made up of the United States, Britain, Canada, Belgium and Greece. Probably reflecting the difficulty of reaching agreement on the composition of the groups, the membership of the various working groups was not officially announced at the time. Nevertheless, the make-up of the three groups was widely reported in the press.[19] As an indicator of status in the area of nuclear policy at this time it can be noted that only the United States and Britain were members of all three groups. Germany of course was a member of the most significant group, that dealing with nuclear planning, but so also was Italy, and it remained to be seen whether this emerging consultative procedure would satisfy the German government's desire for greater access to nuclear weapons. It is noteworthy that the State Department had thought it necessary on 18 October to issue a statement to the effect that the United States continued to show interest in all existing proposals on the alliance nuclear question, including the MLF and ANF;[20] this, despite the fact that in September a committee had been established with the effective purpose of quietly burying the MLF.[21] Apart from Britain and the United States, Canada was the only other ally to be a member of more than one group; a result perhaps of Canada's nuclear claims having been rejected.

The agreement reached on the establishment and composition of the working groups can be seen as representing an emerging consensus in favour of McNamara's approach to the problem of securing allied access to nuclear weapons. The virtual isolation of the French on the nuclear issue following their rejection of the McNamara proposal in July, together with a shift in German policy towards nuclear access following the election in September, made allied acceptance of the McNamara approach easier to achieve. Rather than continue the search for means by which direct allied ownership and control of nuclear weapons could be secured while at the same time ensuring that the United States retained an effective veto over their use, McNamara offered the alternative of greater American consultation with the allies on questions of nuclear policy. McNamara anyway had been sceptical as to the military effectiveness of such 'hardware' approaches, believing that such forces would lack credibility and divert allied energies away from the strengthening of their conventional forces to which McNamara gave highest priority. In addition, McNamara feared that any kind of European or allied nuclear force would derogate from the importance of maintaining a single chain of command over all nuclear weapons, and would compromise the full coordination of nuclear weapons assigned to NATO with external strategic forces. Finally, the establishment of some kind of NATO nuclear force could be interpreted by the Russians and others as constituting proliferation, and by the summer of 1965 the pursuit of a non-proliferation agreement with the Russians had become a major objective of American arms control policy.[22]

Although they had yet to be persuaded, McNamara hoped that by the American initiative the allies could be brought to a thorough understanding of the constraints operating on American nuclear weapons, and by so doing lead them to a more sympathetic response to the thrust of American strategic policy. In particular, it was hoped that the allies could be brought 'to acknowledge their real strategic priorities and adjust their forces accordingly'.[23] Essentially, what the Americans were seeking to do was use the new committee to reinforce their attempts to get the allies to see the strategic problems of the alliance in the same way as they themselves did.

Within three weeks of the meeting of the Special Committee of Defence Ministers a regular ministerial meeting of the NATO Council took place. The meeting occurred during an intensive phase of Atlantic diplomacy, for, as well as the

Council meeting, in December both Wilson and Erhard were to visit Washington. One result of all these meetings was that finally the MLF and ANF were removed from the alliance agenda, although a concern for the *amour propre* of those who had strongly advocated these schemes prevented a public announcement of the fact. The report of the Special Committee was on the agenda of the December Council meeting, and the Secretary General who had acted as chairman of the Committee introduced the discussion of its work. The French prior to the Council meeting had raised doubts as to the legal status of the Special Committee arguing that any attempt to establish a permanent NATO nuclear committee would require the unanimous approval of the Council. These doubts were again expressed at the Council meeting, and it was reported that the French insisted that the work of the Special Committee must end after the NATO Council meeting scheduled for the summer of 1966. Any attempt to institutionalise the new body would be met with a French veto.[24] However, what the legal effect would be of a French attempt to exercise such a veto was open to question, and there was little doubt that the work of the McNamara Committee would be continued whatever the attitude of the French.

Although by the end of 1965 the German government had accepted that any form of direct control of nuclear weapons was ruled out as a current possibility for German policy, there nevertheless remained in Bonn elements who accepted this position only reluctantly. This, when coupled with the weakness at this time of Erhard's own political position, contributed to the ambiguous and uncertain character of German policy towards the nuclear issue in alliance affairs. Thus the German delegation to the Washington talks let it be known that they considered German collaboration essential in the process of alliance nuclear decision-making. Germany, it was said, sought *Mitsprache* (the right of consultation), *Mitbestimmung* (participation in planning) and *Mitbesitz* (participation in any decision as to use). *Miteigentum* (co-ownership) was described as remaining an objective of German policy, but one which for the time being should be left for continued discussion at the official level.[25] In other words the Germans were expressing their acceptance of the relegation of the MLF question to the Continuing Committee which had been set up to deal with it. Still, at the conclusion of the Johnson–Erhard talks it was possible for a German spokesman to interpret the reference in the communiqué to the agreement that 'the Federal Republic of Germany and other interested parties in the Alliance should have an appropriate part in nuclear defence' as meaning a share in the access to nuclear weapons. The spokesman, Herr von Hase was reported as saying that 'in order to defend oneself one has to have nuclear weapons'.[26] This statement echoed one made shortly before by the German Defence Minister who reportedly said, 'Consultation does not imply co-ownership, but co-ownership ensures consultation.'[27]

The communiqué issued at the conclusion of the Johnson–Erhard meeting stressed that Germany neither intended nor desired to acquire national control over nuclear weapons. But, apart from this clear statement which merely reiterated what had been German policy since the Paris Agreements of 1954 and a reference to the McNamara Committee, the remainder of the references to nuclear matters in the communiqué lent themselves to alternative interpretations of which the above references provide examples. It had been a clearly expressed German intention to seek assurances from the United States that a non-proliferation treaty would not rule out the formation in the future of some kind of alliance nuclear force, and the communiqué stated that 'Alliance nuclear arrangements would not constitute proliferation of nuclear weapons and in fact should contribute to the goal of preventing the spread of nuclear weapons.'[28] The question that could be asked here was whether this statement referred to existing alliance arrangements or whether it covered co-ownership arrangements too. The German interpretation was clear. However, there were considerable reservations to such an interpretation on the American side. As the possibility of some sort of multilateral force faded into the indefinite future, German nuclear aspirations became increasingly linked with the diplomatic course of the non-proliferation treaty which was seen by the Germans as the touchstone of American responsiveness to their strategic concerns. Thus the NPT replaced the MLF as the key military and security issue in German–American relations over the next three years.

The first meeting at the ministerial level of the five-power working group on nuclear weapons was held in Washington on 17–18 February 1966. Despite the presence of the Secretary-General, Manlio Brosio, the chairmanship of the meeting was taken by Robert McNamara who took the opportunity to initiate a wide-ranging discussion of the strategic forces available to the alliance and of the strategy by which they were governed. By means of a detailed briefing the American Secretary of Defense sought to introduce the non-nuclear allies in particular to the frustrations and complexities of nuclear planning. To this end McNamara stressed the size and expense of American forces, and balanced them against Soviet capabilities. According to one informed report, McNamara's discussion of Russian strategy and of the forces available to support it was so frank that it disturbed members of the American intelligence community by going much further than any previous briefing.[29]

There is little doubt that the defence ministers of the non-nuclear allies found McNamara's 'seminar' informative, and certainly it was a great change from the previous 'kindergarten briefings' that the Americans had given on the subject of nuclear strategy and weaponry.[30] Although it had been agreed that this meeting would not discuss the question of co-ownership as such, nevertheless there were press reports that the Germans, supported by the Italians, had expressed reservations as to whether a consultative committee could meet the security concerns of the non-nuclear members of the alliance. The view had been put forward, it was said, that no degree of consultation could be really effective and convincing to a potential aggressor unless accompanied by some form of co-ownership of a part of the nuclear potential available to the alliance.[31]

In response to this belated upsurge of German interest in co-ownership of nuclear weapons, the Americans issued a statement seeking to make clear that the McNamara Committee was not a substitute or alternative for a possible allied nuclear force.[32] As Dean Rusk and Robert McNamara were to reiterate in their testimony to the Jackson committee later in the year, the United States remained ready to respond to any agreed European initiative with respect to a system of nuclear sharing, but the United States itself would not undertake any new initiative in this direction.[33] It was indicative of the divisions and lack of direction in the Erhard government that at this time German spokesmen should be leaking to the press their preference for a 'hardware' approach to nuclear sharing as a way of expressing their dissatisfaction with American policy, not only with respect to questions of nuclear strategy, but with the American approach to the NPT as well.

The next meeting of the working group on nuclear weapons took place in London on 28–29 April. It followed the French announcement in March that they were withdrawing from all of the NATO integrated commands and would no longer be participating in the military planning procedures of the alliance. Although the French withdrawal was to make the subsequent development of the new consultative arrangement easier, the French action was not of immediate concern to the operations of the McNamara Committee. Whereas the February meeting had been concerned primarily with strategic weapons, in London attention was directed towards a consideration of the nuclear weapons deployed in the European theatre. The assembled ministers were given briefings on the subject by General Lemnitzer (SACEUR), and by Admiral Moorer (SACLANT), and Denis Healey led a discussion on the results of war games undertaken by the British Defence Operational Analysis Establishment on the effects of waging a long drawn out campaign in Europe using tactical nuclear weapons.[34] According to British sources these studies led to the conclusion that most of the existing alliance doctrine on the tactical use of nuclear weapons was politically unacceptable and militarily unsound.[35] Such a conclusion would be in accordance with the doubts that Healey and other members of the Labour government had concerning the value, dangers and validity of the tactical nuclear posture of the alliance.[36]

Nevertheless, however cogent the arguments against the existing state of affairs in Europe with respect to nuclear weapons, there remained the problem of securing agreement on an alternative approach. The Americans had long been pressing for alliance acceptance of a 'flexible response' doctrine which emphasised the importance of conventional options and the raising of the nuclear threshold. Indeed, largely unilateral decisions on the part of the United States in revising her own strategic posture had done much to raise and exacerbate the issue of nuclear sharing and alliance strategy. Although the French had carried their opposition to American policy to the greatest extremes, resistance to American attempts to bring the strategic posture of the alliance and its military planning into line with the revised American doctrine had come from Germany and the other European allies also.

The British, for example, though unwilling to place too much value on the theatre nuclear weapons deployed in Western Europe, were at the same time also unwilling to commit themselves to any substantial increases in their conventional contributions to the alliance. They argued that NATO military planning was too much concerned with the fighting of a prolonged conventional campaign, and that stockpiles enabling NATO forces to fight a land war in Europe for 90 days were unnecessary. (This was the planning target established under existing alliance military doctrine.) Rather, emphasis should be placed on dealing with ambiguous or unpremeditated threats which could be met with conventional resources and without resort to nuclear weapons. Since a full-scale Soviet conventional attack on Western Europe was in any case extremely unlikely, SACEUR should base his planning on the forces actually available rather than on the basis of 'unrealistic' force goals established by SHAPE on the basis of the minimum capabilities required to deal with an all-out conventional attack by the Soviet Union. Any such attack, the British argued, would quickly go nuclear, and the task of conventional forces would be to give the allies sufficient time to consult on the use of nuclear weapons and to contain the fighting, even after the use of nuclear weapons, to a level from which both sides could withdraw rather than to escalate the fighting further. To this end any initial use of nuclear weapons by the alliance should be limited in scope. The British Minister of Defence used the occasion of the working group meeting in London to express this view further.[37]

There was substantial American agreement on the principle that the alliance's military planning should be based on the forces actually available, but they differed considerably from the British on what constituted an acceptable level of conventional capabilities and on what the role of those forces should be. The Americans argued that the strength of Soviet conventional forces had been over-estimated, and that the allies with reasonable effort could provide an effective non-nuclear defence against them. Increased conventional contributions by the European allies would make this possible and lessen the reliance on nuclear weapons in NATO military planning. A desirable military posture for the alliance was one in which its forces would be able to respond appropriately and effectively to any military action on the part of the Warsaw Pact at both nuclear and conventional levels. Thus the conventional forces available to the alliance should be able to do more than counteract minor or inadvertent Soviet incursions, or simply to impose a 'pause' on invading forces prior to a resort to nuclear weapons.[38]

Germany had built up substantial conventional forces by 1966 but they fell short of the levels originally planned. The Germans resisted American pressure for a greater conventional effort on the two grounds of economic stringency and strategic prudence. Erhard's already vulnerable domestic political position had been further weakened by a downturn in the German economy, and it was not politically expedient to incur additional defence expenditures. Indeed, American pressure on Erhard in September to live up to the offset agreement to purchase American military equipment for the Bundeswehr was a factor contributing to the Chancellor's forced resignation.[39] But, in addition to the reluctance to increase defence expenditures, significantly, the Germans also took the view that greater military flexibility at the conventional level should not lead to a weakening of the threat to use nuclear weapons. Raising the nuclear threshold by providing for a stronger conventional option would simply weaken the credibility of the nuclear commitment. If the Russians sought to exploit the changing strategic balance between themselves and the United States by putting increased pressure on Western Europe, then the risk of escalation should be made plain. The credibility of the deterrent would be enhanced by emphasising the risk of an escalatory response up to that of general nuclear war.[40] Such a posture enhanced in German eyes the importance of the nuclear weapons deployed in the European theatre for tactical purposes and gave to them a crucial position in alliance strategy.

Ironically, at the same time as American policy was downgrading the role of theatre nuclear weapons in its overall strategic posture, there had been a rapid build-up in the number of nuclear warheads available in the European theatre.[41] This seeming contradiction in American policy can be explained in part as the result of two factors operating to reinforce each other. First, military and institutional inertia resulted in the delivery and deployment of weapons programmed under a previous administration and under a different strategic concept. As the weapons became available, the military could find a use for them. In addition, although the Americans could halt the deployment and subsequently withdraw tactical weapons systems which were felt under the new strategic orthodoxy to be excessively vulnerable and destabilising (for example the Davy Crockett), it would have been politically disastrous to reverse the planned deployment of weapons which many Europeans felt to be vital to their security at the same time as McNamara was trying to persuade them to accept the American strategic doctrine of flexible response.

One topic discussed in London was the question of the use of 'defensive' nuclear weapons systems such as atomic demolition munitions (ADMs), nuclear anti-aircraft and nuclear anti-submarine weapons. There were reports that the possibility had been discussed of making such weapons available for limited but virtually automatic use in the event of an attack on NATO territory.[42] The Defense Department quickly denied that the United States had endorsed any such proposal. A statement was issued indicating that 'at no time and in no way did the United States propose a change in the use of nuclear weapons in defense of NATO territory'. The Secretary of Defense, it was stated, had again emphasised 'the belief of the United States Government that NATO must possess both non-nuclear and nuclear forces adequate to deal with the wide range of threats with the power appropriate to each'.[43] However a proposal for a 'nuclear barrier' of ADMs on Germany's eastern frontier had been taken up by the German Defence Minister who claimed that he had discussed the idea with McNamara and the Chairman of the Joint Chiefs of Staff during his visit to Washington the previous November.[44] Subsequently, the German government quickly lost interest in the proposal as the full implications of such a deployment became clear, but von Hassel's sponsorship served to place ADMs on the future agenda of the Nuclear Planning Group. In fact the role of ADMs was to become a major concern of the NPG.

The communiqué issued at the end of the London meeting indicated that there had been a wide-ranging discussion on tactical nuclear forces. The decision was reached to initiate a programme of further studies in this area including the possible modification of the manner of allied participation in the planning and possible decision to use such weapons. Although the ministers accepted that there appeared to be sufficient over-all numbers of tactical nuclear weapons available in the European theatre, problems were perceived as to whether an appropriate 'mix' of weapons existed. The planned studies would consider the various capabilities of the weapons available, their deployment and the circumstances in which they might be used.[45]

The third meeting of the working group on nuclear weapons took place in Paris on 26 July and coincided with a meeting at the Council level of defence ministers: the first in fact since France had announced her intention of withdrawing militarily from the alliance. The presence of the defence ministers in Paris enabled a full meeting of the Special Committee to be held, its membership augmented by the presence of the Portuguese and Norwegian defence ministers, whose governments had now reversed their original decision not to participate. Progress reports were received from the three working groups. In addition, a meeting of the working group on nuclear weapons was held on the same day to review work at the official level in preparation for the next meeting of the group in Rome. It was clear by this time that the outcome of the working group's activities would be a recommendation for some kind of permanent political structure to deal with nuclear planning and consultation in the alliance, and it was anticipated that specific proposals would be considered at the Rome meeting.[46] Thus when the ministers met again on 23 September they had before them a proposed structure for future allied nuclear consultation.

Unlike the Washington and London meetings which had each lasted two days and had ranged widely over questions concerning strategic and tactical nuclear weapons, the meetings of the working group in Paris and Rome were shorter in duration and more concerned with work undertaken at the official level. Further discussion by the ministers of major issues of nuclear consultation and allied participation in the planning for possible use of nuclear weapons would await the setting up of the new consultative arrangements.

The proposals of the working group on nuclear planning were formally accepted at the December ministerial meeting of the NATO Council. A number of significant political developments were of concern to this meeting of the Council and the reports of the McNamara Committee's three working groups were by no means the most important items on the agenda. First, there had been a recent change of government in Bonn. The resignation of Ludwig Erhard had led to the formation of a 'Grand Coalition' between the CDU and SPD, with Willy Brandt as Foreign Minister, and with the former Foreign Minister, Gerhard Schröder, at the Ministry of Defence. The new German government was committed to a more open policy towards the East, and East–West relations was the major topic of discussion at the meeting. A four-power declaration on Berlin had just been issued, and the meeting was in part designed to secure agreement on a general NATO statement on East–West relations (a statement from which France disassociated herself). Finally, by resolution of the Council the so-called 'Harmel Exercise' to study 'the future tasks of the alliance' was authorised.[47]

In October France had agreed to a formula by which she would remain a full member of the NATO Council, but would not participate in discussion on military matters. This involved the establishment of a thirteen-nation Defence Planning Committee by which the allies, meeting without France, would determine the military policy of the alliance. Consequently, it was the newly formed Defence Planning Committee (DPC) which received the reports and recommendations of the three working groups. The report of the working group on data exchange considered matters dealing with the exchange of information relevant to nuclear decision-making, and the follow-up work on information exchange became an important task of the new alliance institutions. The communications working group continued to operate after the Paris Council and its recommendations were a factor in the eventual establishment of the NATO Integrated Communications System.[48]

The recommendations produced by the working group on nuclear planning led to the creation of two permanent bodies to deal with nuclear planning and consultation. A plenary body, the Nuclear Defence Affairs Committee (NDAC) would be open to all interested allies and would receive reports from a seven-member Nuclear Planning Group (NPG). The Nuclear Planning Group would be the body in which the detailed discussion of nuclear matters would take place, and could be regarded as the direct successor to the working group on nuclear planning. This two-tier arrangement was necessary to accommodate two contradictory demands. On the one hand, there was the desire of most members of the alliance to have access to an area of such fundamental importance. On the other hand, against this was the wish of the Americans, buttressed by the successful operation of the working group, to keep discussions on nuclear planning as small and as free-wheeling as possible.

In addition to France, Luxembourg and Iceland chose not to take part in the new bodies, none of these countries having been members of the original McNamara Committee. Norway and Portugal, which had first eschewed membership in the Special Committee, had been represented subsequently at the Paris meeting in July, and they accepted membership in the NDAC. In other words, the NDAC was the successor body to the full Special Committee of Defence Ministers. However, both Norway and Portugal decided not to participate directly in the work of the NPG and did not wish to be considered for membership in it.

As in the case of the original working group, the composition of the Nuclear Planning Group proved to be a matter of contention between the allies. In fact, the communiqué announcing the creation of the two new bodies was subject to a last-minute delay owing to the difficulty of reaching agreement on the precise membership of the NPG. This was finally settled in the new year as a result of a 'gentleman's agreement' which would be adhered to until 1 January 1970, when it would be open to revision. The NPG would be composed of four permanent members, the defence ministers of Germany, Italy, United Kingdom and United States, and three other members of the NDAC serving in rotation. The normal terms of membership for rotating members would be eighteen months, and it was agreed that initially Canada and the Netherlands would serve full terms, while Turkey and Greece would share the first eighteen-month term between them. Turkey would serve the first nine months.[49] At the December 1969 ministerial meeting of the Defence Planning Committee a new rotational formula was established. It took into account the desire of Norway now to be included in the work of the NPG, and enabled Turkey and Greece to serve full eighteen-month terms. A consequence of the new arrangements was that when Norway served on the NPG the membership of the Group was increased to eight.

Thus the pattern of membership in the Nuclear Planning Group and of its nominally superior body, the Nuclear Defence Affairs Committee, followed generally the precedents established by the Special Committee of Defence Ministers. The NDAC was composed of all the allies who had served on the Special Committee, while the NPG, which may be regarded as the successor body to the working group on nuclear planning, was expanded in size from five to seven members. The Secretary-General was to act as chairman of both the NDAC and the NPG. Although Manlio Brosio had acted as chairman of the Special Committee and had been present at the meetings of the working group on nuclear planning, he had not acted as chairman of the latter body, this function having been undertaken by McNamara himself. It was reported that McNamara would have preferred the chairmanship of the NPG to rotate among the ministers constituting the membership, but Brosio was supported by the other allies in his wish to see the position of the Secretary-General in the new body firmly institutionalised. As it happened, Brosio had played a very important part in bringing about allied acceptance of the formula by which the new arrangements had been established. By mediating between the various allies and taking initiatives when no one else was willing to do so, he had ensured that there was a positive alliance response to the American initiative on nuclear consultation.[50]

The Americans considered it very important that the NPG should engage the personal participation of the defence ministers, and that discussion in full meetings of the NPG at the ministerial level should be frank and unfettered. To this end, discussion in the NPG was supposed to be extemporaneous, based on papers circulated and digested in advance. Also, no verbatim or summary records of the meetings were to be circulated although a brief minute describing actions taken would be distributed to all NDAC members and a communiqué issued. Of course, it could be assumed that members of the NDAC not currently on the NPG would be informed of the gist of what went on as part of the normal practice of inter-allied diplomatic exchange. As a further encouragement to informal ministerial discussion, the number of people permitted in the conference room was strictly limited. Typically, a delegation has consisted of a defence minister, the Permanent Representative to the NATO Council, the national Chief of Staff or equivalent, and two other officials. In addition, the Chairman of the NATO Military Committee, SACEUR and SACLANT also attend the ministerial meetings.[51] Suggestions that the representation at ministerial meetings be increased, either by enlarging delegations, or by abandoning the principle of rotating membership were strongly resisted by the Americans as detracting from the object of intimate and relatively informal discussion.

Obviously under this kind of arrangement staff work will be very important. As the NPG developed, in effect two further levels of representation came into being: meetings of the permanent representatives, the main task of which has been to prepare for the half-yearly ministerial meetings, and meetings of what came to be termed the NPG Staff Group. The Staff Group grew up on an *ad hoc* basis and is composed of personnel drawn from the national delegations to NATO as well as personnel from the ministries of defence, foreign offices and armed forces of the allies. In addition, members of the NATO Staff/Secretariat and representatives of SACEUR and SACLANT attend Staff Group meetings. The military authorities and the Staff/Secretariat are present in an advisory capacity only, but this has not prevented them from participating freely in Staff Group discussions. Unlike meetings at the ambassadorial level which are chaired by the Secretary-General, the Staff Group is chaired by the Director of the NATO Nuclear Planning Directorate.[52]

The creation of the Nuclear Planning Group marked a significant turning point in the politics of alliance nuclear policy-making. The attempt to establish an acceptable method of nuclear sharing on the basis of some system of allied ownership and control of nuclear weapons was effectively abandoned in favour of a consultative approach to allied nuclear policy. In the words of a WEU report, the McNamara Committee 'seemed to indicate that the non-nuclear members of the Alliance recognise that, through improved consultation, they will secure a more real share in the planning of nuclear defence of the Alliance as a whole than they could hope to obtain by participating in a small joint nuclear force, the use of which would inevitably be subject to a veto by the United States'.[53] Such a conclusion was premature perhaps in December 1966 in that it was only after experience with the Nuclear Planning Group that all the participating allies became fully reconciled to the new approach. And anyway, after the abandonment of the MLF, the alliance debate on nuclear policy shifted from a concern with mechanisms of control to a more direct involvement with the strategy governing the possible use of nuclear weapons in defence of the alliance area.

The Nuclear Planning Group provided a means by which issues of nuclear planning and doctrine could be isolated from other matters, leaving them to be resolved within the framework of other alliance institutions. What in part had made the nuclear issue so intractable was that questions of nuclear strategy had frequently become mixed up with other disagreements over alliance policy. This tendency for nuclear doctrine to symbolise the broader politics of inter-allied relations did not disappear, of course, with the functioning of the Nuclear Planning Group, but it did help the United States and its European critics to confront directly their differences over nuclear strategy without, as was frequently the case previously, talking at cross-purposes. Among others, Thomas Schelling had taken the position that, as it had been presented, the alliance problem of nuclear sharing was essentially insoluble. In his view the McNamara initiative might enable the problem to be redefined in ways which would be more constructive for the cohesion of the alliance.[54] The Nuclear Planning Group, by offering a new set of institutional diplomatic procedures, altered the context in which alliance nuclear policy was discussed.

The adoption of the new procedures had been greatly aided by changes in the broader alliance political environment affecting allied nuclear politics. First and foremost, the withdrawal of France, which more than any other ally had manipulated the nuclear issue in pursuit of broader foreign policy goals, made allied agreement much easier to achieve. Of course it had been clear that even before these changes the participants in the McNamara Committee had found the exercise very useful and would have been unwilling to abandon the experiment even in the face of a French veto. What the French withdrawal and acceptance of the Defence Planning Committee had done was enable the NDAC and NPG to be set up and begin work without the additional and extraneous burden of a major alliance crisis brought about by French policy. The French action also relieved the pressures on German policy that had been brought about by the contradictory demands being made on it by the French on one hand and the Americans on the other.

In addition, the change of government in Bonn did much to clarify the contradictions of German nuclear policy, and to make a positive German contribution to the NPG possible. The new nuclear arrangements were widely interpreted as giving Germany a voice in the planning of nuclear strategy without giving her access to nuclear hardware or a 'finger on the trigger'. Brandt was reported as having informed the NATO Council that Bonn would not press for anything in the nuclear field which would stir up distrust, thus seeming to rule out future German demand for access to nuclear 'hardware'.[55] A major consequence of Brandt's position was that it was felt to open the way for the non-proliferation treaty, for the Russians had made it clear that there would be no treaty until the NATO nuclear debate had been resolved: a resolution which, as far as the Russians were concerned, would not give the Germans direct access of any kind to nuclear weapons.

The Americans and British in particular were anxious that the NATO debate on nuclear policy should not hinder the pursuit of a major arms control agreement with the Soviet Union. To the extent that the NPG procedures proved satisfactory, to the Germans especially, there would be less stress on the alliance from the non-proliferation treaty negotiations. In fact, the channelling of German nuclear aspirations into a more effective consultative arrangement than had existed in the past became an essential component of American détente diplomacy. Until the alliance nuclear issue had been 'defused' there were definite limits to what the United States could achieve through her policy of pursuing détente through arms control. Although the new German government placed very little value now on direct access to nuclear weapons, it nevertheless remained extremely sensitive to the strategic posture of the alliance and to any changes in it. Thus the Germans were conscious of the broad security implications of the 'negative link' that American diplomacy had forged between allied participation in nuclear policy-making and non-proliferation, and the NPT remained a source of strain on German–American relations. This strain was not entirely removed until yet another change of government had occurred in Bonn. The government of Willy Brandt, by pursuing through the *Ostpolitik* its own version of détente, was able to gain greater freedom of action for German policy than had ever been the case previously. In so doing it became possible for the Germans to separate their concerns with the nuclear strategy of the alliance from the diplomacy of détente. And in the meantime the NPG was available to the 'Grand Coalition' as a means of easing this policy transition.

By the beginning of 1967, then, the alliance had acquired through the Nuclear Planning Group a new set of consultative machinery. Politically and diplomatically the immediate importance of the NPG lay in its successful accommodation of Germany after the demise of the MLF. In the longer term, however, the test of the Nuclear Planning Group's effectiveness and significance would lie in the extent to which the nuclear consultation practised there would satisfy the interests and aspirations of all the various allies in influencing the nuclear policy of the alliance.

Previous attempts at satisfying allied aspirations in this area had been identified with the problems of 'nuclear sharing' and of 'nuclear control'. As such, all of the various proposals for some form of nuclear sharing eventually confronted the question of how a decision to resort to nuclear weapons would be made and, in particular, confronted the stark fact of the American veto. The Nuclear Planning Group represented an attempt to redefine the relationship of the United States to the non-nuclear weapon allies in such a way as to avoid the search for a formula by which the allies could share with the United States *control* over the decision as to whether or not nuclear weapons would be used. The intention was to mitigate through the NPG the impact of the American veto power on the confidence of her allies in the nuclear commitment of the United States by involving the allies more closely in the *process* by which a decision to use nuclear weapons might be reached. However, the logic of sharing the responsibility for saying 'yes' implied in the American approach to the NPG could be extended to a situation in which it was recognised that the allies, or a particular ally, might have to give their consent also as a prerequisite for action. Obviously, the extreme case of this would be where an ally has the ability to say 'no' and to deny any recourse to nuclear weapons. And indeed the Germans by the first meeting of the NPG were raising the question of whether the host country should not have a veto over any decision to use nuclear weapons based on its territory.[56]

Within NATO what constitutes a veto is inevitably bound up with the rule of unanimous consent for action, though in fact there is some ambiguity as to the scope and definition of this rule. Essentially NATO operates on the basis of seeking consensus, attempting by this means to respect the fact that the alliance was founded on the traditional premise of the sovereign equality of its members. A former member of the NATO Secretariat has described the process as follows.

A consensus in NATO does not require unanimous explicit support, but rather the absence of objections to whatever the chairman of a committee determines to be the sense of the meeting. When each speaker on a topic has had his say, and a debate on the question at hand has taken place, the chairman may ask if those who have not already spoken wish to do so, and may then offer a summing-up. He may then specifically ask each country to say whether it accepts his findings, or alternatively, simply close the matter in the absence of objections. Countries may say that they object to part or all of his statement or that they fully support it; and the chairman may adjust his summing-up according to objections if he feels that such a move will broaden support or establish a full consensus.[57]

In this system there is no formal voting as such and the further question arises as to what constitutes a consensus for collective action; whether, in fact, unanimity is required.

It has been asserted, for example, that there is no rule of unanimity operating in NATO at all. At the time of the 'French crisis' a Senate staff report argued that on the basis of article 3 of the Treaty, emphasis was placed on separate and joint action to maintain and develop the individual and collective capacity to resist aggression. In addition, article 5 provided for each ally to respond as it deemed necessary in the event of an attack. Thus, according to this argument the only requirement in the Treaty for unanimity was for the admission of new members.[58] Nevertheless, it is always desirable to seek unanimity, and in certain circumstances unanimity may be politically necessary. Anyway, on a number of occasions the argument that there is no rule of unanimity in NATO has been rejected, most notably by the French.

Basically, the requirement for unanimity can be interpreted in the following ways, all of which are applicable to various aspects of alliance practice. First, it can be argued that unless all are positively in favour no action can be taken. Thus the absence of a positive affirmation of support for a proposal would in effect constitute a veto on alliance action. Essentially, this was the position of the French government when it opposed revisions of alliance strategy in the direction of flexible response, when it opposed the MLF, and when it threatened to veto any attempt to give permanent status to the McNamara Committee. Another interpretation would simply require the absence of positive opposition for action to be taken. In other words, abstention or silence would not stop collective action in the name of the alliance. In this case it is understood that those abstaining are not necessarily required to act themselves. For example, this would conform to the situation of Denmark and Norway not allowing nuclear weapons to be deployed on their territory in peacetime, though they accept that alliance strategy is dependent on the deployment of nuclear weapons in the European theatre.

Even in the absence of the above two conditions, it remains possible for a number of allies to undertake joint action as a sub-group within the alliance without generating significant strain on the alliance as a whole. It is a quite acceptable practice in NATO, for instance, for a minority of allies to form alliance organisations for the purpose of benefiting from joint production or logistics arrangements. However, an attempt by even a majority of the allies to undertake collective action in a sensitive area against the declared opposition of one or more allies would result of course in a great deal of stress. This would be true even if the group in favour of a certain course of action attempted to operate outside the formal framework of the alliance. The examples of France with respect to the MLF and the Special Committee of Defence Ministers have already been cited.

Finally, the situation can exist in which one or more of the allies may have the power to act in ways crucially affecting the interests of the others, but which is not subject to any formal requirement of consensus or unanimity at all. The extreme example of this would be in a crisis involving decisions about the use of nuclear weapons. Circumstances might dictate that the nuclear powers take decisions without attempting to secure allied agreement. Within the framework of alliance there are two typical responses to this situation, neither of which is necessarily mutually exclusive of the other. A government may seek to exercise a veto over particular actions of its allies and, preferably, have this veto power sanctioned by some kind of alliance declaratory policy. Secondly, governments will emphasise the importance of inter-allied consultation. At the heart of the difficulties within NATO on the question of nuclear policy was the fact that in this crucial area the United States was virtually the sole decision-maker. The 'hardware' and collective ownership approaches to the problem of nuclear sharing in the alliance had all, in one way or another, involved the attempt by various allies to obtain some power of veto. The Nuclear Planning Group, on the other hand, stressed the consultative approach, though it should be noted that even then questions concerning the right of veto were to be of major concern to the NPG in the initial period of its operation.

Of course the ability to exercise a veto over the use of nuclear weapons would not give a non-nuclear ally a corresponding ability to ensure that nuclear weapons would in fact be used. The so-called problem of 'how many fingers on the trigger' illustrated the incompatibilities between the desirability of shared decision-making and the requirements of credibility that in a crisis a decision to use nuclear weapons might be taken. It was in order to ensure that their nuclear weapons might be used, as well as to retain control over the right to decide if they would be used, that the Americans gave so much attention to the physical and technical aspects of their command and control. In general it has been the concern of the United States to avoid compromising its power to decide when nuclear weapons would be used. In NATO, this has resulted in the allies of the United States being concerned with two contradictory considerations at the same time, and to which the non-nuclear allies have been particularly sensitive.

On the one hand the allies wish to avoid a situation in which the United States would resort to nuclear weapons in defence of interests which in their view would result in unacceptable costs. On the other hand the allies must be concerned with the credibility of the American nuclear commitment to their security, which means that it should be readily conceivable that the United States would use nuclear weapons in circumstances other than a direct attack on itself. The first concern which, in effect, amounts to a fear that the Americans might too readily resort to nuclear weapons, leads allies to seek an effective veto over their use. The second concern which is that the United States might be unwilling to use her nuclear weapons in support of her allies encourages them to seek ways of reinforcing the credibility of the American guarantee, including ways of circumventing or lessening the impact of the American veto. Naturally these concerns operate differently with allies at different times depending, among other considerations, on the general strategic environment within which the alliance is operating. At the risk of over-simplification it may be said that during the period of 'massive retaliation' the allies tended to be more concerned with the fear that the United States might too readily resort to nuclear weapons. In the changed strategic environment of the sixties, however, the allies were more sensitive to the apparent weakening of the American guarantee.

Under the control arrangements governing American nuclear warheads stockpiled in Europe for possible allied use, the United States has retained the power to decide whether the weapons could be used but not the power to decide that in fact they would be used, since the consent of the allied government controlling the means of delivery would also be required. Nevertheless, a significant proportion of the theatre nuclear weapons available are stockpiled for the use of American forces and so are not subject to such constraints. In addition, virtually all of the strategic forces of the United States remain outside any formal system of alliance control.[59] These forces which are not subject to any form of alliance veto represent the bulk of the American component in the central strategic balance and consequently have a major impact on the level of security enjoyed by the various allies. In recognition of this fact it was anticipated that one of the major tasks of the Nuclear Planning Group would be to open up the deterrent forces of the United States to greater allied influence. On their part the Americans were concerned that their ability to exercise centralised control over the implementation of alliance strategy in the event of conflict was not ultimately affected.

This latter consideration represented a substantial limitation on the likely scope of the Nuclear Planning Group's activities which has been felt particularly in the field of strategic weapons where, by and large, and despite initial expectations, the NPG has had least impact. Additional constraints on the operation of the Nuclear Planning Group were imposed by the United States Atomic Energy Act. In order to maintain nuclear secrecy, the Act has placed a series of injunctions on the administration limiting the amount of information about nuclear matters that can be divulged to the NATO allies.[60] On the eve of the first formal meeting of the NPG, McNamara publicly recognised that these legislative restrictions would have to be adhered to by the Americans when consulting with their allies in the new body. McNamara also drew attention to one further limitation on the consultative scope of the NPG: this was that discussion would be limited to NATO operations.[61] Obviously such a limitation reflected the terms of the North Atlantic Treaty, but the question of to what extent the alliance should recognise linkages between events in the broader international environment outside the North Atlantic area and the concerns of NATO was an old and potentially divisive one. It did not prevent, for example, the Americans from raising issues in connection with Vietnam in subsequent meetings of the NPG. Inevitably what went on in the NPG would be part of the broader processes of alliance political consultation, and the scope of the consultation practised would be determined ultimately by the experience of actually operating the Nuclear Planning Group machinery.

3. THE EARLY YEARS: 1967-9

In a press conference prior to the first meeting of the Nuclear Planning Group (NPG) which was held in Washington on 6–7 April 1967, and in evidence to a Senate sub-committee the previous June, the American Secretary of Defense, Robert McNamara, outlined the administration's view of what the objectives of the NPG should be. In McNamara's view the NPG should continue the process initiated by the original working group on nuclear planning of exposing the non-nuclear allies

more fully and more intimately to the entire spectrum of nuclear activity starting with the analysis of the threat. The consideration of the research and development programmes necessary to assure weapons will be developed to meet that threat effectively, the determination of the size of the force structure, the strategy to provide for the use of that structure and the tactical and operational plans contemplating such use.[1]

In effect McNamara saw the allies as participating in a process of planning how and under what circumstances nuclear weapons might be used, and of considering how allied consultation might be improved should the decision to use nuclear weapons be contemplated. McNamara gave the impression, however, that he was concerned with emphasising the contribution the NPG could make to nuclear planning rather than its contribution to decision-making concerning nuclear weapons. He wished to generate a common understanding of the considerations and factors entering into the determination of nuclear policy. Not merely was the acceptance of a common nuclear doctrine sought (the early meetings of the NPG coincided with the formal acceptance by the alliance of the strategic concept of flexible response), but also shared

69

understanding of the intellectual assumptions and approaches by which American nuclear policy was determined.[2]

Emphasis on allied consultation and participation in planning was politically and operationally more feasible for the United States than was consideration of allied participation in nuclear decision-making. The McNamara initiative which had led to the creation of the NPG represented an attempt to shift the politics of nuclear sharing in the alliance away from 'hardware' and 'collective ownership' solutions to the problems created by the central place occupied by nuclear weapons in the strategy of the alliance. The Americans hoped that the NPG would provide an escape from issues of physical control of nuclear weapons which had previously bedevilled the nuclear debate and which had been brought together in concentrated form in the proposals for a multilateral force.

It was the firm intention of American policy that the work of the NPG would go forward on the premise that the right of the President of the United States to authorise the use of American nuclear weapons was not at issue. The object of American policy was to associate the allies with the process by which consideration was given to the circumstances in which nuclear weapons might possibly be used. In June 1966, explaining the work of the earlier working group on nuclear planning to the Jackson Committee, McNamara was careful to draw a distinction between the power of the United States to exercise a veto over the use of nuclear weapons, which he claimed was not at issue, and the degree of allied participation in the planning for the possible use of nuclear weapons and their participation in consultation regarding a decision to use them. McNamara stated that he believed no allied political leader in NATO had asked the United States to give up its veto power, or had asked that the United States delegate the power of decision over nuclear weapons to any other state or group of states without her own participation. He stated specifically that the United States had no plans for delegating control over nuclear weapons to any other nation or group of nations.[3]

In considering what participation in the NPG might mean with respect to allied consultation on nuclear policy it should be noted that the veto power which the United States was not willing to relinquish was essentially a negative power – the ability to say 'no'. The possession of a veto did not logically or practically rule out the possibility of saying 'yes'. A major task of the NPG as American officials conceived it in April 1967 was to examine ways in which the allies could be associated in a mutually acceptable manner with the processes of nuclear planning affecting the alliance. Following from the work of the working committees that had been established by the Special Committee of Defence Ministers, attention was thus given to ensuring the access of the allies to adequate intelligence data and to considering the technical requirements for effective crisis consultation in a nuclear environment. In addition it was hoped that the NPG would help bring about among the allies a common familiarity with the rationale underlying American strategic doctrine. At root for the United States the NPG was a device for building confidence among the allies that a credible strategic posture existed and could be maintained. Through consultation, the allies would be assured that the nuclear weapons under American control were available for their defence and would be used if necessary. At its simplest, the NPG was seen as a means by which the allies could be persuaded to think alike on questions of nuclear strategy.

The initial meeting of the NPG provided the first occasion since the meeting of the nuclear planning working group in February 1966 for a discussion on the general strategic situation, and also provided an opportunity for the briefing of the Canadians and the Dutch who had not been members of the working group. In fact, the meeting began with the United States Secretary of Defense, Robert McNamara, giving a detailed account of the overall strategic situation as seen by the United States. This established a precedent for the agenda of subsequent meetings. In particular, McNamara led a discussion on the question of the possible deployment of anti-ballistic missile (ABM) systems, raising the technical, strategic and financial aspects of the issue as well as reporting on the state of the Soviet Union's programme. The ABM question was particularly sensitive in the light of the announcement made by President Johnson in March that agreement had been reached with Mr Kosygin that the Soviet Union and the United

States would enter into discussions on limiting defensive as well as offensive nuclear weapons. McNamara reported to the NPG on these discussions and undertook to keep the allies fully advised on future developments.[4] Thus, from the very beginning of the NPG, questions related to the central strategic balance were raised, as were questions related to the strategic policy of the United States towards it. The consequences for nuclear arms control were an important aspect of the interrelationship between the strategic policy of the United States and the central strategic balance, and, again at the very first meeting of the NPG, the United States undertook to keep its allies informed on what was going on. One non-American source was reported as saying that this was the first time that the United States, facing a major bilateral arms control negotiation, had taken its allies fully into its confidence.[5] Implicit in this American commitment was a similar obligation on the part of Britain, the only other nuclear power in the NPG, to keep the allies informed as well.

Issues of more direct concern to the non-nuclear allies were raised by the Turkish and German defence ministers. Discussions concerning the overall strategic balance and the development of American policy towards it were undoubtedly relevant to the nuclear policy of the alliance, but of more immediate concern were the implications of these strategic developments for the security and political options of individual allies. The European allies especially were concerned with the practical consequences for NATO that followed these developments, and with the role to be played by nuclear weapons in the strategic posture of the alliance. Thus the Turks presented a discussion paper on atomic demolition munitions (ADMs) raising, in the words of the communiqué, 'considerations related to the possible use of these weapons in defence of the treaty area'.[6]

The bland words of the communiqué covered what became a lively issue for the NPG, raising strong echoes of an earlier proposal associated with General Trettner for a defence posture based on an 'atomic tripwire'. This proposal had received endorsement from Kai-Uwe von Hassel, Defence Minister in the previous German government, and had aroused considerable controversy in Germany and elsewhere. In an article in *Foreign Affairs*, von Hassel had argued that the concept of flexible response should not be interpreted to mean that the 'so-called' atomic threshold could be raised unduly high without reference to political considerations. 'Apart from the fact that this would lead the potential aggressor to think that he could calculate his risk, it would create a situation in which he could seize pawns for future negotiations.' In order to prevent this, von Hassel proposed that atomic demolition munitions, nuclear air-defence weapons and, if need be, battlefield nuclear weapons be readied for employment in an early phase of a recognisable attack on Europe. Only in this way, it was argued, could a last determined warning be given to the enemy without involving escalation as a consequence. Further, a prolonged conventional war would lead rapidly to the attrition of NATO forces, jeopardise the operational readiness of the nuclear capability and thus shift the balance of power in favour of the enemy.[7] The two most controversial aspects of this proposal were its apparent willingness to envisage a lower nuclear threshold and its implication of the relaxation of American control over the decision to resort to nuclear weapons. According to a report by William M. Beecher in the *New York Times*, the Turkish proposal again suggested a relaxation of American control over nuclear weapons in order to permit the earlier use of ADMs in the event of an attack. Turkey was reported as arguing that the existing arrangements were too slow and suggested as an alternative a carefully spelled-out pre-delegation of authority to SACEUR to release ADMs in the event of a troop build-up and imminent threat along the border, and advance permission to explode them under very specific circumstances.[8]

There was an immediate denial from the Pentagon after the publication of these reports that Turkey had proposed the building of a nuclear mine-belt along her borders. The Pentagon spokesman claimed that the idea of a nuclear tripwire had little appeal, but he added that the possible role that could be played by ADMs in the defence of Europe was being considered.[9] It was clear, however, that the question of revised control and release arrangements with respect to various classes of nuclear weapon located in Europe had been raised at the meeting of the NPG and was to remain on the agenda of subsequent meetings. The importance of this issue was underlined by a report to the Assembly of Western European Union in December. The report stated that existing *political* controls over the selective release of 'even small-yield tactical weapons such as ADMs' were such that these were unlikely to be used until hostile forces had penetrated deep into the territory of the alliance. The report went on to suggest that means should be developed to permit the selective early release of tactical nuclear weapons so that they could be used to their utmost effect against the adversary while his forces were still massed at the early stages of an aggression, rather than being employed only when his forces were dispersed and holding areas and cities which could be damaged or destroyed by the use of such weapons. The suggestion was made that a military solution to a political problem might be for the member governments of the alliance to give prior consent to the use of tactical nuclear weapons in certain circumstances. This would be done by means of a system in which the use of static or small-yield tactical nuclear weapons could be allowed to escalate up to an agreed point once the political go-ahead had been given, but each step in the use of higher-yield weapons would be controlled by separate political decisions.[10] Whatever the merits of such proposals, the report is valuable in indicating the kinds of arguments with which the Americans were being confronted by European spokesmen at this time.

The German Defence Minister, Dr Schröder, had been closely associated with the support for the MLF in the previous German government, and he was thought to be still sympathetic towards this approach to the problems of alliance nuclear policy. At the first meeting he took the opportunity to raise the question of the role of the host country in allied arrangements for the planning and use of nuclear weapons.[11] Schröder was reported as having delineated the problems of a power without nuclear weapons of its own in influencing decisions governing the targeting, deployment and possible use of nuclear weapons on its soil. In effect, Schröder pressed for what amounted to a veto power over the firing of nuclear weapons from German territory.[12] That the Germans should raise this issue now reflected the recent change in government which had brought the Social Democrats into the coalition. The previous German Chancellor, Ludwig Erhard, had been under some domestic pressure to raise the question of a 'host country veto' when he had met with President Johnson in December 1965, but had failed to do so. Now German concerns had been placed explicitly on the alliance agenda.

Apparently the Germans claimed that the existing arrangements for consultation in the event of the possible use of nuclear weapons in defence of the NATO area discriminated against them. One of their concerns was that the United States maintained procedures for consulting with other governments on whose territories nuclear weapons were based, but not with them.[13] Certainly Britain enjoyed a special relationship with the United States in this respect as in other matters concerning nuclear weapons, but it was not clear that Germany was treated differently from any of the other non-nuclear allies. The only general guidelines which existed covering nuclear consultation in the alliance were the 'Athens guidelines' of 1962 which anyway had never been fully implemented. And it was clear by the first meeting of the NPG that these guidelines were by no means adequate to the task of laying down a consistent and comprehensive code of practice covering the consultative relationship between the United States and the various NATO allies hosting its nuclear warheads on their territory. These German concerns were widely shared by the other European allies as was indicated in a report to the Assembly of Western European Union in October 1968. Included in the report was a specific recommendation that the NPG should formulate guidelines concerning the powers of the North Atlantic Council relative to the firing of nuclear weapons by the forces of the alliance.[14] A second German concern, again shared by other European allies, specifically concerned the assent of the host government to the firing of nuclear weapons from its territory. In the German case the problem extended not only to the nuclear-capable forces of the United States, but also to the other allied nuclear-capable forces based on its territory. These latter forces created a somewhat anomalous situation as was noted in the WEU report already cited. In the event of a decision to use these forces the consent of the President of the United States would of course be required as, theoretically, would be the consent of the government of the ally possessing the nuclear-capable forces; however, there was no specific requirement that the German government, from whose territory these or the purely American-controlled weapons would be fired, need give its consent.[15]

Both the German and Turkish presentations raised, albeit in different ways, the political question of how nuclear weapons deployed on behalf of the alliance were to be commanded and controlled. The fundamental questions of how and under what circumstances the alliance might go to nuclear war remained. Although the NPG had not been set up ostensibly as an alternative to the 'hardware' approaches to the problem taken previously, nevertheless how the NPG dealt with these questions would be crucial to its political effectiveness. Anyway, the immediate reaction of the Group was to initiate further studies on the matters introduced by the German and Turkish defence ministers.

According to the communiqué, the British Minister of Defence, Denis Healey, led a discussion on tactical nuclear forces. This followed from British initiatives in this area undertaken at the London meeting of the working group the previous year. Subsequent to this discussion, agreement was reached among those present that the number of tactical nuclear weapons available to the alliance was adequate, but it was also noted that the appropriate distribution of types of weapons should be kept under continuous review. The defence ministers' acceptance of the numbers of tactical nuclear weapons as adequate paralleled their agreement that the size of the strategic forces available and the plans for employing them were adequate to the need.[16] This endorsement of the posture of the strategic forces reiterated one which had already been given in the working group, and it indicates that the United States was concerned with obtaining as many reinforcements of its current strategic policy as possible. This process was to culminate in December with the formal acceptance by the NATO Council of 'flexible response' as the alliance strategic doctrine. A consequence of the acceptance of flexible response, however, was the emphasis on questions concerning the role to be played by tactical nuclear weapons, and it is evident that, unlike the situation with respect to strategic weapons, there was no ready acceptance that the plans concerning them were adequate to the need. Somewhat against the expectations of the Americans at the time of the initial McNamara proposal, it became clear at the first meeting of the NPG that issues concerning what were then termed 'theatre nuclear weapons' were to form a dominant element in the work of the NPG.[17]

A week before the second meeting of the NPG was to be held in Ankara in September 1967, McNamara made a speech in San Francisco announcing the decision of the United States to deploy the Sentinel ABM system against predicted Chinese strategic capabilities. The timing and form of the announcement created considerable resentment among the allies which was reflected during the course of the Ankara meeting. Some of the allies felt that the announcement had been made without sufficient consultation and that the United States had failed to honour its obligations to the NPG. The results of studies into the possibility of a European ABM system were on the agenda of the Ankara meeting and the American action was felt to compromise the forthcoming discussion and to devalue the NPG as a consultative mechanism for the discussion of nuclear policy. The timing of the incident was unfortunate, occurring as it did so early in the development of the NPG, for even if some of the allied response could be described as overreaction, nevertheless, the ABM announcement provided effective ammunition to those who were sceptical as to the value of the NPG.

McNamara attempted to justify the American action at a press conference held on the eve of the Ankara meeting. He maintained that in fact the allies had been kept fully informed of American ABM plans, referring to the discussions which had occurred in Washington in April, and claiming that the subject had been discussed 'during the last two or three weeks' in various NATO Council meetings. He argued also that, although the possibility of a European ABM was about to be discussed, the Sentinel system had no relationship to NATO but was oriented to a possible Chinese strategic threat to the United States emerging in the 1970s.[18] This explanation was not entirely satisfactory to the other members of the NPG; Denis Healey in particular was apparently active in criticising American actions.[19] McNamara was on weak ground anyway, since the decision to deploy an ABM system was one which he accepted with evident reluctance. It ran counter to his publicly stated doubts as to the effectiveness of the ABM and to his concern with the possibly adverse arms control consequences of such a deployment. The fact that he acceded to the decision and the timing of it demonstrated the very great domestic political pressures to which he was subject on this issue.[20] Allied spokesmen, however sympathetic they may have been privately to the embarrassments of McNamara's position, could only point out that a decision with such potentially significant effects on the structure and deployment of American strategic forces was one to be fully discussed in the new NATO body set up in their view for just such a purpose.

It is worth dwelling on the impact of the ABM announcement at Ankara because it is illustrative of the nature and some of the difficulties of the consultative process in NATO. First, the announcement provided an example of the way in which domestic political priorities can run counter to international commitments. Evidently there had been an understanding at the April meeting of the NPG that there was not going to be any sudden decision on the part of the United States concerning the building of an ABM against the Chinese since it would take far longer for China to build an offensive system than it would for the Americans to set up a defence.[21] Thus the September announcement took the allies by surprise, something which consultative procedures are intended to avoid.

McNamara's difficulties with the allied defence ministers arose partly from the tactics he pursued in the domestic debate on the ABM. These were essentially Fabian tactics of delay and small incremental shifts of position. Thus he had held out the possibility of restricting ABM deployment to the protection of the Minutemen missile bases, or of simply deploying a 'thin' system against the Chinese. It was this latter decision which was announced in the San Francisco speech, although McNamara also claimed in that speech that the proposed deployment would have the additional advantage of protecting the Minutemen sites against Soviet attack.[22] But as part of his delaying tactics McNamara had also argued that any firm decision should not anticipate arms control negotiations with the Soviet Union. At the April NPG meeting he had briefed the allies on this point, reporting that the March Kosygin–Johnson summit had led to the inclusion of defensive weapons in proposed arms limitation discussions. However, in the meantime Kosygin had met with Johnson at Glassboro in June and rejected any mutual limitations on ABM development. This rejection undermined McNamara's tactic of delaying a decision in the expectation of arms limitation talks with the Soviet Union.[23] Somewhat surprisingly, there is little evidence that McNamara sought to use his commitments to the NPG on the ABM issue as additional ammunition in Washington although there is some evidence that as a result of the allied discussions at Ankara he was able to declare, despite his San Francisco speech, that no decision had been made as to whether the option would now be exercised to extend the proposed Sentinel system to defend the Minutemen sites.[24] Like the proposed arms limitation talks with the Russians, the NPG was available for a similar tactical use in the Washington debate.

The ABM issue had domestic political consequences for some of the allies too, and affected their responses to the American decision. The Canadian government, for example, was immediately sensitive to McNamara's announcement. Apart from the possible implications of ABM deployment for continental defence and the Canadian strategic position, the Canadian government was embarrassed by the manner of the announcement in the light of the inevitably negative response to the American decision from sections of Canadian opinion. The decision, seemingly taken without adequate consultation, exposed the Canadian government to the adverse criticism of those critical of the Canadian defence relationship with the United States anyway, and made it difficult for Ottawa to be supportive publicly of American policy. Again, the deployment of an ABM system by the United States, whatever its proposed form, could always be interpreted in Europe as providing strategic options for the United States which would not necessarily enhance European security. It could be argued that undesirable consequences for the overall level of strategic stability flowed from what could be presented as a unilateral American decision. Such responses were doubtless in some cases disingenuous, or the result of immediate and unreflective reaction rather than strategic analysis; nevertheless, they represented political realities that had to be taken into account by the various allied governments. In effect, European critics of the United States were able to usurp arguments put forward by American opponents of Washington's position. Political sensitivities were particularly great in West Germany where divisions on defence policy existed in the new coalition government, divisions which could be exacerbated by the ABM issue. The allied response to the ABM announcement reconfirmed that in matters of nuclear policy their interests were both strategic and political in character. McNamara's general briefing to the NPG, then, on the American decision respecting the Sentinel system had a political significance beyond that which would normally be associated with the informing of allies about national decisions. His task was to allay allied doubts about the adequacy of the NPG as a means by which the United States would consult with its allies on strategic decisions which could affect their interests. To this end McNamara again committed the United States to keep her allies informed on the course of arms limitation discussions with the Soviet Union and briefed the allies on the current state of these discussions.[25]

In addition to discussing the question of anti-ballistic missile defence in the context of McNamara's briefing on the ABM decision and his defence of it, the Ankara meeting of the NPG also considered a study in connection with the possible deployment of an ABM system in Europe. The consideration of this study was led by Healey, who held the view that a

European system would not be particularly useful or viable, and that any attempt to develop such a system would have unfortunate consequences for the prospects for arms control and détente. In the view of one participant in the meeting, the fact that the NPG did not immediately endorse this view was a reflection of European dissatisfaction with the manner in which the American decision had been made.[26] Thus it was not until the following spring that the NPG agreed that an ABM system was not viable for Europe.

The rest of the agenda of the Ankara meeting was dominated by issues concerning theatre nuclear weapons. Issues raised in April were again considered in the form of interim reports on the studies which had been initiated at the Washington meeting of the NPG. The whole question of theatre nuclear weapons, their role, credibility, and political control, was to form the centrepiece of the work and agenda of the NPG and guidance was given for the continuation of studies in all these areas. One new element was added however, in the form of an Italian-led discussion of the role of national participation in the process of alliance military nuclear planning. It was agreed that suggested improvements in this respect in connection with the work of the Military Committee would be dealt with in a more comprehensive report to be presented to the next meeting of the NPG which was to be held in the Hague in April 1968.[27]

The Hague meeting was marked by a significant change in personnel: the new United States Secretary of Defense, Clark Clifford, attended for the first time. The absence of McNamara was significant in that he had been the major sponsor of the NPG and his successor was neither as influential nor as committed to the success of the NPG as McNamara had been. Clifford himself was to be replaced by Melvin Laird a year later, and it has been claimed that during this period Denis Healey played the major role in maintaining the momentum of the work of the NPG.[28] Certainly at this time American foreign policy was preoccupied with Vietnam and it was difficult to obtain any priority of attention for alliance problems in Washington. In these circumstances an American Secretary of Defense, new to the post and not enjoying the weight in the administration possessed by his predecessor, might have been tempted to downgrade the importance of the NPG and the American commitment to nuclear consultation through it.

The occasion of the Hague meeting of the NPG provided Clifford with the opportunity to familiarise himself with his colleagues through a series of bilateral meetings. A major topic of discussion was the Non-Proliferation Treaty of which the complete draft agreed by the Soviet Union and the United States had been tabled in Geneva in January, and which was shortly to be presented to the United Nations. The Non-Proliferation Treaty was essentially the product of bilateral negotiation between the Soviet Union and the United States, and one of the American objectives in the NPG as in other alliance institutions was to meet European concerns that the United States and Soviet Union would be able to reach a series of understandings over their heads. European governments were concerned not only with the terms of the Non-Proliferation Treaty as such (though the treaty posed problems enough for the non-nuclear European allies), but also with the implications of the Treaty for Soviet–American relations and with their relations with the United States. American policy towards détente with the Soviet Union at this time was centred on the development of mutually acceptable arms control and arms limitation measures designed to stabilise the central strategic balance and enhance the security position of the United States. Essentially, the United States was taking a position with respect to its European allies that the security of the West was indivisible and that consequently American policy would have beneficial effects on the security of all. However, although it was clear that the effect of American policy would be to transform the established pattern of military confrontation, there were European doubts as to the consequences for them, and a perception that the interests of the United States and its European allies in détente could diverge.[29] In particular, the Europeans were concerned that they be fully consulted with respect to any arrangements made for Europe. And as the emerging *Ostpolitik* of the Kiesinger government was to make clear, West Germany by following her own version of détente was determined to ensure that 'consultation' in effect included a German power of veto. One manifestation of this which was of direct consequence to the work of the NPG was the German desire to establish clearly the rights of the host country over the decision to use nuclear weapons deployed on its territory.

The implications of détente and the associated issues concerning East–West relations over arms limitation and arms control were matters central to the activities of the NATO Council and its subordinate structures, and to inter-allied diplomacy generally. The Declaration on Mutual and Balanced Force Reductions produced at Reykjavik in June, and the more comprehensive Declaration on East–West Relations in December the following year, represented products of the general process of alliance consultation taking place on these matters. As will emerge, the role of the NPG in all this was a restricted one; but one, nevertheless, salient and intimately bound up with the political and security consequences of the changing strategic relationship between East and West. The Non-Proliferation Treaty was a part of this changing strategic relationship. Of immediate and particular concern to the allied defence ministers at the Hague, however, was the compatibility of the Treaty with the operations and functions of the NPG and its impact on the possibility of developing some European nuclear defence identity in the future.

A major stumbling block to the negotiation of the Non-Proliferation Treaty had been the proposed multilateral force (MLF). The Russians had refused to accept any treaty compatible with the MLF, being concerned with preventing the Germans in particular from gaining any significant control over elements of strategic nuclear power and wishing to ensure through the provisions of the Non-Proliferation Treaty that proposals to share ownership and control of nuclear hardware would be ruled out. It was central to the Russian position on arms control that there be no diminution of the American veto on the use of nuclear weapons even in the rather spurious form proposed in the MLF. The effect of the stand taken by the Russians was not only to delay the conclusion of an arms control agreement, which the United States regarded as crucial to its view of détente, but also to complicate inter-allied relations generally, and those of Germany and the United States in particular. Thus, the United States supported by Britain sought to assure the allies that the procedures for consultation on alliance nuclear policy and planning embodied in the NPG were compatible with the Non-Proliferation Treaty and not compromised by it. At the same time, in order to get final Russian acceptance of the Treaty, the Americans were assuring the Russians that nothing that the NPG was doing was in any way incompatible with it. Undoubtedly, however, the Treaty established limits to the kinds of proposals that the NPG could make with respect to nuclear sharing in the alliance, ruling out hardware suggestions such as the MLF and inhibiting any proposal that could be construed as constituting proliferation. But already the American loss of interest in the MLF and the initiative that led to the NPG had clearly indicated that the new consultative body was to be seen as an alternative to proliferation.[30] By participating in the NPG, the allies had accepted this too. What was of concern to allied capitals was the fact that a United States–Soviet agreement effectively imposed limits on the scope of inter-allied solutions to the political problems of alliance nuclear policy, in effect giving the Soviet Union a claim to exercise a veto on certain kinds of policy alternative and providing a basis on which it could subsequently seek to establish a precedent for intervening politically in Western European policy debates.

A rather peripheral issue raised at this time, but one reflecting both European doubts and European aspirations, was the question of whether the NPT ruled out a future European defence entity from possessing nuclear weapons. The official alliance view with respect to this question, and with respect to the position of the NPG, was reflected in an answer given in a parliamentary question by British Minister of State for Foreign Affairs, Fred Mulley, later in the summer. In his view, articles I and II of the NPT were not to be interpreted as prohibiting NATO nuclear consultation and planning or the 'permanent committee established for this purpose'. Nor did the Treaty disturb existing bilateral arrangements for deployment of nuclear weapons within allied territory, or the transfer of nuclear-capable delivery vehicles and, in the view of the British government, the Treaty could not be interpreted as barring any future federated European state from succeeding to the former nuclear status of one of its components.[31]

Apart from the discussions arising from the NPT and the general strategic overview from the Americans which had become an established feature of the NPG agenda, the allied defence ministers had a wide range of business to deal with. As had been anticipated in Ankara, the ministers concluded that the deployment of a European ABM system was not justified. The Dutch Minister of Defence summed up the conclusions of the meeting in a statement in which he indicated that a European ABM would be too costly, not totally effective, and might compromise arms limitation discussions between the United States and Soviet Union.[32] The persistent issue of atomic demolition munitions, initially raised by Turkey at the Washington meeting, again achieved prominence. This time the issue was raised by Greece which had replaced Turkey on the NPG. The Turks were reported as being no longer willing to place high priority on the question of how ADMs should be deployed and possibly used. Participation in the discussions and studies conducted within the NPG had served to 'educate' the participants in the difficulties of command and control and the tactical limitations of these weapons.[33] Greece, however, was not only new to the NPG, but could be expected to display an interest in a topic to which Turkey had devoted so much attention. The whole question of the possible tactical use of nuclear weapons in Europe continued to be of major concern to the NPG, and the role of ADMs was included in the studies on theatre nuclear weapons which the four permanent members of the NPG were commissioned to present to the next meeting.

The attitude of the Greeks and Turks to the work of the NPG and to the whole question of nuclear sharing in NATO could be characterised as a desire for access to nuclear weapons without having given a great deal of thought to the consequences of doing so. From their point of view, access was desirable because it seemed to involve little or no political or financial cost and, anyway, it would have been unthinkable for one to gain some kind of access to nuclear weapons without the other doing so as well. Actually, for all the smaller NATO allies, participation in the NPG had elements of satisfying demands for formal recognition of status in the alliance without necessarily involving them in any new commitments and responsibilities. Of course there were also many differences in attitude towards the NPG which can be seen as having arisen from differences in their political and strategic situations. With respect to nuclear weapons, those countries involved with the Central Front clearly had a greater and more immediate interest in alliance nuclear policy than did the Scandinavians or those involved with the southern flank. This greater concern arose not only from the fact that the Central Front was considered to be the key area in the overall European security system, but also because this was the area where the bulk of the nuclear-capable forces in Europe were deployed and where the most extensive plans for their use existed. Nevertheless, of all the matters considered by the NPG, those connected with theatre nuclear weapons were likely to engage the greatest interest of all the smaller allies in the sense of their wishing consultation to amount to something more than a one-way briefing on strategic developments. In particular, all those countries possessing nuclear-capable forces and hosting American nuclear warheads wanted a genuine input into the processes by which policy affecting those forces was determined. For the smaller powers on the Central Front, however, the strategic environment in which they operated was far more complex and the nuclear component more significant than it was for the other smaller allies.[34]

The major allies of the United States participating in the NPG could hope to secure more from consultation than formal recognition of status and some influence on policy regarding theatre nuclear weapons. For Germany and the United Kingdom at least, though each in different ways and with different interests in view, there was the possibility of having an impact on the pattern of military confrontation that underlaid the structure of international security in Europe, and of making policy choices which could affect the political relationships between East and West which flowed from that security structure. But the position of Italy in all this was somewhat anomalous when compared with that of either Britain or Germany. Though accorded formal equality of status as a permanent member of the NPG, Italy possessed nothing like the military and political influence of its two major European allies over alliance policy. And whatever its aspirations in this respect it was difficult for Italian spokesmen to overcome the handicaps imposed by the weaknesses and instabilities of their domestic political system.

Following from an Italian initiative at the previous meeting of the NPG, the defence ministers at the Hague agreed to make recommendations to the Nuclear Defence Affairs Committee for increasing national participation in military nuclear planning.[35] What these recommendations were was never formally made public but it is known that at the end of 1968 revised procedures were introduced governing allied representation at the Joint Strategic Targeting Centre at Omaha. As a result of decisions reached at the Ottawa meeting of the NATO Council in 1963, allied officers had been assigned to the Joint Strategic Target Planning Staff. From 1963 to 1966 officers from Italy, Britain, Germany and France were assigned on the assumption that these positions would be rotated among countries contributing forces to the various nuclear missions of the alliance, and when France withdrew in 1966 Belgium took her place. In 1968 Britain, Germany and Italy were given permanent representation at Omaha with a fourth position to be rotated among the other allies that qualified. The tour was to be of three years and it was understood that the officers assigned to the Joint Strategic Target Planning Staff would be concerned only with material linked with the command responsibilities of SACEUR, and would have access only to strategic plans connected with NATO.[36]

Whatever the details of the recommendations stemming from the Italian initiative, any attempt to increase national participation in the military aspects of nuclear planning would amount to very little in substance. In the first place, given the weaknesses of the Italian Ministry of Defence, Italian initiatives in the alliance have tended to be discounted anyway, and any impact that Italian spokesmen might have had has depended on the presence from time to time of particularly strong minded individual representatives.[37] Secondly, it is character-istic of NATO that decision-making structures made up of national military representatives tend not to produce collective military views of any consequence for the political authorities of the alliance. Rather, the task of such bodies (for example the Military Committee) has been to act as sounding boards for politically considered national military positions. The working out of politically acceptable common positions on military and strategic matters is the task of the political authorities in such bodies as the Council. Any attempt by a military body made up of national representatives to put a common view would be regarded as irrelevant and politically naive. This is not to suggest that national military representatives do not establish a rapport based on a common appreciation of military contingencies, or on agreement as to the military implications of agreed alliance strategy, but it is not their task to present a common 'military' view of matters which are politically sensitive.[38]

The Hague meeting of the NPG marked the end of the first rotation period under the system of representation which had been agreed at the ministerial meeting of the NATO Council in December 1966. Canada and the Netherlands, whose term had ended, were reluctant to disassociate themselves from the continuing work of the NPG. Under pressure from them the so-called 'Hague formula' was agreed by which countries whose terms had ended could continue to participate at the official level in meetings of the permanent representatives and the Staff Group. Originally it was agreed that participation at the official level would be restricted to those matters which had previously been of concern to them as full members of the NPG. However, subsequently it proved too cumbersome to determine which countries should be involved with which issues, and by the end of 1968 the Hague formula was being interpreted as allowing any member of the NPG to participate fully in the work of the two official levels regardless of its current status at the ministerial level.[39]

With the departure of Canada and the Netherlands, Belgium and Denmark were represented for the first time at the ministerial level of the NPG when it met in Bonn on the 10–11

October 1968. The meeting was almost entirely concerned with the four reports on various aspects of theatre nuclear weapons that had been commissioned at the Hague, and the brevity of the subsequent communiqué was indicative of the widely reported differences of opinion which these reports had aroused among the allied defence ministers.[40] The British paper dealt with the maritime use of nuclear weapons, the Italian with the use of ADMs and with nuclear anti-aircraft weapons, the Germans considered the role of nuclear weapons on the battlefield and the Americans discussed the demonstration use of nuclear weapons for bargaining purposes.[41]

Three broad themes can be seen as emerging from the discussions on the role of theatre nuclear weapons that were taking place in the NPG. These were first; how and under what circumstances the alliance might have recourse to nuclear weapons, particularly the circumstances in which the alliance might contemplate first use; secondly, consideration was given to the objectives that might be served by the use of nuclear weapons in the European theatre, including the types of weapon that might be best suited to achieve these purposes; thirdly, what kinds of consultation should take place in circumstances in which resort to nuclear weapons might be contemplated and what, if any, power of veto could be exercised by a NATO ally over the use of nuclear weapons in its defence even if such use had been authorised through the existing NATO command structure. From its inception the NPG had been exploring the implications of these themes and clarifying where possible the nature of allied differences with respect to them. The favoured method of doing this was by the preparation of studies at the official level as a basis for discussion and debate during ministerial meetings of the NPG. In the light of the differences revealed by the presentations made in Bonn, it was to be expected that the response would be to require further studies of the question.

A novel approach was taken in this case, however. Germany and Britain were charged with the preparation of draft guidelines for the possible use of theatre nuclear weapons within the alliance strategy of flexible response. The initiative for this cooperative undertaking apparently came from Denis

Healey, who allegedly saw this Anglo-German project as a way of outflanking some of the political consequences of the continuing French veto on British membership of the European Community.[42] However, this Anglo-German collaboration could also be seen as indicating the increased status of Germany with respect to the nuclear policy of the alliance. By cooperating in an area in which previously the United Kingdom had had privileged access to the United States, Germany was able to pursue more effectively immediate objectives concerning such aspects of nuclear policy as the rights of the host nation with respect to nuclear weapons stored on her territory. Be that as it may, the initiative was undeniably an important one in that it confronted directly the ability of the NPG to deal with highly sensitive strategic issues in a manner which was both constructive and politically feasible.

Following from the election of President Nixon in November, a new American Secretary of Defense, Melvin Laird, was in London for the fifth meeting of the NPG which was held in May 1969. As at the previous meeting, the work of the assembled ministers of defence was concerned primarily with questions concerning theatre nuclear weapons, in this case the Anglo-German report commissioned in Bonn. The Healey–Schröder proposals reflected long-standing European concerns and developed points which had already emerged through the work of the NPG. The 65-page paper suggested a number of general principles which should be included in the proposed guidelines governing resort to nuclear weapons in defence of the NATO area. Among them, one, clearly reflecting German interests, was that any decision to use nuclear weapons should be taken in the last resort by those immediately concerned. This was understood to mean the possessor of the warhead, the possessor of the launcher and the country from which the weapon would be fired. However, again as a general principle, the likely issues, circumstances and consequences surrounding a decision to use nuclear weapons should be fully discussed and, where possible, agreed by the allies in advance. Another proposal was that initially nuclear weapons should be used very sparingly, the report stressing that nuclear weapons used tactically were not to be conceived simply as an extreme form of artillery, but rather as a means of demonstrating resolve and the willingness of the allies to escalate the level of conflict further if necessary. The overall intention of the paper was not to extend the authority or responsibilities of the NATO military commanders, but to provide the basis for political guidance in a crisis, and to indicate the underlying tactical and technical problems that needed to be resolved, including the problem of rapid consultation in an emergency.[43]

Although there was apparently a broad degree of acceptance for the proposals contained in the Anglo-German paper, agreement seemed closer on questions involving arrangements for consultation in the event of the possible use of nuclear weapons being considered than on questions involving what stage in a conflict such weapons might be used and on what scale. The joint paper seemed to suggest a rather earlier resort to nuclear weapons in the event of conflict in central Europe than was envisaged by the Americans. In addition, the Anglo-German approach seemed to favour in these circumstances a limited demonstration use rather than the more massive use favoured by the Americans in order to secure a definite, if only temporary, military advantage.[44] In essence the difference was the old one between the Europeans who argued that forward defence could only be accomplished by the deterrent threat to use nuclear weapons at a relatively early stage in a conflict, and the Americans who continued to seek a higher nuclear threshold through increased conventional force contributions from the European allies. No firm guidelines were suggested as to where the nuclear threshold might occur. It was widely appreciated that this would depend on the circumstances and scale of any attack, and no allied government would commit itself to any firm course of action in advance. No definitive action with respect to the Anglo-German proposals was taken at London. Guidance for further work on the guidelines was given, and the discussion was to be continued at the next meeting of the NPG.[45]

The work of the NPG at this time was to be seen within the context of the formal adoption by the alliance of flexible response as its official strategic doctrine. In effect, by accepting flexible response, the allies had endorsed American strategic policies. These policies clearly recognised the increased risks of a nuclear commitment to Europe brought about by a changing strategic environment. Nevertheless, many Europeans were not really prepared to accept the consequences of this endorsement, and one response to this was an attempt to spell out what flexible response might mean in the event of war. In particular, attention was focussed on the role of theatre nuclear weapons, and the debate on the proposed guidelines governing them reflected continuing tensions with respect to alliance nuclear policy.

One view of what was meant by the alliance doctrine of flexible response was developed by the Secretary-General, Manlio Brosio, in a series of addresses to the Assembly of Western European Union.[46] These speeches are particularly worth noting since they were made during the period in which the NPG was actively developing guidelines affecting theatre nuclear weapons, and may be taken as a compromise view designed to accommodate as much as possible alliance differences over how nuclear weapons might be used. Brosio stressed the escalatory use of nuclear weapons as part of the strategy of flexible response which, in his view, implied a very close connection and interaction between deterrence, defence and deliberate escalation. The alliance should show a readiness to use the appropriate conventional and nuclear weapons, but flexible response should not be interpreted to mean that a conventional attack could and should be countered exclusively with conventional weapons, for without the will to use nuclear weapons effectively and appropriately there could be no deterrent effect. 'Under the present strategy the selective and limited use of tactical nuclear weapons would not be deferred until our conventional defences were reduced to a desperate situation. By that time, it would be neither feasible nor effective to use them. The enemy would already have advanced too far and there would be a danger of hitting our own troops along with his or, worse still, the civilian population.'[47] Although the will to initiate the use of nuclear weapons must be made manifest, nevertheless the actual response, whether conventional or nuclear in form, limited or extensive in scale, must be uncertain. Brosio argued that the essence of the strategy of flexible response was that it was not hard and fast and could not be anticipated by a potential aggressor and would thus keep him in a state of uncertainty.

In the event of an initial use of nuclear weapons by NATO, Brosio dealt with the question of the likely response of the enemy by asserting that if the enemy responded in kind or raised the level of use to that of mutual destruction, then the responsibility for so doing would be his. That is, the aggressor would be made clearly aware of the risks involved in continuing the aggression. An adequate strategy for the tactical use of nuclear weapons would be designed to prevent this coming about, however, by facing a potential opponent with the risk of escalation. One clear function of theatre nuclear weapons, then, was to deter by providing a variety of options for escalation. There was the problem, of course, of the collateral effects on the allies of any such use of nuclear weapons. 'Yet these deadly weapons will invariably be used only to a limited extent, for in employing any weapon, be it nuclear or conventional, we should stop short of sacrificing the lives and property of civilian populations and undefended towns.'[48] The Secretary-General showed himself to be aware of the problem, but was hardly in a position to confront it given the difficulties it created for any attempt to secure alliance agreement on the way in which theatre nuclear weapons might ultimately be employed. The collateral effects of anything other than the most restrained use of nuclear weapons on allied territory, quite apart from any enemy retaliation that might occur, would be such as to cast serious doubts on the political feasibility, and therefore the credibility, of any widespread defensive use of nuclear weapons.[49] The tactical use of nuclear weapons, as Brosio recognised, was not a substitute for adequate conventional forces, although, as the debate between the Americans and Europeans over conventional force levels indicated, this begged the question of what level was adequate for what purpose. In other words, whether deterrence or defence was being sought. On the other hand, conventional forces were not a substitute for theatre nuclear weapons. The difficulties of reconciling the not always compatible elements of conventional and nuclear escalation, deterrence and defence, within the confines of a purely strategic doctrine reinforced the political significance of the consultations on the subject that were occurring within the NPG. They also encouraged the search for political solutions outside a purely alliance framework, particularly in the case of Germany, which was the ally whose security was most immediately affected by the new strategic posture.

The German policy of *Ostpolitik* which was developing at this time was not simply a response to the new strategy, but German doubts about it, together with the new direction in foreign policy, may be taken as symptomatic of a changed perception of the conditions underpinning German security. In fact, there were considerable differences in the German government between the Defence Ministry under Schröder and the Foreign Ministry under Brandt as to what course should be taken by German security policy. Brandt was very much the architect of the policy of seeking security by political means through the *Ostpolitik*, whereas Schröder represented the established CDU policy of seeking to reinforce the *status quo* by influencing the character of the American strategic commitment. The German contribution to the paper on nuclear guidelines took place within the context of internal policy differences which at times had led to the German delegation to NATO receiving conflicting instructions from the defence and foreign ministries. Nevertheless, the German component in the joint paper was very much the product of the Defence Ministry under Schröder.

The German view of what flexible response meant for the defence of the NATO area had been made clear at the time of its formal adoption by the NATO Council. Schröder, in an address to the Bundestag, had indicated his preference for a forward strategy based on the availability to SACEUR of a 'graduated deterrent' which would include tactical nuclear weapons capable of being delivered by allied forces, including, of course, German means of delivery.[50] As stated, this strategic preference roughly coincided with the situation then existing in Western Europe. German concerns, however, were directed to how such a strategy might be implemented and, in particular, to the stage in a conflict at which resort to nuclear weapons might occur, how they might be used and their targets. Furthermore, two aspects of American policy reinforced these concerns. One was the renewed emphasis on the importance of the European allies increasing their conventional capabilities which now was coupled with congressional pressure for significant American troop reductions in Europe. Secondly, there was the concern with the possibility of Soviet–American arms control negotiations leading to restricted defence options for the European allies of the United States. Justification for this concern could be found in the willingness of the Americans to meet Russian demands that a non-proliferation treaty rule out the possibility of the Americans sharing ownership of nuclear weapons with their allies which, of course, had been the basis of the MLF proposal.

Schröder continued to stress the importance of forward defence in a speech to the Assembly of Western European Union in October of the following year.[51] By reaffirming the alliance commitment to forward defence he wished to ensure that, should the necessity arise, theatre nuclear weapons would be used in good time and as far forward as possible in order to avoid loss and destruction of NATO territory. The American emphasis on conventional capabilities suggested that nuclear weapons might be used only after a relatively lengthy period of conventional fighting with the consequence that to be militarily effective they would have to be used on an extensive scale and on German territory. Though accepting the need for effective conventional forces, neither the Germans nor the other European members of the alliance accepted the possibility or indeed the desirability of building conventional forces capable of fighting a major conventional war on the Central Front. German policy sought to avoid the adoption by the alliance of a declaratory strategic posture in which too much emphasis was placed on raising the nuclear threshold and in which too great a distinction was made between the use of conventional and nuclear weapons. Thus Schröder, while accepting that nuclear weapons were completely different in nature from conventional armaments, nevertheless stressed the well-established CDU position that conventional and nuclear weapons had to be seen as an inseparable whole for deterrence to be maintained under a strategy of flexible response.[52] The Germans were the major European critics of that element in American strategic policy which sought to provide a major conventional war-fighting option in Europe. In Schröder's opinion, conventional forces should be sufficiently strong to be able to react without delay in the event of an attack, especially one directed against Central Europe, and to hold even a superior conventional assault long enough to enable alliance consultation to take place concerning the possible use of nuclear weapons.[53] What, in effect, Schröder suggested was that conventional forces should be capable of serving a crisis-management function..

Denis Healey had reached essentially the same conclusion as to the role of conventional forces in the alliance, although he had done so on the basis of a somewhat different argument. For Healey, a large-scale conventional assault on Western Europe was an extremely unlikely contingency. A more likely danger to be guarded against was the possibility of some local incident getting out of hand which would require the capability to deploy effective conventional forces on the spot. The alliance needed the capacity to deal with 'ambiguous' situations without resort to nuclear weapons.[54] Healey could agree with the Germans that the important test of the relationship of conventional forces to the nuclear weapons available in the European theatre was whether or not it contributed to a more credible threat of controlled nuclear escalation in the event of an attack.[55]

Basically, what the Europeans sought from the strategic posture of the alliance was not a credible war-fighting posture, which they suspected was the American objective in applying the strategy of flexible response to NATO, but a posture of deterrence by punishment. Instead of seeking to convince a potential aggressor that he would not be militarily successful, they sought deterrence by confronting the aggressor with an unacceptable risk of nuclear escalation. In Germany itself both coalition parties, the CDU and the SPD were agreed on this. However, whereas the CDU reacted to American initiatives concerning alliance strategy by pressing for reassurance that nuclear weapons would be released early enough for them to be employed sufficiently far forward to minimise any collateral effects on Germany, the SPD stressed the necessity of securing German control over the employment of any nuclear weapons on German territory. The thrust of the SPD position was that, given American policy, there was no guarantee that the United States would release nuclear weapons in circumstances which would enable unacceptable damage to be avoided.

The position of the United States in the alliance debate was necessarily somewhat ambiguous. Ambiguity was inherent in the subject-matter of the debate of course, but also it arose partly from the different policy tendencies in Washington itself and partly from the necessity of the United States avoiding public positions which were too much at variance with the views of its European allies. American public statements nevertheless revealed clear differences of emphasis with respect to the circumstances in which nuclear weapons in the European theatre might be used, and they were far less sanguine as to their deterrent effectiveness. The essence of the American position with respect to the tactical use of nuclear weapons was that the decision to employ them should not be forced upon the alliance simply because there were no other means available. It was necessary to recognise that there were many possible situations in which it would not be advisable or feasible to use such weapons.[56] Although McNamara, for example, could agree with Healey that the most likely kind of conflict in the NATO area was one arising from miscalculation in a period of tension, rather different conclusions were drawn with respect to the role of conventional forces and the level of the nuclear threshold. The Americans pointed out the need for balanced alliance forces capable of meeting any Soviet threat at an appropriate level of response. This included the need for balanced conventional forces. While not denying the deterrent effect of theatre nuclear weapons, McNamara wished to convince the allies that nuclear forces, no matter how versatile and powerful they might be, did not by themselves constitute a credible deterrent to all kinds of aggression. He argued that only the existence of balanced forces would convince an aggressor that whatever effort he might make, he would be matched by the alliance. Only under such conditions would it be clear to the aggressor that military force of any kind at any level would not secure political ends because every means of military pressure would be met by an appropriate measured response.[57]

American spokesmen placed much greater emphasis than did the Europeans on the possibility of limited conventional probes against NATO positions. Indeed, undue reliance on the tactical use of nuclear weapons would not only be an unsound cure for inadequate conventional forces in these circumstances, it was argued, but it could also tempt the Soviet Union to consider limited conventional probes designed to secure local gains and to divide the alliance.[58] Apart from the fundamental American concern to minimise the risks inherent in the nuclear commitment to the defence of Western Europe, it was clear that the Americans were also worried at the possible bargaining disadvantages they might face in a situation in which it would be impossible for the alliance to meet the threat of a major conventional assault except by threatening resort to nuclear weapons in return. A source of difference between the American and European points of view on this was that, even though the possibility of the Soviet Union being able to threaten a large-scale conventional assault might give them a bargaining advantage in a crisis, there was no agreement on the extent to which it was worthwhile bearing the costs of insuring against it.

Undoubtedly, one concern shared by many Europeans was that as European conventional capabilities increased, the more dubious would the American nuclear commitment to Europe become. It was argued that the emphasis on conventional defence possibilities in the American approach to flexible response could serve to indicate to a potential aggressor that a conventional attack could be initiated with little risk of a nuclear response. As for the possibility of limited conventional probes against NATO positions, it was pointed out that any local conventional success by an attacker would confront the alliance with the problem of expelling him at acceptable military or political cost. German and French critics of the American position in particular, argued that the conventional phase of any conflict would necessarily be of short duration since few allies were willing to plan on the basis of accepting the risk of heavy conventional casualties and local defeats without the prospect of rapid retaliation against the aggressor. Anyway, it was argued, flexible response envisaged the use of nuclear weapons at some stage in any major conflict in Europe, and a case could be made that it was better from the European point of view to use them early in a campaign before confronting the consequences of conventional defeats rather than after.[59] Although, in many cases, the European allies accepted the cogency of arguments put forward that resort to nuclear weapons in the European theatre would not necessarily aid the defence (the NPG had been an important vehicle for achieving this), they were still not willing to accept the political or military credibility of a purely conventional counter to the conventional forces of the Warsaw Pact. The strategic dilemma thus created was one reason why the European allies were so sensitive to any American action which could be construed as 'decoupling' the American strategic deterrent from the defence of Western Europe.

By the spring of 1969, alliance discussion of the implications for nuclear policy of the doctrine of flexible response had become focussed on the guidelines proposed in the Anglo-German paper on the use of theatre nuclear weapons. It was clear that the strategic posture of the alliance rested on the proposition that in certain circumstances the alliance would be faced with the decision to resort to the initial use of nuclear weapons. In order to contain the stresses on the alliance generated by this situation, any guidelines covering the use by the alliance of nuclear weapons would have to confront the very great interest of the United States in limiting the risk that any resort to theatre nuclear weapons would lead to a retaliatory strike on her territory. To the extent that any guidelines were successful in holding out the prospect of limiting this risk, then the threat of the President authorising resort to theatre nuclear weapons in defence of Western Europe, even if this meant initial use, was of increased credibility. On the other hand, European members of the alliance would need to be assured that any guidelines adopted did not condone any weakening of the link between the nuclear weapons deployed in the European theatre and the strategic deterrent forces of the United States. The problem was to consider how nuclear weapons might be used by NATO in defence of alliance territory without necessarily forcing the Russians to escalate to the full extent of their nuclear ability and also without committing NATO itself to further use.

It was against the background of considerations such as these that the discussions concerning guidelines on the tactical use of nuclear weapons continued at the sixth ministerial meeting of the NPG at Warrington, Virginia on the 11 and 12 November 1969. Following the general election held in October there had been a change in government in Bonn and the new Defence Minister, Helmut Schmidt, represented the Federal Republic. Prior to the meeting, Healey had met with his new German counterpart and they had reaffirmed their commitment to the joint proposals contained in the Anglo-German paper. Such a reaffirmation was necessary because there had been differences of view with respect to defence policy between the SPD and CDU in the previous German government, and the new government was about to initiate a review of defence policy. Admittedly, given the short time involved since taking office, Schmidt had little choice but to accept the proposals which had been agreed by his predecessor. Nevertheless, the new Defence Minister would place a some-what different interpretation on them, and German policy would reflect greater ambivalence with respect to theatre nuclear weapons than had previously been the case. Indicative of the thrust of the new government's concerns was Schmidt's call for a bigger European say on the use of tactical nuclear weapons and his claim to the press on the eve of the Warrington meeting that the Anglo-German paper which formed the main item on the agenda was designed to give the European allies of the United States substantial influence in the nuclear sector.[60] A further indication of Schmidt's thinking on these matters had recently appeared with the publication of his book, *The Balance of Power*. In it, Schmidt had argued that the adoption by the alliance of flexible response had reduced the degree of automaticity of nuclear retaliation in the military posture of NATO, and had emphasised the role of the leading power in any decision to make a calculated and limited use of nuclear weapons in defence of the European theatre. Thus the United States, the only power in the alliance with sizeable nuclear forces, had gained an overwhelmingly preponderant role not only in the determination of the military posture of the alliance, but also in the possible management of crises through the controlled threat or use of nuclear weapons, the possibility of which the strategy of flexible response had supposedly increased.[61]

At Warrington, agreement was reached on two documents which were forwarded to the NATO Council and approved at the December ministerial meeting. One document consisted of provisional political guidelines for the initial tactical defensive use of nuclear weapons, and the other of guidelines covering consultation procedures in the event of the possible use of nuclear weapons in the defence of the NATO area being considered.[62] The guidelines on initial use sought to offer political guidance to the military authorities of the alliance as to the circumstances in which the initial tactical use of nuclear weapons might be authorised.

The value of such guidance would depend in part on the extent to which the tensions in the strategic relationship between the United States and her allies could be reconciled with the requirements of effective operational planning. The guidelines were the product of an established method of working; that is, they were developed from detailed staff papers which in turn led to more general considerations being incorporated capable of covering various possible eventualities and capable of securing everyone's agreement.[63] In the latter case, if allied differences concerning strategic doctrine and defence planning were too great, then agreement would only be possible at the expense of considerable ambiguity. Although the guidelines were not to be construed as contingency plans, but rather as a means of developing a common approach and way of looking at things, too much ambiguity would make the guidelines valueless as a way of directing political guidance to military planning. It remains open to debate as to how far these guidelines, together with the subsequent attention that the NPG gave to the possible follow-on use of nuclear weapons, extended the role of the allies concerning the possible use of theatre nuclear weapons. Nevertheless, it is possible to argue that a major function of the consultative processes practised in the NPG is the political one of continuously involving the allies in a review of the strategic premises underlying the deployment of nuclear weapons in the defence of the alliance. Thus the guidelines on the initial tactical use of nuclear weapons could be seen as a further refinement or restatement of the nature of the allied consensus on the strategy of flexible response.

Allied agreement on the guidelines had been made easier by the relaxation of American pressure on the allies to increase their conventional capabilities in order that a significant raising of the nuclear threshold in the event of a conventional attack could be achieved. Melvin Laird, compared with his predecessors in the previous administration, was more willing to admit that the Europeans could not be persuaded to increase their conventional capabilities to the extent required. The result was that inevitably the strategic posture of the alliance continued to stress deterrence rather than defence. The task of the conventional component in the NATO triad of forces became that of offering a 'stalwart' defence capable of imposing a pause on any conventional attacker. Congressional pressures and the demands of Vietnam had resulted in a shift in the rationale behind American policy. From a policy designed to buttress an American conception of flexible response, it changed to one designed to ensure that the Europeans undertook a greater share of the defence burden in Europe in order to facilitate cuts in the size and costs of American forces there.

The guidelines for consultation procedures on the use of nuclear weapons in some respects can be considered as elaborations of the Athens guidelines of 1962. At the May ministerial meeting of the NATO Council that year the United States and Britain committed themselves to continue to make nuclear weapons available to NATO in case of aggression and to consult the allies before using such weapons. One of the measures agreed to at Athens, the creation of a group called the Nuclear Committee, proved to be of little long-term significance, but certain basic principles of consultation were suggested. The guidelines developed at Athens indicated the kinds of action that would be necessary in various circumstances in which the alliance might have recourse to nuclear weapons. In the event of a nuclear attack on a member state there would be provision for an immediate, automatic response even without consultation among the membership. In the case of a conventional attack, however, the nuclear weapon states would consult with their allies before using nuclear weapons if time permitted.[64] The French refused to cooperate in all this, rejecting any element of 'automaticity' in the nuclear posture of the alliance, and serious doubts were expressed in Germany too. In some ways the attitude to the use of nuclear weapons in defence of NATO exhibited at Athens by all the major allies, the United States included, had already been outdated by various policy and strategic developments. Many of these developments were the subject of an important statement by McNamara at the meeting and were later enshrined in what became known as the doctrine of flexible response. Indeed, it was the formal adoption of flexible response as the alliance strategy that subsequently led to the attempt to draft further guidelines.

There was agreement at Warrington that no consultation procedure would be credible unless the whole process was considerably speeded up. Under the Athens arrangements a number of exercises were held to test the system of political consultation and the command and control arrangements of the alliance with respect to a decision to use nuclear weapons. It seems that there was considerable scepticism among a number of the participants as to their likelihood of working in any relevant fashion in time of war. The arrangements adopted at Warrington placed much greater emphasis on the allies discussing a wide range of likely contingencies in advance, but leaving the final decision to those countries directly involved. As reported at the London meeting, these would be the country owning the nuclear weapon, the country supplying the delivery vehicle and the country from whose territory the aircraft or missile used as a means of delivery would be launched.[65] The draft guidelines on nuclear consultation presented at Warrington were the product, apparently, of a joint Belgian–American effort which pulled together in a way similar to the Anglo-German paper on initial use, the results of previous allied discussions on the various areas of concern about the adequacy of the alliance's consultative arrangements.[66]

A key new development in the guidelines was that, whereas those countries actually possessing nuclear weapons or the means of delivery could always have denied consent to their use, under the new arrangements the consent of the host country was to be sought specifically as well. Such a provision was of most immediate concern to Germany on whose territory was deployed the largest number of United States nuclear warheads in Europe and whose territory was within the most likely area for a tactical nuclear battle. In addition, Germany was host to the nuclear-capable forces of allies other than the United States. Not that the new arrangements amounted to the 'host country veto' which had been an element in German policy since 1966 – it was explicitly understood that agreed consultation procedures would be used, 'time and circumstances permitting', and that inflexible or over-elaborate procedures might inhibit action and reduce the credibility of the deterrent posture. There was nothing in the guidelines to compromise the release authority of the nuclear powers.[67]

In the case of the American President, as a congressional study has pointed out, a commitment to consult with the NATO allies, while undoubtedly a factor the President would consider, hardly constitutes a constraint on his authority. Rather, the obligation to consult would serve to influence any decision made. It can be argued that there is little reason to doubt that the President would consult with the allies of the United States if such consultations were not prejudicial to the American national interest; nevertheless, the time available for such consultation might be extremely short. Undoubtedly, the same considerations would apply to the British Prime Minister as well. Again, as the same study also pointed out, time limitation is not the only exception to the obligation on the part of the nuclear allies to consult. They are not obliged to consult if, 'upon their consideration of the attendant circumstances it is deemed necessary to order the use of nuclear weapons without such consultation'. Thus every nuclear power has the option to forego consultation if in its considered judgement circumstances do not permit such consultation. An example of such circumstances might be provided by the necessity for surprise. One important result of the drafting of the guidelines on consultation was that there would be little doubt that these exceptions to the commitment to consult by the nuclear allies were known and understood by all members of the alliance.[68]

Accordingly, the problem for Germany if it wished to exercise full control over the employment of nuclear weapons either on or from its territory was that, like any host country, unless it could physically deny the use by its allies of the nuclear weapons available to them by some means, a permissive action link (PAL), for example, then its right to be consulted if circumstances permitted would not necessarily constitute an effective veto over the use of nuclear weapons on its territory. With the rather special possible exception of the Thor and Jupiter missiles deployed in Europe between 1958 and 1962, the policy of the United States has been never to allow its allies a physical veto over the release of nuclear warheads to its own and allied nuclear-capable forces deployed in the European theatre. In order for a comprehensive host country veto to operate, the country concerned would require a physical 'finger on the trigger' of all nuclear warheads based on its territory, and this is something which American policy has always denied. Nevertheless, all political and military planning in NATO for the possible use of nuclear weapons has to take into account the 'constraints' inherent in the situation. In the event of nuclear weapons on its territory being fired without its consent, the host country always has the sanction of withdrawing from the battle and announcing that it will not fight. And, of course, in the event of the alliance attempting to fight a defensive battle in Central Europe, German participation would be absolutely essential.

The difficulty for a country like Germany, to which Schmidt

was far more sensitive than his predecessor, was that there was a danger of its being defended with nuclear weapons against its will. The fear was not so much that the United States and the other allies would disregard its wishes, for which there would be little reason, as that in a crisis the deployment and command and control arrangements would not allow sufficient time for consultation before the decision to use nuclear weapons was taken. This consideration was at the root of many of the German hesitancies and ambiguities of policy towards theatre nuclear weapons. On the one hand the Germans had a committed interest in being defended as far forward as possible, but on the other hand many of the nuclear weapons which would allow this to be done were of a type and deployment which would allow the least time for decision if they were to be effectively used. This explains, for example, the increasing German doubts as to the value of atomic demolition munitions (ADMs) and the reluctance of the new German government to allow 'pre-chambering' to take place. For a host country like Germany, whose territory would likely become part of any battlefield in Central Europe, the problem extends not only to the nuclear-capable forces deployed there, but also to those weapons capable of being used tactically in the battle which could be launched from outside its territory. Hence for Germany arose the very great concern with being consulted adequately in advance as to the circumstances and manner in which the use of nuclear weapons in the European theatre might be contemplated. Such considerations as these affected to a similar or lesser extent the policies of all the allies of the United States participating in the work of the NPG.

The evolution of the consultative activities of the NPG can be seen as a response to these allied policy considerations and interests. The allies sought some control over the nuclear policy of the alliance through consultation as to possible use and some input into the plans according to which nuclear weapons would be targeted and the scale of their use determined. Consequently, the two sets of guidelines agreed at Warrington were complementary in their effect. The guidelines on the initial defensive tactical use of nuclear weapons represented a compromise formula as to how, possibly, and under what circumstances the initial use of nuclear weapons tactically might occur. In turn, the guidelines on consultation outlined the procedures, channels and priorities that the allies would endeavour to follow prior to a decision by a nuclear power on whether to release a nuclear weapon for use. Typically, the guidelines were designed to operate in times of crisis, but it was understood that their ability to do so effectively would depend on the effectiveness of the continuing dialogue on nuclear matters conducted by the NPG. A further test of their effectiveness, however, was the extent to which the process of political compromise, which had enabled agreement on the guidelines to be achieved, had resulted in formulae capable of being operationally applied in a credible fashion. The guidelines had to serve both military and political purposes, the weight accorded to each varying from ally to ally and from time to time. In this respect, they could be considered an incomplete but positive response to the continuing demands being made on the alliance by its members for a satisfactory system of sharing in the making of nuclear policy.

The revised consultative procedures and the guidelines on the initial use of nuclear weapons were designed to reinforce the credibility of the threat to use nuclear weapons in defence of the NATO area while at the same time seeking to ensure that the interests of the allies most directly affected were protected. In order to do this it was necessary for the allies to consult on how they might go to nuclear war. The consultation procedures might prove too cumbersome, but as long as it remained possible for the United States to cut the Gordian knot in time of crisis and act unilaterally with respect to the use of theatre nuclear weapons in defence of its forces in Europe, then other things being equal there would be sufficient uncertainty of response to maintain credibility in an alliance strategic posture dependent on theatre nuclear weapons. However, to the extent that in order for nuclear weapons to be used the positive assent of two or more allies would be required (in circumstances in which the consequences for both would be very dangerous and very possibly disastrous), the credibility of the use of nuclear weapons being authorised is very much reduced. In these circumstances the value of prior guidelines on consultation and the initial use of nuclear weapons is problematic. The procedures agreed at Warrington represented an implicit compromise between the need to ensure for the purposes of deterrence that in certain circumstances there was a credible expectation that nuclear weapons would be used, and the need for the purposes of alliance cohesion that the allies had reasonable assurance that they would not be involved in nuclear war against their will.

The difficulties inherent in such a compromise were well summed up by a former United States ambassador to NATO.

Sovereign governments do not and cannot decide ahead of time how they will act or even whom they will consult; that depends on time and circumstance. At every stage of NATO's life as an organization, the smaller countries have quite naturally tried to maximise the influence which their status as allies can bring to bear on the actions of the larger members. The nub of the issue is whether in an emergency some members might act in the name of the Alliance as a whole, even if all had not agreed to do so. By common consent, this constitutional issue is never brought to a head, for there is potential conflict between two NATO dogmas which can both be traced back to the Treaty itself: that NATO actions are taken by unanimous consent, and that any 'number can fight'. No member can concede in peacetime that its opinion in a life-or-death emergency might be ignored by others. But neither can any member concede in peacetime that what it decides to do about its NATO obligations might be restrained by the contrary views of its allies. The presumption of cooperation is not *that* strong.[69]

The agreement on the guidelines may be said to mark the end of the initial phase of the work of the NPG. The ability of the members of the NPG to reach agreements of this kind indicated that the Group had proved to be of some success as a consultative mechanism for the inter-allied discussion of nuclear policy. In so far as the NPG was able to operate on the basis of a 'common universe of discourse' with respect to the analysis of nuclear issues, it had met one of the major objectives of McNamara when he had initiated the Special Committee in 1965. By its operation in practice, the NPG had helped define for the allies the nature and limits of consultation in the alliance as it concerned nuclear policy. Mutual comprehension, however, was not in itself sufficient to resolve

lifferences of perception and interest among the allies, and
oetween the United States and the Europeans in particular.
Nevertheless, the NPG had eased the process of reaching
agreements, however limited, in an issue-area which had been
previously marked by divisiveness and a high level of stress on
he alliance political system. In addition, even where firm
agreement had not been possible, the operation of the NPG
had helped minimise the political consequences. Consultation
within its framework had helped demonstrate that many
nuclear issues 'yield to study but not neat conclusions'. In
contrast to the situation prior to 1967, a situation had been
created in which there was a greater sense of allied participation
in the process of nuclear policy-making, and the boundaries of
consultation concerning nuclear weapons had been extended.

4. THE EVOLUTION OF THE NUCLEAR PLANNING GROUP: 1970–4

The seventh meeting of the Nuclear Planning Group which took place in Venice on 8 and 9 June 1970 was the first to be held under the revised membership arrangements that had been accepted at the ministerial meetings of the NATO Council the previous December. The 'gentleman's agreement' which had hitherto governed membership in the NPG expired at the end of 1969, and the new arrangements accommodated the desire of Norway to participate directly in the work of the NPG. Previously, Norway had simply monitored the work of the NPG from its seat on the Nuclear Defence Affairs Committee (NDAC). It was agreed that all the non-permanent members of the NPG would serve full eighteen-month terms and that membership of the Group would be expanded to eight whenever it was necessary to accommodate the additional member. Thus the Venice meeting was the first that Norway attended; a total of eight countries participated.[1]

Much of the time of the Venice meeting was taken up with the continuing discussion of the role of tactical nuclear weapons in the European theatre. In particular, attention was directed towards the role of atomic demolition munitions (ADMs) in alliance strategy and to the number and variety of nuclear weapons available for use in the defence of the NATO area. The object of these discussions was to extend the area of common allied understanding of the issues raised and to seek allied agreement on policy with respect to them. The meeting gave the attending defence ministers the opportunity to review a series of studies which had been undertaken by the alliance and national authorities on matters connected with theatre nuclear weapons and to issue directions for further work in this field.[2]

110

The guidelines formulated at Warrington, Virginia in November 1969 had settled one set of issues concerning alliance policy towards theatre nuclear weapons only to pose others concerning the strategy they were supposed to serve, and how political control was to be exercised over them once the decision to undertake initial use had been made. For example, the German Defence Minister, Helmut Schmidt, continued to voice German concern about alliance plans to use nuclear weapons in certain circumstances on German territory. In particular, Schmidt was reported as being doubtful of proposals to deploy ADMs along the frontier between the two Germanies to be used possibly as 'follow-on' weapons in the event that an initial use of nuclear weapons failed to halt an attacker.[3]

The work of the meeting was not completely restricted to theatre nuclear weapons. As at previous meetings of the Nuclear Planning Group, the American Secretary of Defense gave a briefing on the overall strategic balance. This briefing apparently was linked to the one delivered to the Defence Planning Committee in December 1969, and was to be continued at the next meeting of the DPC scheduled to take place in Brussels almost immediately following the conclusion of the Venice meeting of the NPG.[4] These briefings were delivered against the developing background of American foreign policy under President Nixon. After a year in office, the new administration had produced a major foreign policy statement in the form of a presidential report to Congress on 18 February 1970. This statement entitled *United States Foreign Policy for the 1970s: A New Strategy for Peace*, and incorporating the so-called 'Nixon doctrine', attempted to pull together many strands of American foreign policy. Of immediate consequence to the NATO allies was the attempt to re-establish the coherence of American policy after the stresses to which it had been subjected by the involvement in Vietnam. This was to be achieved by a highly centralised control on the formulation of policy being exercised by the President and his Special Advisor for National Security Affairs, Henry Kissinger.[5] The diplomatic style of the Nixon administration was one which was congenial to the continued pursuit of a bilateral relationship with the Soviet Union on an expanding range of issues. Despite the strong commitment to consultation with the allies in NATO on matters affecting East–West relations offered by the President in February and April 1969, there were inevitably concerns on the part of the allies that the extent and nature of the consultation practised would not be sufficient to protect their interests.[6] The tensions generated were clearly demonstrated by the inter-allied disputes of 1973. Ironically, this was the year which had been heralded in American policy as the 'Year of Europe'.

In fact, with respect to the politics of the inter-allied security relationship, attention in general had moved away from a central focus on issues of nuclear strategy to broader issues concerning the implications of détente, and to the consideration of immediate matters such as the continuing congressional pressure for a reduction in the size of American forces deployed in Europe. Although these were matters of consequence for the nuclear posture of the alliance, their impact tended to be indirect and the role of the NPG with respect to them was a marginal one. The loci of decision-making and consultation for these issues were to be found in other alliance institutions. Although there were no firm rules which determined what could be placed on the agenda of the NPG, clearly what was discussed would be limited by the general 'brief' given to the Group to consider alliance nuclear policy, and by the various interpretations put upon this brief by the defence ministers. In this, the views of the American Secretary of Defense were the most important. Thus, what constituted consultation on policy concerning the strategic deterrent was largely determined by the content of the general strategic briefing by the Secretary of Defense.

By and large, the response of the allies to these briefings has been the relatively passive one of taking note of them as statements of American strategic policy. Initially, it had been anticipated that the NPG machinery would have a contribution to make to the desire of some allies of the United States to have greater involvement in questions concerning the strategic deterrent. In practice, however, the NPG had concentrated on the problems of theatre nuclear weapons. This shift in emphasis largely resulted from the appreciation that, under a strategy of flexible response, if nuclear weapons were to be used the crucial political decisions would likely concern their limited tactical use in the European theatre.[7]

Nevertheless, from time to time contentious issues have been raised in the NPG following the Secretary of Defense's briefing on American strategic policy. A noted example was that of the decision to deploy the Sentinel ABM system which generated considerable heat during the Ankara meeting of the NPG in September 1967.[8] In contrast, the announcement by the United States in March 1969, that an extended ABM system called Safeguard was to be deployed appeared to have excited little comment in the NPG. A number of factors can be held to account for this. At Ankara, the defence ministers were still unsure of the new body's role, and thus were likely to be particularly sensitive to any decision by the United States affecting nuclear weapons taken with what seemed to be inadequate consultation. But, by the spring of 1969, the Nuclear Planning Group was engaged in a major series of studies concerning theatre nuclear weapons, and already they had been established as the area of greatest allied input into alliance nuclear policy. Strategic weapons decisions were recognised as being largely the responsibility of the United States, and it was also recognised that the allies could reasonably expect to be consulted concerning them only to the extent of being informed of the development of American policy.[9] With respect to the Safeguard decision, the degree of consultation by the United States with her allies seems to have been adequate since it did not lead to open dispute. Finally, the Safeguard decision simply did not generate the same degree of political interest as had the original ABM proposal, and consequently there was not the same temptation for politicians to take public stands concerning it.

The next meeting of the NPG took place in Ottawa on the 29 and 30 October 1970 and was particularly significant in that, like the Warrington meeting, it marked the conclusion of a stage in the work of the NPG concerning theatre nuclear weapons. According to the communiqué, the ministers undertook a general strategic review, and discussed the balance of strategic forces and the changes which had occurred since the previous meeting. In addition, the ministers dealt with a number of papers concerning the defensive use of nuclear weapons, and with other policy issues concerning 'the whole of the alliance's nuclear forces'.[10] Apparently one paper was concerned with the consequences of the deployment of the 400-mile-range Pershing missile which would allow a reduction in the number of tactical aircraft maintained on special alert for nuclear missions.[11] However, with respect to theatre nuclear weapons, the major result of the Ottawa meeting was the acceptance by the ministers of two documents. One concerned the concepts governing the role of nuclear strike forces in the European theatre: the other developed political guidelines governing the possible use of atomic demolition munitions.

The document entitled 'Concepts for the role of theatre nuclear strike forces in Allied Command Europe (ACE)' represented an addition to the area of allied agreement on the guidance that could be offered the military authorities of the alliance responsible for nuclear planning. For really the first time at the alliance level, an attempt was made to define where theatre nuclear weapons fitted into NATO strategy and what kinds of weapons were needed to implement it. The 'Concepts' document added a definite alliance component to the direction given by American authorities to the Nuclear Activities Branch of SHAPE, the body responsible for formulating the operational plans for the possible use of nuclear weapons in defence of the European theatre.[12] In effect, the elaboration of concepts governing the theatre nuclear strike forces involved consideration of the various weapons available for the implementation of the alliance's strategy. Also, it involved the evaluation of their various technical characteristics, deployment and numbers, and an evaluation of their ability to conform to the political guidelines already adopted. It could be expected that such a document would need revision in the light of changes in the overall character of nuclear weapons deployment in Europe, and in fact formal amendments were adopted in 1972 as the result of subsequent work by the NPG.

However, significance of the adoption by the alliance of the

'Concepts' document extended beyond that of providing formal alliance guidance to SHAPE on nuclear planning. It provided a further occasion for allied consultation on the character of the American nuclear guarantee. If nothing else, the development of agreed concepts concerning the nuclear strike forces in Europe helped ensure that the character of the nuclear arsenal would not be unilaterally altered by the United States without consulting its allies in the NPG.[13] Psychologically at least, such a formal reinforcement of the commitment to consult helped strengthen the credibility of the American nuclear commitment.[14]

The draft guidelines on atomic demolition munitions drawn up by the NPG which were to be sent on to the next meeting of the Defence Planning Committee for approval, were an attempt to resolve allied differences over a class of theatre nuclear weapon which had turned out to be particularly controversial. ADMs, which have been popularly described as 'nuclear landmines', are weapons with relatively low yields designed to be emplaced in such a fashion that when detonated they would create major barriers to an invading force, and so 'canalise' the enemy's attack as to make it easier for defending forces to respond effectively. It appears that there are two types of ADM currently deployed in the European theatre, one of which is portable, and the other transportable by truck.[15] Teams consisting of five or six men are assigned to deploy and detonate the weapons.[16] The fact of ADM deployment had been made public in the early 1960s in connection with the Trettner proposals for a nuclear barrier between the two Germanies. Immediately, debate had arisen as to the usefulness and desirability of the weapons, and of the effectiveness and credibility of the proposed strategies concerning their deployment and use. Like many debates of this kind, this one involved confusion between the character of the weapons themselves and the strategies governing them.

The NPG became concerned with atomic demolitions munitions at its very first meeting when questions concerning their role in alliance strategy were raised by the Turkish Minister of Defence. As a result, the Group sought to elucidate the issues involved and to draft politically acceptable guidelines on their possible use for the military authorities of the alliance. Although it appeared that ADMs had been deployed in the European theatre since the 1950s, the draft guidelines adopted by the NPG at the Ottawa meeting seem to have provided for the first time specific alliance authority for military commanders to plan for the movement of ADMs from their storage areas to points where they might be used in the event of conflict. One intention in drafting the guidelines was to reduce the time between a military request to employ ADMs, and the implementation of any properly authorised decision to do so.[17] Also, it was reportedly made clear that military commanders would require specific authorisation from the President of the United States before they could actually put the weapons in place.[18]

These measures were far from meeting the call by the Turks in 1967 for a relaxation of American controls on ADMs in order to speed up decisions with respect to their use.[19] In fact, it was made clear that ADMs were subject to the same controls as all other American theatre nuclear weapons in Europe, and the guidelines underscored this point. Although the suggestion that controls over ADMs might be relaxed had been responsible for the initial public controversy over them, the apparent resolution of this issue by the guidelines had not settled a number of other doubts and reservations that had been expressed in connection with their presence in the European theatre. In part, these reservations were of the same kind as those raised in connection with theatre nuclear weapons generally; nevertheless, certain political and strategic problems were highlighted by the existence of ADMs in the NATO armoury.

Given the commitment to a strategy of forward defence, the military effectiveness of the ADMs on the central front of the alliance is dependent on their emplacement far forward on the border with East Germany. From the American point of view in particular, such a deployment poses acute problems of command and control. In the event of a major attack, the time available for a decision to emplace and subsequently to detonate an ADM before it was over-run by advancing enemy forces would be very short indeed. It was awareness of this which had led to the original suggestion for a relaxation of

American control. One approach to the problem was to suggest increasing the 'real-time' available for the employment of these weapons by introducing a 'modernised' ADM.[20] Another, which did not involve the application of new technology, simply proposed the precautionary digging of holes suitable for the emplacement of ADMs. This 'pre-chambering', however, has not taken place, at least not on the Central Front.[21] Still, even if there was a possibility of significant increases in the time available for decision, major difficulties concerning atomic demolition munitions would remain.

One set of difficulties arises from the fact that these weapons inevitably would be exploded on friendly territory which on the Central Front, of course, means German territory. Quite understandably, West German governments have shown considerable reluctance in countenancing a strategy which would greatly increase the likelihood that, in the event of theatre nuclear conflict, there would be early use of nuclear weapons on West German soil. This concern exists quite apart from the fact that the actual emplacement of ADMs would increase the risk of a conventional conflict being escalated to the nuclear level prematurely. The danger here lies in the possibility that, in the event of a successful conventional assault, the nuclear authorities of the alliance would be faced with the choice of either authorising the early use of ADMs (and other short-range, forward-deployed weapons), or permitting their capture by the enemy and the loss of the opportunity to use them in a militarily effective way. It is for reasons such as these that the Germans did not allow pre-chambering to take place, and thus reduced the potential military usefulness of the ADM arsenal in Germany. It is not clear whether there has been any pre-chambering anywhere in NATO Europe, though it is known that ADM teams have been stationed in Italy, and there have been suggestions that pre-chambering may have taken place in Turkey.[22] In the light of Turkish initiatives with respect to atomic demolition munitions it is tempting to infer that such preparations had indeed been made.

The refusal of the German government to allow sites to be prepared for the possible deployment of ADMs is indicative of the considerable shift in attitude to theatre nuclear weapons which occurred after the 1969 election and the coming to office of an SPD-dominated coalition government. SPD spokesmen had been active in criticising the earlier Trettner/von Hassel proposals, but the attitude of the Brandt government to ADM deployment reflected general ambivalence towards the whole question of the role and value of the nuclear weapons deployed in Europe.

Nevertheless, despite the many doubts expressed concerning ADMs, arguments have continued to be advanced favouring their deployment. It has been claimed, for example, that these weapons could serve militarily useful purposes and enhance the war-fighting capability of the alliance. Essentially, such arguments date back to the initial deployment of tactical nuclear weapons in the European theatre in the 1950s, when it was felt that they would compensate for the deficiencies of the alliance's conventional forces. Doubts as to the feasibility and desirability of theatre nuclear weapons as a substitute for conventional forces in a war-fighting role are widely shared among the NATO allies. Nevertheless, it has been suggested that ADMs are inherently defensive in character (thus reducing the risk of escalation following their use) and could be used to slow enemy movements, particularly in places where it would be difficult to bypass natural barriers and where, as in the case of a surprise attack or unexpected breakthrough, there is no time to erect effective defensive barriers by conventional means. Of course, such use would depend on the early authorisation of the release and employment of these weapons.[23] It is this need for early release which made the possible use of atomic demolition munitions particularly sensitive politically, and which cast doubt on their suitability for the kind of 'second gesture' role that, apparently, had been suggested for them at the Venice meeting of the NPG.

Quite apart from their value as defensive weapons, it is possible to make a case for ADMs on the basis of their possible contribution to a posture of 'deterrence by threat of punishment'. This, in effect, has been the role suggested for them as part of a nuclear 'barrier' and 'tripwire'. Central to their purported deterrent effect is the fact that, in most circumstances, in order to be effective they must be used quickly. Thus, it can be argued, a barrier of ADMs positioned at critical invasion points along the borders of the NATO area would serve notice that, in the event of a major attack, nuclear weapons would very likely be used. Such a premeditated deployment of ADMs would reinforce the credibility of the alliance's theatre nuclear posture because although they would be detonated on NATO territory, the collateral effects of properly emplaced and designed weapons would be relatively low. And since their use would not have any direct impact on the territory of the invader (except for possible fallout effects) the detonation of ADMs would not necessarily invite a nuclear response. In a sense, the construction of a nuclear 'tripwire' would place the responsibility for initiating nuclear warfare on the invader since, given the commitment to employ nuclear weapons in defence of the alliance, and given the reinforcement of that commitment by the forward deployment of ADMs, it would be the actions of the invader which would initiate nuclear warfare.[24] However, despite the supposedly non-escalatory character of ADMs, the threat of 'punishment' in such a posture is contained in the unpredictable, but probably disastrous consequences (to all concerned) of any outbreak of nuclear warfare in Europe. Thus the value of a 'tripwire' as a deterrent device is related as much to the degree of 'uncertainty' it creates for an attacker as to the consequences of testing it.[25]

Unfortunately, in a nuclear environment, a tripwire strategy can be considered plausible only by the weak when confronting the strong. The weaker party leaves itself no alternative but to initiate nuclear war in certain defined circumstances. In effect, the defenders 'burn their boats' and leave no room for manoeuvre. However, apart from any doubts as to the credibility of any commitment to the automatic initiation of nuclear war, such a strategy runs entirely counter to the official alliance doctrine of flexible response. It is also incompatible with the centralised control over the conduct of nuclear war necessary for the implementation of this doctrine. Given the difficulty of securing alliance agreement to flexible response, it is unlikely that the allies generally, let alone the Americans, would readily abandon a strategic posture that had been so difficult to achieve. At any rate, the adoption of a strategic posture which explicitly advertised military weakness would undermine the political and diplomatic position of the alliance.

Doubts arise then as to the effectiveness of atomic demolition munitions in both a war-fighting and deterrent role, doubts which have been reflected in the uncertain approach to ADMs taken by the allies. In particular, the 'automatic' quality of these weapons has provided grounds for increasing expressions of concern. Thus, on the American side, these weapons have been held to be incompatible with a policy of raising the nuclear threshold as high as possible. On the other hand, for the SPD government of Germany, commitment to the deployment of ADMs would seem to indicate acceptance of nuclear war in Germany at the early stage of any conflict on the Central Front. Although the Germans favoured the deployment of theatre nuclear weapons as part of an overall strategy of nuclear deterrence, they have been extremely reluctant to confront the possibility of nuclear warfare on their territory, and have accepted that the advantages to the defender of such warfare are at best dubious. Consequently, it has been the policy of the German government to stress the importance of the link that theatre nuclear weapons provide with the strategic deterrent of the United States. The presence of theatre nuclear weapons has been seen as 'more a political than a military means in the strategy of deterrence'.[26] In this context, atomic demolition munitions have appeared to the German government as a political liability and, if anything, as undermining the link between the American strategic deterrent and the security of Europe.

One might wonder why ADMs continued to be deployed in the European theatre at all. In part, their deployment can be understood as the compromise result of conflicting pressures from the allies with respect to their possible use, and the consequent response of the United States. After all, public debate on ADMs had been occasioned originally by the positive attitude taken to them by leading German authorities. Subsequently, the NPG debate had been initiated by the Turks, and taken up by the Greeks and the Italians. However, another factor seems to have been at work as well. There appears to have been an incomplete correspondence between a desire on the part of military authorities for ADMs in order that their planning options might be expanded, and the machinery of political decision-making concerning nuclear weapons. This is something that often seems to have been the case in connection with the acquisition of theatre nuclear weapons. Atomic demolition munitions were deployed in Europe because they were available and a military use could be found for them. It was not until the NPG attempted to formulate guidelines governing them that full consideration of their strategic implications was undertaken by the alliance at the political level.

One additional matter was dealt with at the Ottawa meeting. The official communiqué contained the statement that the ministers 'reaffirmed the importance of the NPG in providing a continuing forum for allied consultation on nuclear matters in which political and military considerations are closely inter-related'.[27] It seems that at the conclusion of the lengthy process of drafting a series of important alliance documents on nuclear strategy the Group took stock of itself checking to see what had to be done, whether its role should be modified, and whether this role could be better served by alternative methods.[28] The result of this review was that the NPG should continue along the same lines as before.

The next stage of the work of the NPG involved the further refinement of the process of alliance consultation on nuclear policy. Thus at the next meeting, which took place at Mittenwald, Germany in May the following year, a new series of studies on the tactical use of nuclear weapons was initiated.[29] There was also the usual consideration of the overall strategic balance which followed from the briefing given by the United States Secretary of Defense. This took place against the background of a number of important political and strategic changes which were affecting the alliance. Consideration of these changes had formed a substantial part of the agenda of the Ministerial Meeting of the NATO Council in December 1970. The Council had reiterated the continuing alliance interest in mutual and balanced force reductions (MBFR) and in the convening of a conference on security and cooperation in Europe (CSCE). In addition, the results of the alliance defence for the seventies (AD70) study were reported. Among other things, the study concluded that the alliance approach to security would continue to be based on the 'twin concepts of defence and détente', and that the 'present NATO defence strategy of deterrence and defence, with its constituent concepts of flexibility in response and forward defence' would remain valid with an appropriate mix of nuclear and conventional forces.[30] The Council had also noted the signature by the Federal Republic of treaties with the Soviet Union and with Poland on the renunciation of force, treaties which represented significant stages in the development of Germany's *Ostpolitik*.

Alliance decisions in connection with these changes were being taken largely elsewhere than in the Nuclear Planning Group. For example, the development of alliance positions on force reductions was the responsibility of the MBFR Working Group, a joint military–civilian committee that had been established in 1969, and the Senior Political Committee of the NATO Council. The Senior Political Committee was also the main vehicle for the inter-allied working out of agreed papers and analyses on the security conference.[31] Nevertheless, these political and strategic developments affected the operation of the NPG in two broad ways. First, they affected the salience of the Group's work by directing the attention of the allies away from questions of nuclear strategy to the political and diplo-matic implications of détente. In turn, détente was affecting not only the structure of the East–West relationship, but also the pattern of inter-allied relations. As a result, issues of nuclear strategy were downgraded on the alliance agenda. The second general impact on the NPG of the changing environ-ment in which it operated concerned the European response to American pressures for a redistribution of what was increasingly seen in the United States as the burden of Western security. In particular, there was an American demand for a greater defence effort by the Europeans which was backed by the threat of further substantial cuts in the numbers of American troops in Europe. Although American policy no longer placed as much emphasis on the expansion of the alliance's conventional option as it had previously, the concern with burden-sharing had the effect of directing attention to the conventional component of the forces available to the alliance. One response was the development through the Eurogroup of the European Defence Improvement Programme (EDIP) which was concerned exclusively with the upgrading of conventional capabilities. The cumulative effect of all these changes was to reduce the relative political significance of the Nuclear Planning Group.

Even though the overt political sensitivity of issues of nuclear strategy to alliance politics had declined, the work of the NPG as means of providing for allied consultation on nuclear policy remained significant. The Nuclear Planning Group, after all, was the only alliance institution at the political level exclusively concerned with nuclear strategy and, in connection with theatre nuclear weapons in particular, provided opportunities for a genuine input from the allies of the United States into the nuclear policy process. The studies on the tactical use of nuclear weapons within the framework of a strategy of flexible response considered at Mittenwald formed part of an ongoing series which was to constitute an important part of the agenda of future meetings. It was anticipated that these studies would assist in the development of further policy recommendations concerning the defensive and deterrent posture of the alliance.[32] The documents adopted at Warrington in 1969 and at Ottawa the following year indicated that the allies had been able to reach at least some consensus concerning how and under what circumstances the alliance might resort to the initial use of nuclear weapons. Now they were engaged on the possibly more difficult task of trying to develop agreed policy on how theatre nuclear weapons would be used in a follow-on role should the initial use fail to halt an attack. Basically this involved consideration of how alliance control could be exercised over the conduct of theatre nuclear war.

The NPG meeting at Mittenwald was the last to be chaired by Manlio Brosio. At the next meeting of the Group, which was held in Brussels in October, the new Secretary-General, Joseph Luns, was in the chair. At Brussels, the strategic briefing given by Melvin Laird seems to have been especially wide-ranging in its content. Apart from dealing with the American assessment of the changes that had occurred in the overall strategic balance between NATO and the Warsaw Pact since the previous meeting of the NPG, which was a regular feature of these briefings, the Secretary of Defense dealt with the implementation of the 'Nixon doctrine' as it affected Europe. President Nixon's forthcoming visits to Moscow and Peking were also discussed, as were the implications for Europe of the American programme of 'Vietnamisation' in Indo-China. Finally, questions were raised concerning SALT and MBFR.[33] While the broad political and diplomatic background against which the alliance functioned was relevant to the work of the NPG of course, it was not part of the usual operations of the Group to give any close consideration to matters such as these. The briefing given on this occasion can be understood in part as an American attempt to reinforce messages which also were being delivered through other alliance and regular bilateral diplomatic channels, the objects of such diplomacy being to allay allied fears concerning the direction of American policy and, if possible, to secure positive allied support for it.

More central to the usual activities of the NPG was the review presented by SACEUR of the military procedures developed in conformity with the provisional political guidelines on the initial tactical use of nuclear weapons adopted in 1969. In the light of this review the ministers were able to exchange views on the experience gained in the operation of the guidelines concerning theatre nuclear weapons over the previous two years. Such experience was relevant not only to any possible further development of the existing guidelines, but also to the exploration of the large number of factors which might affect the course of a nuclear conflict. These factors included the types of weapon available (the implications of which had been examined in the preparation of the 'Concepts' document adopted in Ottawa), the choice of targets and the estimation of the likely response of the enemy to various stages of any nuclear escalation of conflict in Europe. As a result of discussions at this and previous meetings of the NPG, the assembled ministers were able to address a number of specific problems related to tactical nuclear defence and issue instructions for their further investigation.[34] In this respect, particular attention was given to a German–American study, which was presented jointly by Helmut Schmidt and Melvin Laird, setting out a variety of options for the tactical employment of nuclear weapons.[35] A joint presentation such as this followed precedents which had been established at previous meetings of the NPG, and which had proved to be a useful diplomatic device. In this case allies having particular interests in an issue might, through joint study, seek to reconcile any differences they might have; an important consideration given the differing German and American approaches to the role of theatre nuclear weapons on the Central Front.

In December, after a lengthy period of gestation, the German government published a major statement on its defence policy. Apart from affirming that the alliance's nuclear forces were adequate for their strategic mission under the strategic concept of deterrence, the White Paper was remarkably silent as to the role that theatre nuclear weapons were envisioned as playing in German defence policy.[36] At the same time the German government recognised that the concept of flexible response and the principle of forward defence were vital to German security.[37] And, of course, the deployment of theatre nuclear weapons by the alliance was essential to the very possibility of flexible response and to the hope of implementing forward defence. As already indicated, given that public attention was directed towards the implications of détente for Europe and to the *Ostpolitik*, this downplaying of nuclear weapons was not entirely surprising. But it can be suggested that an additional factor was operating as well: that the German government wished to avoid raising issues that were politically sensitive, not only in Germany itself (particularly within the ranks of the SPD), but also within the context of inter-allied relations. Consequently, it was not in the interest of any of the participants to publicise unduly the issues that were being discussed in the NPG.

The follow-on use of theatre nuclear weapons continued to form a substantial part of the agenda at the subsequent two meetings of the Nuclear Planning Group. These took place in Copenhagen in May 1972, and in London in October. The year 1972 was a very eventful one diplomatically for the alliance, and the various developments in East–West relations continued to overshadow the work of the NPG. Between 22 and 29 May, President Nixon was in Moscow for the signing of the agreements limiting offensive and defensive strategic weapons which marked the conclusion of SALT I. Also in May, the Bundestag ratified the Moscow and Warsaw treaties on the renunciation of force which effectively settled the question of the western boundaries of Poland and the Soviet Union. In June the final protocol to the Berlin agreement was signed by the four powers responsible (Britain, France, USA and USSR). The conclusion of all these agreements prepared the way for the next stage of East–West diplomacy. This involved the preparatory talks for a European security conference which got underway in Helsinki in November, and the exploratory talks on mutual force reductions which opened in Vienna in January 1973. In Geneva, also in November, the United States and Soviet Union began a further series of strategic arms limitation talks. Although purely bilateral in form, SALT II can be seen as linked to these other multilateral diplomatic undertakings.

At Copenhagen, the ministers continued their examination of the programme of studies initiated in 1970 concerning the defensive use of nuclear weapons. In addition to studies dealing with various aspects of the problem prepared by various member countries, follow-up reports prepared at the Staff Group level to the SACEUR study presented at Mittenwald were also considered.[38] Further development of this study programme led the defence ministers at the twelfth meeting of the NPG in London to consider a report from the alliance's Military Committee considering the ability of NATO to conduct operations in situations in which nuclear weapons might be employed. Admiral Duncan, the Supreme Allied Commander Atlantic (SACLANT), presented a study concerned with the implications of a hypothetical initial defensive use at sea of tactical nuclear weapons, which led to a general discussion among the ministers of the possible military and political consequences. According to the communiqué, the NPG also 'examined in some detail the arrangements, procedures and facilities for consultation among member governments' if the use of nuclear weapons became necessary.[39] Clearly the issue of how and under what circumstances the allies would be consulted by the nuclear powers had not been resolved entirely by the 1969 guidelines on the subject. However, perhaps the main substantive achievement of the 1972 meetings of the NPG concerning theatre nuclear weapons was the revision of the 'Concepts for the Role of Theatre Nuclear Strike Forces in ACE' which had been accepted in Ottawa two years earlier.[40]

However, in estimating the significance of this revision to the work of the NPG, the following should be considered. In effect, the policy of the alliance with respect to theatre nuclear weapons was constantly changing in the light of altered political circumstances and developing technical capabilities. First of all, military authorities in SHAPE, in drawing-up their 'General Strike Plan' (GSP), necessarily had to respond to changes in American policy and strategic doctrine since the GSP was linked to the 'Single Integrated Operations Plan' (SIOP) developed under the authority of the US Joint Chiefs of Staff.[41] Secondly, much NATO planning for the operational use of nuclear weapons was in the hands of American officers who, whatever their relationship to the US command structure, naturally were sensitive to changes in the direction of American military policy respecting nuclear weapons. Thirdly, the very process of consultation within the NPG structure had the effect of making the various allies aware of how they all perceived changes in the strategic environment, and required of them appropriate policy responses. These policy responses in turn entered into the political process by which the overall strategic policy of the alliance was determined. Thus the revision of the concepts governing the role of theatre nuclear weapons in Europe, though a significant product of the consultative processes of the NPG, simply represented a particular statement, at a given time, of agreed alliance policy concerning certain aspects of theatre nuclear weapons. Two major developments after 1970 concerning the nuclear arsenal available in the European theatre had occasioned, presumably, the revision of the 'Concepts' document. These were the deployment, beginning in 1972, of Lance short-range ballistic missiles (SRBMs) as replacements for some of the Sergeant missiles that were currently available and, as of January 1972, the abandonment of any nuclear role by the Canadian forces based in Europe.[42]

One consequence of the signature by the United States of the Moscow Agreements had been the formal acceptance by the Americans of the fact of strategic parity with the Soviet Union. Such an acceptance had been implicit in the policy of 'strategic sufficiency' announced by the Nixon administration within a year of taking office, but, apart from clearly indicating that the United States would not accept a position of strategic inferiority, what would be accepted by the United States as parity and therefore determine the criteria of sufficiency was by no means clear. Prior to the conclusion of SALT I, the criteria for sufficiency had been identified as, first, maintaining an adequate second-strike capability able to deter an all-out surprise attack on US strategic forces; secondly, providing no incentive for the Soviet Union to strike first in a crisis; thirdly, preventing the Soviet Union from acquiring the ability to cause greater damage to the United States than could be inflicted on the Soviet Union by the Americans in a nuclear war; fourthly, defending against damage from small attacks or accidental launches.[43] Further, it has been suggested that two additional criteria governed the defence policy of the Nixon administration at this time. There was a desire to develop more flexible targeting options, and a determination to ensure that the overall numerical balance of strategic forces between the United States and Soviet Union could not be seen as disadvantageous to the United States.[44] In all, these criteria amounted to a requirement for a large, various and modernised strategic arsenal which many critics of the Nixon administration held to be incompatible with any effective stabilisation of the arms race.

Indeed, a common criticism of the SALT I agreements was that, rather than contributing to any slow-down in the pace of Soviet–American arms rivalry, they simply directed the arms race into new channels. Nevertheless, the Moscow Agreements did close certain options with respect to the development of strategic forces, and the United States recognised this in its defence policy by dropping the slogan 'sufficiency' and replacing it with the notion of 'essential equivalence'.[45] The explanation and justification of these changes in American strategic policy to the allies was a major function of the strategic briefings given to the NPG by the United States Secretary of Defense. In particular, it was necessary in these briefings to assure the allies that the course of American policy was compatible with their own interests. Thus among the tasks facing Melvin Laird at Copenhagen and London was that of seeking alliance acceptance of the American strategic position as it evolved from 'assured destruction' through 'sufficiency' to 'essential equivalence'. And linked to this was the need to demonstrate that theatre nuclear weapons had a positive and acceptable role to play in Europe. Certainly, within the overall framework of its strategic policy, the Nixon administration, unlike some of its critics, continued to see theatre nuclear weapons as having such a role. Despite the many ambiguities and difficulties associated with the nuclear weapons designed for tactical use in support of NATO, it was essential for the existence of allied military cohesion that an agreed doctrine concerning TNWs exist. Allied differences with respect to theatre nuclear weapons arose not from any disagreement as to the desirability of their presence in the European theatre, but from differences as to how and under what circumstances they would be used. It is to these latter concerns that American policy towards the strategy of the alliance has had repeatedly to address itself.

American defence policy as it developed under the Nixon administration had to respond to the reluctance in Congress and elsewhere to support policies that emphasised the possibility of direct American military involvement in conflict. The whole thrust of the 'Nixon doctrine' had been to emphasise the responsibilities of friends and allies in undertaking the burden of their own security. Thus successive defence statements by the administration emphasised the need to deter conflict at whatever level it occurred and played down war-fighting capabilities. Laird argued that previous national security policies had not focussed sufficiently on lowering the probability of all forms of war through deterrence. Instead, the effect of these policies had been to lower the probability of nuclear war while stressing a growing American capability to engage and to fight in other types of conflict.[46] The policy of the Nixon administration was to adopt a 'total force approach' with the object of deterring four distinct levels of warfare: strategic nuclear war, theatre nuclear war, theatre conventional war and sub-theatre or localised warfare. In the deterrence of theatre and sub-theatre conventional warfare, emphasis was placed on the contribution of local forces.[47] It was to be the task of American forces to support the efforts of others but not to assume the primary burden. The allies of the United States were warned that they would have to assume increasing responsibility for their own defence.[48] Nevertheless, the special responsibilities of the United States for nuclear deterrence continued to be recognised.

Understandably, the Nixon administration overstated the differences between its strategic policies and those of its predecessors. However, this restatement of American strategic policy did have implications for the NATO strategy of flexible response. At the level of conventional forces it provided an additional rationale for American pressure on the allies to increase their share of the burden of conditional defence, and to which the foundation of the Eurogroup and the announcement of the European Defence Improvement Programme had already been a partial response.[49] Although the successors to McNamara as American Secretary of Defense had reduced the emphasis on the desirability of the alliance possessing a full conventional war-fighting option, the definition of four discrete types of warfare, including theatre conventional war, inevitably reinforced doubts as to the scope of the nuclear deterrent. The new policy could be interpreted as strengthening the barriers to escalation from one level of conflict to another higher level. On the other hand the role of nuclear weapons in the deterrence of non-nuclear conflict was still considered to be relevant.[50] Thus Laird argued that a realistic strategy called for the planning of forces sufficient to cope with each level of potential conflict. Theatre nuclear weapons should be related to the conventional posture in such a way as to provide realistic options without having to rely solely on strategic nuclear weapons. 'In other words we plan to maintain tactical nuclear capabilities that contribute to realistic deterrence while allowing for maximum flexibility of response in every major contingency we plan for, should deterrence fail.'[51]

The aspirations reflected in this argument were no different from those previously associated with the strategy of flexible response. The essential problem of ensuring the credibility of the American nuclear guarantee also remained the same. While discerning a clear interest in strengthened conventional capabilities, the United States also recognised the political constraints on any great increase in the size of either its own or allied conventional forces. Parity with the Soviet Union at the strategic level had, in the view of the Nixon administration, made it increasingly undesirable to rely on the deterrent threat of American strategic weapons. Yet, in the European theatre, the strategic commitment was necessary for the credibility of the tactical nuclear weapons' deployment there. Consequently, it is not surprising that at least one observer has been led to conclude that the role of nuclear weapons in the security policies of the United States was ambiguous.[52]

As a possible way of escaping from these nuclear dilemmas, attention was directed to the possibilities and prospects for the modernisation of the theatre nuclear arsenal. Research and development and weapon improvement programmes were planned in order to ensure that the theatre nuclear weapons and their associated command and control systems would have both adequate capability and a minimal chance of accidental or unauthorised use.[53] The implications for alliance strategy of such a modernised arsenal was one of the topics discussed at the Ankara meeting of the NPG in May 1973.

Public discussion of the possibilities of modernised tactical nuclear weapons at this time became focussed on the so-called 'mini-nukes': a somewhat misleading term that was usually applied to weapons characterised by a combination of high accuracy and refined, low-yield warheads.[54] Proposals for a new generation of tactical nuclear warheads suggested the marriage of precision guidance and miniaturised, low-yield warheads that would be carefully 'tailored' for specific blast and radiation effects. The accuracy of the new weapons would compensate for the lower yields of the warheads and, it was argued, make defensive operations on a nuclear battlefield more feasible. In fact the 'mini-nuke' debate rehearsed the arguments that were to take place later in the decade over enhanced radiation weapons: weapons which were popularly to be known under the soubriquet of 'neutron bomb'.

The advocates of 'mini-nukes' stressed the enhanced war-fighting capability they would give to the alliance's nuclear forces.[55] The combination of accuracy and low-yield would reduce the undesirable collateral effects of any recourse to nuclear weapons by NATO in the European theatre and thus make the threat to use nuclear weapons more credible. It was argued that these weapons, given an appropriate tactical doctrine and military deployment, would enhance the position of the defence against the 'blitzkrieg' threat posed by the forces of the Warsaw Pact. By favouring the defence, the introduction of 'mini-nukes' would strengthen the overall deterrent posture of the alliance. In effect, this argument paralleled those of the 1950s which suggested that the introduction into Europe of theatre nuclear weapons would reinforce the defensive capabilities of NATO forces. However, an additional consideration that has been held to favour the development of modernised tactical weapons was the supposed reduction in the risk of escalation should they be used. By virtue of their low yields and limited collateral effects, their controlled use would have less destructive effect in many cases than the use of conventional explosives. Consequently, it could be argued that their use should not be considered as crossing a decisive escalation threshold in the same way as would resort to the existing arsenal of theatre nuclear weapons. Furthermore, modernised low-yield nuclear weapons should be used in such a way as to avoid escalation. Their deterrent value would lie in their very military effectiveness and would avoid the creation of a nuclear battlefield characterised by the high levels of radiation and physical destruction associated with the theatre nuclear weapons currently deployed, and which would severely hamper the conduct of defensive military operations. Therefore, it would be in the interest of the defenders that they should exploit the military advantages of 'mini-nukes' without generating levels of destruction which would make their use self-deterring. The possession by the alliance of a modernised stock of theatre nuclear weapons would in fact create an additional firebreak against escalation to even greater levels of violence.[56]

On the other hand, counter-arguments to the deployment of low-yield battlefield nuclear weapons have emphasised the importance of maintaining an unambiguous distinction between the use of conventional and nuclear weapons. Any crossing of the nuclear threshold would have incalculable and probably disastrous consequences, and it is the temptation to make early and widespread use of them that would make the introduction of such weapons so dangerous. Also, it is not possible to assume that the enemy would view the employment of 'mini-nukes' as constituting a special category to which a response with existing kinds of theatre nuclear weapon would be inappropriate.[57] Critics also evidenced concern with the command and control implications of these weapons. It was suggested, for example, that their deployment would increase the probability that nuclear weapons might be used without the specific authority of the President of the United States.[58] And anyway, unless the decision to fire these weapons at targets of opportunity (which would be a major military rationale for them) were to be delegated to politically unacceptably low levels of military command, battlefield communications would have to be dramatically improved in order to give higher authority the 'real-time' in which to make a decision. Essentially, what the critics of 'mini-nuke' deployment objected to was the attempt to increase the 'acceptability' of the battlefield use of nuclear weapons. The possible deterrent effect of a nuclear war-fighting capability was downplayed in favour of reliance on the 'deterrence through fear of escalation' which was implicit in the current nuclear posture of the alliance.[59]

The question of 'mini-nukes' was specifically addressed by the ministers present at the Ankara meeting of the NPG.[60]

Awareness of this fact, together with the contemporary request to Congress by the American administration for funds for the new nuclear artillery shells, served to stimulate public debate on the merits of possible 'mini-nuke' deployment. Yet, ironically, it became clear that the administration had no intention of producing in the near future weapons with anything like the range of characteristics advocated by the strongest supporters of 'mini-nuke' deployment. What the administration was seeking from Congress was funding for improved artillery shells which would feature better control mechanisms and more 'tailored' warheads as replacements for some of the existing and aging stockpile. Nevertheless, military spokesmen before congressional hearings in the spring and early summer of 1973 did indicate a general need for an improved and up-dated theatre nuclear weapon arsenal.[61] At that time both the request and the statement of need were received unsympathetically.

It has been reported that at Ankara, despite the importance of the topic, the Americans were somewhat unresponsive to the interest of the Europeans in the whole 'mini-nuke' issue.[62] This unresponsiveness seems to have been a result of the political sensitivity of the issue, but also of differences in view between the military, who by-and-large favoured the development of new weapons, and the State Department, which was more conscious of the political difficulties. Anyway, the American delegation fell back on the not unfamiliar tactic of avoiding embarrassing discussion by claiming that the law and policy of the United States precluded the discussion of new weapons before deployment was a practical possibility. Subsequently, the United States issued a public statement to the effect that a new family of precision-guided and miniaturised nuclear weapons had not been developed or deployed, and that the United States would only undertake such a decision after full consultation with its allies.[63]

As it emerged, the position of the American administration with respect to a modernised tactical nuclear arsenal was that the very term 'mini-nuke' was misleading. No accepted definition of what constituted a mini-nuke existed and, anyway, the arsenal of theatre nuclear weapons already contained low-yield warheads. Nevertheless, the United States continued to seek reduced yield and improved accuracy in tactical nuclear weapons in order to decrease unwanted damage and yet possess the capability for target destruction. But a new 'mini-nuke' programme as such did not exist.[64] On the one hand the need for a continuous review and updating of the theatre nuclear arsenal was stressed, and on the other hand it was asserted that no plans existed for the introduction of a new generation of low-yield weapons. The ambiguity of the American position was apparent. A clarification of American policy in this area was attempted in a statement to the UN Conference of the Committee on Disarmament in Geneva. In this statement it was pointed out that the term 'mini-nuke' falsely conveyed the impression that a 'radically new and futuristic family of weapons' was being talked about, and that such miniature weapons could be handled and used in the same fashion as conventional weapons. Nothing of the kind was contemplated. What the United States was involved in (as it had been for many years) was a gradual process of moderately upgrading the tactical nuclear stockpile. It was not the policy of the American government to treat any tactical nuclear system as interchangeable with conventional arms, or to blur the distinction between conventional and nuclear weapons. The command and control procedures that the United States applied to nuclear weapons in general had always applied to small-yield weapons as well, and it was not the intention to change this policy.[65]

As in the case of atomic demolition munitions, the issue of 'mini-nukes' was particularly sensitive for the Germans. After the Ankara meeting on 22 July, the German Defence Minister, Georg Leber, had announced at a press conference his understanding of the American position by stating that the United States was not thinking of equipping its troops with these weapons. In his view the first use of nuclear weapons would mean a change in the kind of war being fought, and important distinctions between the various kinds of nuclear weapons should not be drawn. The use of a 'single atomic hand grenade' would cause escalation to the most powerful nuclear weapons.[66] When confronted with this statement,

Secretary of Defense Schlesinger admitted that there was a 'natural ambivalence' in Germany regarding the first use of nuclear weapons. But the Secretary of Defense went on to assert that the Germans, including Georg Leber, had always been interested in receiving reassurance from the United States that tactical and strategic weapons would be available for use in the event of a threat. While distinguishing 'between circumstances in the employment of nuclear weapons', according to Schlesinger 'there had been no change in the German desire throughout CDU or SPD dominated governments for assurance that nuclear weapons will be used in defense of Germany under these circumstances'.[67]

As German policy towards theatre nuclear weapons had developed under the SPD, there had been increased emphasis on the importance of raising the nuclear threshold. In contrast to the German position at the time of the drafting of the 1969 guidelines on initial use, there was far greater reluctance to contemplate resort to nuclear weapons by the alliance fairly early in any campaign on the Central Front. It could be surmised, however, that, like the previous German government, the current administration favoured relatively long-range interdiction strikes which avoided German territory in the event that the alliance was forced to consider the use of theatre nuclear weapons. It followed that for the Germans the problem with 'mini-nukes' (and ADMs as well) was the implication that they would be used early in any conflict on the Central Front and on German territory. Nevertheless, the Germans had to face the fact that, given the forces deployed on both sides in Central Europe, it was likely that at some stage of a major battle on the central front it would be necessary to use nuclear weapons if German territory were to be defended. Thus a primary concern of the German government was to ensure that adequate consultation take place before nuclear weapons were used, and that the German government be able to exercise effective political control over the circumstances and manner of their use involving Germany. The fear of the German government concerning ADMs and 'mini-nukes' was that their deployment would lessen the time available for consultation and make it even more difficult for any degree of

German control over the use of theatre nuclear weapons to be exercised. In other words, the deployment of these weapons would increase the likelihood of the conduct of a nuclear campaign slipping from a political control in which the nuclear host country could genuinely share.[68]

At Ankara in May 1973, apart from the question of 'mini-nukes', the ministers discussed a range of topics within the framework of the established pattern of the agenda of the ministerial meetings of the Nuclear Planning Group. As at previous meetings, the United States briefed the allied ministers on the current balance of strategic forces and on the latest trends in that balance. For the first time, however, the briefing was not given by the American Secretary of Defense. A new Secretary of Defense, Elliot L. Richardson, had just been appointed and he was represented by the United States Permanent Representative, Dirk P. Spierenburg and by Assistant Secretary of Defense, Robert C. Hill. In the light of an examination of the implications of strategic developments for the strategic posture of the alliance, the ministers agreed that the strategic forces of the alliance would be adequate for the foreseeable future.[69] Basically, as on previous occasions when statements of this kind had emerged from the NPG, the ministerial agreement simply represented another formal alliance endorsement of American strategic policy.

It was announced in the communiqué that the series of studies dealing with the possible follow-up use of theatre nuclear weapons in deteriorating situations after initial use had occurred, had been concluded. This series of studies represented the first phase of a work programme that had been initiated in 1970 and was one way in which the alliance, through the NPG, had attempted to deal with some of the many issues concerning the possible use of theatre nuclear weapons which had not been covered by the 1969 guidelines. The final study, which was jointly presented by the Netherlands and Britain, dealt with questions of nuclear defence in a maritime context. This study, although arising from the attempt to refine political guidelines, can be seen as complementary to Admiral Duncan's presentation to the previous meeting of the NPG. At Ankara, General Goodpaster, as

SACEUR, following on from SACLANT's presentation at Copenhagen put forward a hypothetical scenario to illustrate a particular option for the initial defensive tactical employment of nuclear weapons. The ministers were reported as having discussed the political and military factors that would have to be taken into account in reaching decisions in a crisis, and as having clarified the procedural questions that would be involved. In similar vein an exchange of views took place on the preliminary impressions gained during the WINTEX-73 NATO exercise with particular reference to the process of political consultation.[70]

Finally at Ankara, the next phase of the work of the NPG in connection with the possible use of theatre nuclear weapons was announced. This would be involved with the comparative analysis of the various studies that had been undertaken 'for the purpose of gaining deeper insight into policy matters pertaining to the defensive tactical use of nuclear weapons'. This process was expected to contribute to the refinement and elaboration of existing political guidelines concerning this area.[71]

Between the conclusion of the NPG meeting in Ankara and the next meeting, which was held in The Hague in November, events in the Middle East and developments in Soviet–American relations placed a great deal of strain on inter-allied relations. In particular, relations between the United States and Germany were adversely affected. President Nixon's meeting with Brezhnev in Washington and San Clemente in June produced several agreements which were felt by a number of the allies, in addition to Germany, to have been reached without adequate consultation. The agreement between the USSR and USA on the prevention of nuclear war was especially disturbing since it had been negotiated secretly, without prior allied consultation or indeed without prior notice.[72] Not only was the lack of consultation resented by the allies, but the terms of the agreement could be interpreted as giving precedence to the super-power relationship at the expense of alliance consultation. Moreover, it was possible to see in article 2 of the agreement the implication of a 'no first use of nuclear force' doctrine that, if made explicit, would completely undermine the strategic premises on which the alliance was built.[73] This agreement, when coupled with American concessions on the timing and form of the CSCE, and on the dropping of 'mutual' from the proposed force reduction negotiations in Vienna, did little to further European willingness to cooperate with the United States on the creation of the new 'Atlantic Charter' called for by Dr Kissinger in his 'Year of Europe' speech of 23 April 1973.[74]

The nadir of inter-allied relations in this period was reached in October when the Arab–Israeli war created acute differences between the United States and its allies. The alliance response to the Middle East crisis underlined all the doubts which existed as to the effectiveness of the alliance as an agency for crisis management. Even though the Middle East was outside the scope of the North Atlantic Treaty, nevertheless the crisis exposed limitations in the process of political consultation among the allies which inevitably affected the confidence that would be placed in those consultative arrangements more directly concerned with the responsibilities of NATO. One particular incident is reported as having occurred which clearly demonstrates the limitations of alliance consultation as a safeguard for the interests of a weaker ally when these directly confront those of the dominant alliance power. When the German government requested that the United States cease moving military supplies from Germany for shipment to Israel, the American ambassador, Martin Hillenbrand, is said to have stated that the United States regarded Germany's sovereignty as limited, and reserved the right to take any action it deemed proper in the interests of international security. This message was reinforced in Washington by the Secretary of State in an interview with the German ambassador.[75]

Although these matters were not of direct concern to the work of the NPG, inevitably it was sensitive to the background political environment in which it operated, and the implications for the alliance of the recent crisis were discussed at The Hague.[76] However, despite the existence of serious inter-allied tensions, the ministers were able to continue discussion of the work programme that had been laid down previously. It seems that James Schlesinger, the new Secretary of Defense, who had succeeded Elliot Richardson's short tenure of office, was determined to limit as much as possible any adverse effects of the crisis on the operation of the Nuclear Planning Group. At a press conference following the meeting, Mr Schlesinger indicated that the United States did not want allied differences over the Middle East crisis to spill over into the area of European security. It was important that any tendency towards recrimination over recent events should be avoided, and that any observed failings be corrected. The Secretary of Defense was concerned, however, with pointing out that the American pledge to come to the defence of the alliance rested on the European nations providing the minimum of support necessary to maintain the American commitment. In Schlesinger's view, the minimum level of support required was increasing, at least in the military field, and it was necessary for the alliance 'to show more vigour' in terms of what it was accomplishing than had been the case in the past.[77] Schlesinger stressed the requirement for greater military effort on the part of the allies, but it was possible to infer that in the view of the United States a minimum of political support was necessary as well. As far as the NPG was concerned, all this simply illustrated the fact that its functioning ultimately depended on the operation of the larger alliance political system of which it was part.

Of course, by the end of 1973 the working of the Nuclear Planning Group had become sufficiently institutionalised, its routines well enough established to be able to continue functioning through institutional inertia. One way in which a political system like NATO can cope with the stress generated by inter-allied divisions is to continue established patterns of consultation and cooperation. The continuation of alliance consultation on matters of nuclear policy through the NPG served to demonstrate that the allies were still capable of dealing constructively with matters of great intrinsic importance to them. Whether or not the consultative process led to substantive agreements of any significance, the fact that consultation occurred served the important political function of supporting alliance cohesion in a volatile and divisive international environment. Thus the continuing work of the

NPG in such well-established areas of concern as the implementation of the strategy of flexible response and the political
and military implications of the tactical employment of
nuclear weapons at various stages of a possible conflict, helped
the allies overcome their larger political differences.

Indeed, at The Hague and at the subsequent meeting of the
NPG in Bergen in June 1974, further agreements on alliance
nuclear policy were achieved and a reaffirmation of the value
of the work of the Nuclear Planning Group was made.
Specifically at The Hague the ministers discussed a report by
the military authorities on the operational concepts and
doctrine that were currently governing their military planning.
Consideration was given as well to a number of measures that
had been taken in the light of experience concerning political
consultation on the use of nuclear weapons, and the progress
made in implementing the political guidelines on atomic
demolition munitions was reviewed.[78] In Bergen, the ministers
again discussed arrangements for effective consultation between
member governments in time of crisis. This time a report on
the involvement of the Military Committee in the consultative
process was considered and this report together with a
number of comments on it was passed on to the Defence
Planning Committee. In addition to the usual appraisal of
Soviet capabilities, a six-nation report on 'Warsaw Pact politico-
military strategy and military doctrine bearing on the possible
tactical use of nuclear weapons' was discussed. Of more
immediate impact on alliance nuclear policy, however, was
the briefing by the Secretary of Defense on a number of
technological developments that could affect the tactical
nuclear capability of the alliance. These technological developments included a briefing on enhanced radiation weapons
and led the NPG to initiate a major review of their political and
military implications.[79] The Secretary of Defense was responsible also for introducing a discussion of developments in
American targeting doctrine which could have an impact on
the nuclear posture of the alliance. The development by
Schlesinger of a doctrine of 'limited nuclear options' and the
controversy that it aroused was a factor in reviving the salience
of nuclear issues as the implications of the new doctrine for the

alliance were examined. Finally, the Norwegian Defence Minister made a statement attempting to clarify his government's nuclear and base policy.[80]

Although differences in the allied approach to nuclear weapons remained, after Bergen it might have seemed that the work of the NPG could proceed along its clearly defined paths of consultation without any immediate prospect of issues arising which were sufficiently divisive to compromise its continued ability to function. However, the final meeting of the NPG scheduled for 1974 was directly affected by developments in the broader political environment of the alliance. Events in Portugal resulted in a situation which challenged the ability of the Nuclear Planning Group to continue functioning as a vehicle for allied nuclear consultation. Whereas it could be said of the earlier history of the NPG that the Group itself generated divisive issues for the alliance, now it seemed that more and more political developments outside the terms of reference of the NPG and beyond its control constrained the manner of its operation.

It had been planned that the sixteenth meeting of the Nuclear Planning Group should take place in Rome on 7 and 8 November. The Rome meeting would have been the occasion for the beginning of a new cycle of membership rotation. Prior to 1974, Portugal though a member of the NDAC had never participated directly in the work of the NPG, and was the only member of the NDAC not to do so. However, in the early months of 1974 the Portuguese Permanent Representative to the North Atlantic Council began participating in the work of the NPG, as did his representative on the Staff Group, and it was anticipated that Portugal would be represented at the ministerial level in Rome. In the meantime, on 25 April, the Caetano government fell and the arrangements by which Portugal was to participate fully in the work of the NPG collapsed with it.[81]

Basically the position was that the United States government was unwilling to discuss extremely sensitive issues of nuclear policy with an allied government which was both unstable and included communists. The future character of the Portuguese regime was a matter of major concern to all the allies, but the

West Europeans in particular were concerned that no actions be taken which might damage the forces of the democratic centre in Portugal. The United States refused to release nuclear information to a government which it regarded as an unacceptable security risk. Thus the participation of Portugal in the work of the NPG, when coupled with the attempts of the United States to unseat her, was acutely embarrassing for the European allies. The Rome meeting of the NPG did not take place, it being put about that the defence ministers had found it inconvenient to meet at that time. Instead, the meeting was held in Brussels on 10 December and coincided with a meeting of the Defence Planning Committee. This meeting had been made possible by a decision of the Portuguese government, in the light of the American attitude towards it, to abstain from future meetings of the NPG.[82]

Although the immediate problems posed by the change of regime in Portugal were successfully circumvented, they served to indicate a number of difficulties that challenged the Nuclear Planning Group as a mechanism for effective allied consultation on nuclear policy. For consultation on particularly sensitive issues such as these, the Portuguese incident demonstrated that the degree of political homogeneity required was far greater than for the operation of the plenary alliance institutions. Thus Portugal could be accommodated on the NDAC, a purely rubber-stamping body, but not on the NPG where elements of real consultation occurred. In this respect the case of Portugal provided a possible clue to the implications of any success that 'Eurocommunism' might have on the operation of the alliance political system. The question of Portuguese representation also pointed out the degree to which the NPG had moved away from the original conception of a select high-level body able to discuss nuclear matters on an intimate and relatively informal basis. As the membership and procedures of the NPG increasingly paralleled those operating in the alliance at large, it was increasingly likely that it would reflect the cumbersome political processes characteristic of a multilateral alliance institution such as NATO. Finally, it was again shown that the attitude of the United States was crucial in determining the ground rules under which consultation on nuclear policy would operate, and it highlighted the essentially unilateral character of the consultative processes at work in the NPG.

5. NEW DIRECTIONS: 1975–80

By the end of 1974 it was clear that nuclear consultation in the alliance was taking place in a political and strategic environment far different from that which had existed when the Nuclear Planning Group had been established in 1967. That the NPG had been able to survive the appearance of new political issues and dramatic changes in the strategic balance while continuing to serve as a useful vehicle for nuclear consultation was testimony to both institutional adaptability and persistence. Indeed, SALT, the proposed revisions in American targeting doctrine, the possibilities suggested by new weapons technologies, and the political review of the role of theatre nuclear weapons (TNW) initiated in the United States by the so-called 'Nunn Amendment' of August 1974 had all served to increase the salience of nuclear issues in the alliance and consequently gave increased importance to the work of the NPG. However, in the previous several years the work of the NPG had become increasingly routine, and it was not clear that the circumstances were propitious for new departures. Yet, in retrospect, it was probably the routine character of its work that helped the NPG to overcome the impact on its operations of the political vicissitudes being experienced by the alliance at this time and of the adverse developments in its strategic environment.

In addition to the upheaval in Portugal, the summer of 1974 had seen the Cyprus crisis bring Greece and Turkey to the brink of war, and the Turkish invasion of the island in July and August led the Greeks to emulate France and withdraw from the alliance's integrated military command structure. However, unlike France, Greece continued to participate in the nuclear consultation processes of the alliance by retaining her membership in the NPG. In terms of the strategic environment, the

145

increasing concern being given to the implications of new technologies can be understood as one response to changes in the alliance's military environment and to shifts in the European military balance. By the beginning of 1975 it was becoming clear that strategic parity and the steady improvement in Soviet conventional and theatre nuclear forces were challenging many of the assumptions on which the alliance's military posture was based.

Thus, at the beginning of 1975 the consultative mechanism was working, but it was not clear to what extent, in the light of the strains to which the alliance was subject, consultation would help resolve in the long run the inevitable allied conflicts of interest over nuclear strategy. In the past, the Nuclear Planning Group had been effective inasmuch as the processes of nuclear consultation practised there produced outcomes that were sufficiently acceptable to the various allies for them to sustain a strategic posture that was politically as well as strategically credible. Ultimately, of course, this would continue to depend on the unfolding of the total political environment in which the alliance existed, but at the level of the NPG it would depend more immediately on the nature of the consultation undertaken. The next few years were to see the NPG more and more exercised by issues of theatre nuclear force modernisation and by the linking of modernisation to issues of détente and arms control. Not that the NPG concerned itself much more directly with arms control and détente than it had in the past, but that national positions in the NPG were more clearly determined by attitudes towards them. Overall, questions concerning the modernisation of the alliance's theatre nuclear forces served to re-open many of the issues of nuclear policy that the setting up of the Nuclear Planning Group in the first place had done so much to resolve. One result was that by the end of the decade the whole structure of nuclear consultation in the alliance was to undergo change.

A good example of the linking of broader political and security concerns with the work of the NPG was provided by a Dutch proposal that tactical nuclear weapons be included in the deadlocked MBFR negotiations in Vienna. In essence, the

Dutch suggested that NATO should offer to trade a reduction in its theatre nuclear weapons against Soviet tanks deployed in Eastern Europe.[1] This suggestion was made public on the eve of the Brussels meeting of the NPG that had been postponed as a result of the difficulties over Portuguese representation and, from the point of view of a number of the participants, the Dutch initiative was considered to be singularly ill-timed. This was because it was seen as undermining a delicate balance in the alliance over theatre nuclear weapons. In November President Ford had met with his Russian counterpart in Vladivostok and they had reached an understanding on overall ceilings for strategic forces within the context of negotiations on SALT II. As part of this understanding the Russians had dropped their insistence that 'forward based systems (FBS) be included in any future agreement limiting Soviet and American strategic forces'. Although what the Russians have meant by forward based systems has tended to be rather elastic, the concept has usually encompassed those European-based systems that have an operational radius sufficient to strike targets in the Soviet Union. The American resistance to including NATO's longer-range strike forces (which consisted solely of aircraft) in SALT was supported by continual European representations on the subject. The Germans in particular were concerned that any future bilateral agreement between the Americans and the Russians was not made at the expense of the European balance. By raising the issue of the possible inclusion of theatre nuclear weapons in the Vienna talks so soon after Vladivostok, the Dutch seemed to invite the Russians to keep the FBS issue alive to their own advantage and to the embarrassment of NATO. Both the British and German defence ministers were reported to have been upset by the Dutch actions, and Georg Leber was said to have quite bluntly described the proposal as 'foolish'.[2]

The Dutch proposal also entailed a major modification of the agreed alliance position on MBFR. The NATO position was that the first phase of any reductions should be restricted to conventional ground forces and that subsequent reductions should be phased so as to produce a common manpower ceiling in the 'agreed reductions area'. This had been rejected by the Russians who insisted that tactical air forces should be included from the very beginning and that entire units should be withdrawn along with their associated conventional and nuclear weaponry. In other words, the Russians pressed the FBS issue at the theatre level at the same time as they were pressing their case that forward based systems should form part of the agenda for SALT II. As already noted, this demand for the inclusion of FBS in the second round of SALT had been dropped at Vladivostok, but the Soviet position on MBFR remained unchanged. The Dutch proposal could thus be interpreted as a concession to the Soviet negotiating position. On the other hand, the Dutch proposal was not exactly novel. In 1973 the Americans had circulated among their NATO allies three alternative proposals for possible force reductions in Europe, and the third option involved the offer of withdrawing NATO nuclear forces against the withdrawal of a Soviet tank army.[3] Thus, although the initial Western position on MBFR involved conventional forces only, the possibility of trading off NATO theatre nuclear forces had been discussed and was subsequently revived in what became known as 'Option III'.

Dutch spokesmen justified their initiative by arguing that it might provide a means of achieving some significant movement in the Vienna talks, but a more fundamental motivation lay in the growing importance of nuclear issues in Dutch domestic politics which was increasingly leading the Dutch to question the alliance's theatre nuclear posture and their own place within it.[4] In this the Dutch, like other Europeans, were monitoring the renewed debate in the United States on the role of theatre nuclear weapons. A suggestion from a former member of the Kennedy administration that, given a more effective conventional posture, a European stockpile of 1,000 warheads would be sufficient for deterrent purposes had attracted considerable publicity in the spring, and was part of a widespread feeling in the American strategic community that the NATO arsenal was too large and not well tailored to the strategic doctrine it was designed to support.[5] This feeling was reflected in the Nunn Amendment which called upon the Secretary of Defense to undertake a study of the 'overall concept for use of tactical nuclear weapons in Europe' and the 'reduction in the number and type of nuclear warheads which are not essential for the defense structure for Western Europe'.[6] The suggestion that there were too many warheads of too many different types in the NATO nuclear stockpile was examined in the review that subsequently took place.

At the Brussels meeting of the NPG in December 1974 both the Vladivostok agreement and the Nunn Amendment were on the agenda, and it was apparently within the general discussion of various aspects of theatre nuclear weapons that these agenda items aroused that the Dutch proposal concerning MBFR was considered. Following the meeting the US Secretary of Defense claimed that no specific proposal had been considered, merely that the possibilities had been explored, but he did indicate that he would oppose any significant reduction in US nuclear forces in Europe without matching concessions from the Soviet Union.[7] In taking this position, the Secretary of Defense stated what was to be a persistent theme as the question of theatre nuclear force (TNF) arms control became increasingly important on the agenda of alliance nuclear policy.

As part of the continuing attention that the Nuclear Planning Group was giving to the possible follow-on use of nuclear weapons if initial use had failed to achieve its purpose, the Brussels meeting received briefings from SACEUR and SACLANT on some of the planning options involving nuclear weapons that were open to the alliance.[8] Following the adoption of the provisional political guidelines on initial use in 1969, the NPG had initiated a series of studies on various aspects of the possible tactical use of nuclear weapons under the concept of flexible response, and the first series had been completed by the Ankara meeting in May 1973. The second phase of this series of studies was completed for the seventeenth meeting of the NPG at Monterey in June 1975. At Monterey, apparently at the suggestion of the British, it was decided to initiate a third series of studies which would be directed to the production of a consolidated set of guidelines governing the use of nuclear weapons in the European theatre.[9]

Of more immediate significance, however, was that the United States was now suggesting to the allies that theatre nuclear weapons indeed be contained in the Western offer of first phase reductions in the Vienna MBFR negotiations. The allied ministers now had available Schlesinger's report to Congress on the theatre nuclear posture in Europe, and this formed an important item on the agenda. The report in a sense vindicated the Dutch position that it would be possible for NATO to trade nuclear weapons for tanks without diminishing the security of the alliance. Certainly, the other allies were now prepared to accept this modification of their bargaining position in MBFR, and the major concern now became that of determining what systems should be included in the offer. This became the subject of subsequent allied discussions at the official level and when the new Western offer (Option III) was tabled in Vienna in December, it included 1,000 nuclear warheads, 54 nuclear-capable F-4 aircraft and 36 Pershing missiles.[10]

Schlesinger's report to Congress opened up in a very direct way for the NPG the whole question of the composition and adequacy of the alliance's theatre nuclear arsenal. The report itself had given considerable attention to the need to modernise all aspects of the theatre nuclear posture including the weapons themselves, and had stressed the need for the continued development of selective and controlled options that would enable the alliance to deal with major penetrations and achieve a quick and decisive reversal of the tactical situation, and to engage if necessary in a discriminating interdiction campaign against enemy forces and lines of communication.[11] In this latter respect, the report reflected at the theatre level the ideas that the Secretary of Defense had publicised in a series of statements the previous year under the general notion of 'limited nuclear options', and which had already been discussed at the Bergen meeting of the NPG in June 1974.[12] By now the discussion of theatre nuclear force modernisation in the Nuclear Planning Group had moved on from consideration of such matters as improved site security and measures to ensure against unauthorised use, to include consideration of the wide range of possibilities for the introduction of new weapons into the alliance's theatre nuclear arsenal. The prospect of dealing with some of the alliance's nuclear problems through technological innovation had been presaged in the earlier discussion of 'mini-nukes', but now the alliance was beginning to consider the implications of specific innovations. Thus, for example, the NPG was examining the possibility of overcoming some of the tactical, control and, significantly, political difficulties associated with the ADMs by the use of 'earth penetrator' warheads delivered by new missiles. At Monterey, the NPG ministers agreed on a work programme that would examine the implications of techno-logical improvements for the deterrent posture of the alliance. However, not only were the possibilities of technological innovation for nuclear weapons to be examined, but the implications for conventional defence were to be looked into as well. [13]

This resulted in the 'new technology study' by two *ad hoc* groups under the auspices of the NPG. One group was to examine the political implications of the new technology (the 'Political Implications Team'), and the other the military implications (the 'Military Implications Team'). It should be noted that the new technology study was concerned with the implications and possibilities of a wide range of new techno-logies, and was by no means concerned primarily with nuclear weapons. Rather, the emphasis was on the application of new technologies for conventional warfare and with the implications of these technologies for the nuclear posture of the alliance. Thus, by way of example, consideration was given to the extent to which the development of conventional precision-guided munitions (PGMs) could be substituted for roles currently assigned to nuclear weapons. [14] The reports of these teams were to be considered nearly two years later, but their establishment both paralleled and reflected alliance concern with a changing strategic and military balance; a concern that was evidenced in the 'Long-Range Defence Concept' that formed the basis of the Defence Planning Committee's 1975 ministerial guidance for future defence planning. [15]

As always when Americans have undertaken a review of their policies and doctrine concerning nuclear weapons, it served to reveal underlying European uncertainties and insecurities concerning them. 'Limited nuclear options' and the possibility of modernisation were no exception in this respect, and were themselves but responses to a transformed strategic situation. The various allied assessments of the political and strategic consequences of both SALT I and of any SALT II were very much affecting allied discussion of nuclear policy and, in addition, there was emerging in NATO circles a genuine concern with the cumulative impact on the military balance of improvements in the conventional and nuclear capabilities of the Warsaw Pact. In the United States, critics of the direction that the SALT process was taking questioned whether, on the basis of existing trends, the United States would emerge the stronger in any counterforce exchange with the Soviet Union, and therefore in effect questioned whether the United States would have the strategic capability to implement a strategy of limited nuclear options.[16]

This suggestion that the United States faced an adverse 'exchange ratio' was certainly noted by the Germans, who were raising the question of the impact of growing Soviet capabilities on European security in a situation of strategic parity, and who were seeking reassurance that the United States still had the capacity to meet the threat of Soviet medium and intermediate-range nuclear weapons targeted against Western Europe. American officials argued in response that the United States retained under the SALT agreements a strategic arsenal sufficient to provide for both assured destruction in the event of a Soviet disarming attack on the United States and the capacity to cover targets of more immediate European concern. Indeed, one important objective of Schlesinger's doctrine of limited nuclear options was to ensure the continued credibility of the 'coupling' of American strategic forces directly to European security. Nevertheless, there was a growing feeling in Europe that the SALT process was not giving enough attention to the theatre nuclear balance and to European interests in it. Thus there were suspicions in Germany over the nature of the understanding that the United States had reached with the Soviet Union over the FBS issue at Vladivostok. It was suspected that the Russians had secured from the Americans an undertaking not to do anything to upset the *status quo* concerning the strength of its theatre nuclear forces deployed in Western Europe. From the German point of view, in so far as the Soviet Union insisted upon a definition of 'equal security' with the United States aimed at limiting, if not eradicating, the strategic options that longer-range theatre nuclear weapons provided for the United States, it disregarded any security interests that Western Europe might have in the deployment of these weapons.[17] Once SALT began to impinge on theatre systems, Europeans generally, and the Germans in particular, were bound to be sensitive to the implication that agreement on what constituted a satisfactory global balance would be determined by the Soviet Union and the United States bilaterally without providing for any direct input from those who might be affected by the regional implications of such a balance.

The decision to increase the number of Poseidon warheads assigned to SACEUR for targeting purposes and the stationing of an additional wing of F-111 strike aircraft in England can be seen as one American response to these concerns.[18] Despite this, questions concerning the implications of SALT for the theatre nuclear balance persisted and manifested themselves throughout the negotiations that led to the signing of the SALT II agreement in Vienna in June 1979. These questions centred on such elements in SALT II as the non-circumvention clause and the limits placed on cruise missile deployment by the Protocol to the treaty, but they were also to become part of the more wide-reaching debate on theatre nuclear force modernisation in NATO. As the political debate widened, however, the original grounds for European concern with TNF modernisation were to be largely lost, and the content and context of alliance discussion of the subject moved beyond the more narrowly technical confines of allied consultation on nuclear policy. In other words, as the political salience of nuclear issues increased, so the ability of the allies to settle matters through such routine forms of consultation as the NPG declined. Nevertheless, at the end of 1975 the multilateral discussion of nuclear policy could still be largely contained within the Nuclear Planning Group as the primary alliance forum for questions concerning theatre nuclear weapons. And so at the next ministerial meeting of the NPG at Hamburg in

January 1976, the new US Secretary of Defense, Donald Rumsfeld, provided a major briefing on the development of enhanced radiation (neutron) warheads.[19]

This briefing confirmed that the NPG had now, in effect, embarked on a new phase in its work. Two earlier phases can be distinguished: first, the drafting of the original provisional political guidelines for initial use and the establishment of consultative procedures in the event that resort to nuclear weapons was contemplated; and second, the elaboration of concepts governing nuclear use in the European theatre. This activity went beyond the 'Concepts' document in 1970, and beyond the formal amendment of that document two years later; it can be seen as involving the whole series of studies on possible follow-on use in the event that initial use failed to secure its purpose. Now, the work of the NPG was very much focussing on the implications of the deployment of new warheads and means of delivery. This involvement with the implications of new technology for the nuclear posture in Europe was to constitute a major element of the Nuclear Planning Group's work over succeeding years.

Although allied recognition that SALT had important implications for the alliance's theatre nuclear posture had done much to stimulate allied interest in the possibilities opened up by TNF modernisation, the more immediate catalyst was provided by the mounting concern of the alliance's military authorities with the growing conventional and nuclear capabilities of the Warsaw Pact. These concerns about the military balance in Europe were now being paralleled at the political level, and it was necessary to address the question as to how far the alliance could continue to rest its deterrent posture on the concept of flexible response without changes in the character and composition of its nuclear arsenal. Thus, at the nineteenth meeting of the NPG in June there was discussion of an American paper dealing with various ways in which the effectiveness of the alliance's theatre nuclear forces could be improved, and the allies received a further briefing from the Secretary of Defense on the status of enhanced radiation warhead programmes.[20] There is no evidence that the participants in the work of the NPG were particularly aware of the political difficulties that were to be generated by TNF modernisation; they were conscious, of course, of the general sensitivity of nuclear issues, and had always tended to be circumspect in their handling of them but, in retrospect, the resulting lack of publicity given to the issues involved seems to have made the task of allied governments more rather than less difficult in persuading reluctant publics of the necessity of theatre nuclear force modernisation.

At the Brussels meeting of the NPG in June and at subsequent meetings, the main focus of allied discussion on modernisation was on the possibility of providing enhanced radiation warheads for some of the alliance's battlefield systems. But, in addition, the ministers were also beginning to be made aware of developments also affecting longer-range theatre nuclear weapons. Although as yet no reference had been made to it in any NATO communiqué, the prospective deployment by the Soviet Union of the new SS-20 missile was being regarded with some anxiety in NATO circles. The mobility and range of the SS-20, when coupled with the performance of the Soviet Union's new Backfire bomber, would considerably augment the range of 'Eurostrategic' options possessed by the Soviet Union, and simply underlined growing doubts in a number of European governments of the adequacy of the theatre nuclear balance in Europe.

The increased Poseidon commitment to SACEUR and the decision to deploy additional F-111 aircraft in Europe have already been noted as actions taken by the United States to bolster NATO's theatre nuclear capabilities. Although these measures were subject to allied consultation, it can also be noted that they could be undertaken by the United States without requiring much in the way of positive decision or action on the part of the allies. The new deployments, basically, either replaced or augmented existing systems and did not represent any major shift in the nuclear posture of the alliance. As if to reinforce this point, the NATO Secretary-General, Joseph Luns, felt it necessary to state publicly that the deployment of additional F-111s should not be interpreted as an alliance response to the SS-20.[21] One effect of the new deployments, however, was to reverse a trend towards the reduction in the number of the alliance's nuclear-capable delivery systems in the European theatre. On taking up the post of SACEUR at the end of 1974, General Haig was reported as saying that he found that conventionally armed aircraft were replacing dual-capable ones 'in a mindless way'. Subsequently, he gave priority to reversing this trend, and one reflection of this was the decision to equip the American F-16 aircraft that were about to be deployed to deliver both conventional and nuclear munitions.[22]

In May 1977 the meeting of the North Atlantic Council that was held in London took place at the summit level and addressed itself to the changing defence needs of the alliance in the 1980s. The Defence Planning Committee was called upon to initiate and develop a long-term defence programme in accordance with these needs. As a result, ten areas were selected for special attention and task forces were established to deal with each one. Task force 10 was charged with the examination of the alliance's theatre nuclear forces, and the Nuclear Planning Group, as the already existing alliance body with responsibilities in this area, undertook the task.[23] But, although priority had been given to questions of theatre nuclear force modernisation at the highest political level, there had been no allied agreement on many aspects of the actual form that modernisation should take. In particular, there was as yet no agreement on the immediate issue of the possible deployment of enhanced radiation weapons.

An article in the *Washington Post* on 4 June publicised the fact that the American administration had requested Congress for appropriations to build neutron warheads for the 8″ Howitzer and the Lance missile, two battlefield systems currently deployed in Europe. The publicity generated by the *Post*'s article helped elevate the question of the 'neutron bomb' to one of central political importance for the alliance, although the discussion of the issue that occurred in the Nuclear Planning Group meeting in Ottawa a few days later was able to take place in an atmosphere that was still largely unaffected by the emerging public debate. In fact, the Ottawa meeting continued to range over a wide variety of topics concerning theatre nuclear weapons: from air defence weapons to 'quick-reaction alert' (QRA) aircraft, from the Soviet deployment of the SS-20 to improvements in the consultative machinery in the event of the possible use of nuclear weapons in defence of NATO. Despite the move on the part of the US administration to appropriate funds for the production of enhanced radiation warheads, no allied decision on their deployment had been taken. Finally, the Ottawa meeting of the NPG also received the reports of the 'new technology study' which, according to the communiqué, concluded that 'while not offering a low-cost and easy means of maintaining a credible and effective deterrent' the efficient application of the new technology 'could enhance NATO's capacity to implement its strategy if deployed in a timely, integrated manner and exploited imaginatively'.[24] In short, the new conventional technologies, while enhancing conventional defence capabilities, and in some cases providing a possible substitute for roles currently assigned to nuclear weapons, nonetheless were neither a substitute for them, nor an answer to the problems posed by their deployment.

The prospect of deploying major new weapons systems in Western Europe as part of the modernisation of the alliance's nuclear forces was reviving all the doubts and dilemmas that were inherent in the very deployment of nuclear weapons in Europe. During the summer of 1977, there was a major debate on neutron weapons in the US Congress which both stimulated and was paralleled by one in Western Europe. The publicity and controversy aroused by the 'neutron bomb' altered the political environment within which the alliance considered its possible deployment. Whereas the Ottawa meeting of the NPG had been able to treat the question of enhanced radiation weapons as a routine item on its agenda, by the next meeting of the Group at Bari in the autumn it was difficult to accommodate this issue within the regular processes of alliance consultation. These had ensured that the defence ministers had been fully apprised of the possibility of deploying these weapons and there had been considerable ventilation of the implications of neutron weapons for allied defence planning at the official and NATO command levels, but there was no firm consensus on deployment, or on the political and diplomatic consequences of so doing.

One broad issue raised was the likely impact on East–West

relations of a decision to go ahead with the production and deployment of enhanced radiation weapons. Given the Carter administration's proclaimed commitment to arms control, there were fears that a positive decision might compromise ongoing SALT negotiations, undermine attempts to curb nuclear proliferation, and hinder the attempt to achieve a comprehensive test ban. The Soviet Union was sending out strong warning signals that arms control negotiations might be brought to a standstill if a positive decision on deployment was made. To the extent that the Soviet Union succeeded in linking NATO's decision on neutron weapons with negative consequences in terms of arms control, and to the extent that the allies were responsive to the linkage, the Soviet Union had, in the view of some, succeeded in intervening in an alliance decision on the military requirements of its own security.[25] The Russian attempt to establish a seeming *droit de regard* over the alliance's decisions on modernisation was, in retrospect, one of the more significant features of the whole neutron bomb controversy, and one which later affected the allied approach to the deployment of modernised long-range theatre nuclear forces.

In Western Europe no government was more sensitive to the political and military implications of enhanced radiation weapon deployment than was the German. In so far as the military rationale for neutron weapons rested on their effectiveness against armoured forces, the implication that they would enable the alliance to adopt a more explicitly war-fighting posture in Europe was bound to pose clear problems for the Germans. In addition, the adverse effect that deployment might have on relations with the Soviet Union was an important consideration for a government that placed high value on the continuation of its *Ostpolitik* and the pursuit of détente. Considerable opposition to deployment arose within the ranks of the SPD, and it was not surprising that the Germans in the summer and autumn of 1977, like most of the other European allies, preferred to take a 'wait and see' attitude to deployment. However, Helmut Schmidt did establish as an important principle of German policy at this time that Germany alone should not be the host for these weapons, and that responsibility for deployment should be shared with other allies.

By and large, what the Germans and other allies were doing was looking for the United States to take the lead (and the opprobrium) in reaching a decision on the neutron bomb. This was something that the Carter administration was reluctant to do in the light of the controversy aroused and in the light of the importance that the administration was now placing on negotiating a SALT II agreement with the Soviet Union. The Americans argued that since the weapons would be deployed in Europe it must first be necessary to secure the agreement of the Europeans. However, it was not clear what would constitute a satisfactory measure of agreement. Would the passive acquiescence of the major allies be enough, and could the opposition of some of the smaller allies, the Dutch for example, be discounted? As it turned out, President Carter, for domestic political reasons, wanted more than simply allied acceptance of some form of deployment; what he wanted was a direct endorsement from the major allies involved. In effect, the Carter administration was attempting to deflect domestic opposition and avoid allied recrimination by placing the onus of decision on the European allies and seeking from them a 'substantial consensus' in favour of enhanced radiation weapons.

At a press conference prior to the Bari meeting of the NPG, the Secretary of Defense suggested that a unanimous decision in favour of the deployment of enhanced radiation weapons was not necessary for the United States to go ahead with production, and that the United States would give most weight to those allies on whose territory the weapon would be deployed. In the meantime, allied consultation on the matter would continue as part of the process of sounding out allied views and dealing with unresolved political questions.[26] Among these unresolved political questions was that of the sort of political costs that leaders on both sides of the Atlantic might be willing to bear for the sake of enhanced radiation weapon deployment. Certainly the European allies were unwilling to accept the burden of political decision that the Americans sought to place on them. The Carter approach marked a considerable change from alliance precedents in the nuclear field in that previously the initiative for change had always come from the Americans. Although such initiatives were not always welcomed by the allies nor were policy changes accepted by them, nonetheless it had always been accepted that it was for the Americans to exercise leadership. By attempting to shift the initiative for decision on to its allies, the United States was in effect trying to avoid the position of *demandeur*. But, however much the United States might seek to avoid this position, the experience of the neutron bomb issue and later the question of deploying modernised long-range theatre nuclear forces demonstrated how difficult it was for the United States to abdicate its leadership in this field. In fact, as subsequent decisions by the Americans showed, the United States was completely unwilling to do so, there being no way that the final responsibility for decisions over American nuclear weapons could be shared.

The transatlantic tensions generated by the neutron bomb issue were open to diplomatic and propaganda exploitation by the Soviet Union, and throughout the latter part of 1977 and into the new year a major Soviet campaign against neutron bomb deployment was mounted. In response, it was suggested that NATO link a decision on production and deployment to some compensating Soviet concessions on arms control. During 1977, the possibility was raised in Vienna within the context of the MBFR negotiations, but this approach was rejected by the Russians who were unwilling to offer more than a mutual ban on deployment. Despite this, it was reported that Leslie Gelb, Head of the State Department's Bureau of Political and Military Affairs, suggested such a 'bargaining chip' approach to the NATO ambassadors in February 1978. Apparently the argument was put forward that if the linkage were to be rejected by the Russians, as there was every reason to expect, then it would be much easier for a decision to go ahead with production to be made since the failure of the Russians to offer a *quid pro quo* would help defuse opposition both in the United States and in Europe.[27]

Although the allies generally favoured using the neutron bomb as a bargaining counter, it was not clear that a Russian rejection would necessarily make a decision to deploy enhanced radiation weapons any easier. What the tactic did do was provide various allied governments with a further excuse for temporising on the issue. Thus most of the allies took the position that the neutron bomb should not be looked at in isolation, but should be linked to more general arms control considerations. But even this position did not lessen the difficulties for a number of European governments, as was evidenced in March when the Dutch Defence Minister resigned over the failure of his cabinet to declare outright opposition to the deployment of the neutron bomb in Western Europe.

The political salience of the issue had moved the main focus of allied consultation on enhanced radiation weapons away from the Nuclear Planning Group and into bilateral channels. Washington sought to influence its allies through direct representations and, in particular, tried to persuade London and Bonn to come out in favour of deployment. Although with evident reluctance, both Helmut Schmidt and James Callaghan began to do so. In turn, Washington also appeared to be moving towards a positive commitment. A special meeting of the NATO Council was scheduled for 23 March, but was cancelled at the last moment at the instigation of the Americans amid growing rumours that President Carter was moving towards a negative decision on production and deployment. This set in train an intense phase of inter-allied diplomacy between Washington, Bonn and London. Both Callaghan and Schmidt felt that they had exposed themselves politically in their qualified support for deployment, and now they were being let down by the President. The German Foreign Minister flew to Washington in order to make last moment representations and to underline the German position that it would support deployment if one other continental country would accept deployment also. Consequently, when President Carter made his public announcement on 7 April, he did not announce the outright cancellation of the programme; rather, the decision was made not to go ahead with production at that time. The option of later installing enhanced radiation elements in the Lance and 8″ artillery warheads that were to be modernised anyway was to be kept open in the event that the Russians did not reciprocate in some way.[28]

An important factor in President Carter's decision was the hope for some breakthrough in Soviet–American relations, but after the relative failure of the Vance mission to Moscow in April, it was clear that no sudden improvement in Soviet–American relations was about to occur and that the Russians were not willing to respond to the American decision on the neutron bomb with any concessions regarding their own theatre nuclear weapons. Partly in response to this disappointing state of affairs, it was publicly announced in October that the United States would produce the components for enhanced radiation warheads, but would not assemble them. With this decision, until President Reagan's announcement in the autumn of 1981 that the United States would produce and stockpile them, the issue of the neutron bomb disappeared from the political agenda of the alliance. Nonetheless, allied relations had been soured by the experience, and it served to reinforce the many doubts in Europe about the direction of policy in Washington. All were agreed, however, that the whole episode had been salutary as to how not to determine alliance policy on nuclear weapons.

Certainly, this experience coloured the handling of a further and also controversial nuclear modernisation issue that was emerging at this time. This was the possibility of deploying new long-range theatre nuclear forces in Western Europe. Having been charged with the task of examining the alliance's nuclear force posture at the London summit, the Bari meeting of the NPG decided to set up an *ad hoc* group for the purpose. At American urging, the Nuclear Planning Group departed somewhat from previous practice by setting up a 'High Level Group' (HLG) of senior officials drawn from all the countries participating in the work of the NPG. This expert body operated at a level of representation senior to that found usually in NPG meetings at the Staff level, and it was hoped by this means to give an urgency and authority to its proceedings that it otherwise might not have. The High Level Group was instructed at Bari to examine the role of theatre nuclear forces in alliance strategy, the implications of recent Soviet theatre nuclear force deployments, and the technical, military and political implications of alternative NATO theatre nuclear force postures.[29]

From its inception, the HLG concerned itself almost exclusively with long-range theatre nuclear weapons. Despite the controversy surrounding the neutron bomb, the HLG did not become involved, but concentrated instead on the implications of the Soviet Union's modernisation of its own long-range theatre nuclear forces. The current deployment by the Soviet Union of the Backfire bomber and the SS-20 mobile intermediate-range ballistic missile were of particular concern, and the HLG from its initial meetings began to develop proposals for the introduction in turn of a modernised force of long-range nuclear weapons into the alliance's arsenal.

This concentration on what the alliance currently terms 'intermediate-range nuclear forces' reflected European preoccupations that had been most forcefully expressed over the previous several years by the Germans. These were re-stated by Helmut Schmidt in October 1977 in a widely reported lecture to the International Institute for Strategic Studies in London. In this lecture, the Chancellor drew attention to the implications of parity at the level of strategic nuclear weapons for European security, arguing that the strategic balance resulting from the SALT process had neutralised the strategic capabilities of the two superpowers, and that as a consequence the significance of disparities between East and West in the area of conventional and tactical weapons had been magnified. In these circumstances, Europeans should be careful to ensure that the SALT process did not neglect other components of the alliance's deterrence strategy. In the Chancellor's view, parity should apply to all categories of weapons in the European balance. Underlying these remarks was the fear that Soviet–American agreement on strategic forces might have the effect of ignoring nuclear systems of particular concern to Europe (the Backfire bomber for example), and of shifting the focus of the arms race to European-based systems.[30] Following his address, the Chancellor was widely interpreted as having advocated the creation of a distinct 'Eurostrategic' balance, but given the implication that the establishment of such a balance could have the effect of 'decoupling' the security of Europe from American strategic forces, German spokesmen were quick to deny this interpretation. Rather, it was emphasised that the European balance should be evaluated only within the framework of the overall global balance of nuclear forces.[31]

This general sensitivity to the impact of the SALT process on European security concerns found particular expression over two features of the negotiations on SALT II. First, there was the possibility of range and deployment constraints being placed on cruise missiles and on the transfer of technology relevant to them. The British and Germans especially took the view that it was important that the United States retain the option of sharing a technology that was seen as having a potentially valuable application to European defence.[32] Secondly, there was the question of the interpretation of what came to be known as the 'non-circumvention' clause in the SALT II agreement. This appeared originally in response to Soviet pressure on the FBS issue and was an attempt by the Russians to secure from the Americans a commitment not to circumvent the spirit of any agreement by augmenting their forward based systems. In the event, the Americans rejected a 'non-transfer' clause that would have limited American freedom to sell or otherwise transfer advanced technology to its allies, and in agreeing to the non-circumvention provisions of article XII of the SALT agreement that was finally signed in Vienna in June 1979, the Americans regarded their commitment as basically redundant, being no more than an obligation not to violate what had been agreed to either directly or indirectly.

Initially in response to European concerns about SALT, the Americans had argued that it was unrealistic to separate the theatre and strategic balances, and they offered reassurance that the United States had a strategic arsenal that was sufficient to cover all targets of interest to Europe and that the Moscow Agreements of 1972 in no way undermined this capability.[33] Nevertheless, as already noted, the decision in 1976 to increase the size of the Poseidon commitment to SACEUR and to deploy additional F-111s in England could be interpreted as reflecting the reality of European concerns about the theatre nuclear balance. Indeed, the increasing chorus of criticism that was emerging in the United States over the direction being taken by the SALT process and its consequences for the American strategic position, served only to reinforce the doubts of those in Europe who were concerned with the implications for European security.

By the next meeting of the NPG in April 1978, what were variously known as 'grey-area' and 'Eurostrategic' weapons were at the forefront of its agenda. The High Level Group had already met twice and had prepared an initial report for the NPG which suggested that there be an 'evolutionary' adjustment of NATO's theatre nuclear forces that would provide the alliance with an increased long-range theatre nuclear capability. For the purposes of arms control, these weapons were considered to fall into a grey-area, because, by virtue of their range and other operational characteristics, they could not be considered tactical in that their military purpose would not be immediately to affect operations on the battlefield, nor could they be considered strategic in the same sense as the central strategic forces of the two superpowers, and which were governed by the SALT definitions. One definition offered at this time was that grey-area weapons were those with a range of between 400 and 2,000 or more nautical miles, and which were not covered by the main East–West arms control negotiations.[34] These range parameters reflected the fact that the shortest range from which a weapon deployed right forward in West Germany could reach the Soviet Union is about 400 n.m. and that weapons with a range not much greater than the 2,500 n.m. of the SS-20 conceivably could reach militarily significant targets on the territory of one superpower when launched from the other. From the point of view of NATO, the grey-area weapon of greatest concern was the SS-20, and it was the ability that this would give to the Soviet Union to threaten military targets all over Western Europe more flexibly and more effectively than ever before that was a primary element in allied discussions on the changing nuclear balance in Europe.

In June, the administration in Washington issued a Presidential Research Memorandum (PRM-38) calling for a study of long-range theatre nuclear force (LRTNF) modernisation, the eventual outcome of which was a decision to produce two new long-range missiles for deployment in Europe.[35] These were the Pershing II, an improved long-range version of the Pershing Ia missile already deployed in West Germany, and a new long-range, ground-launched cruise missile (GLCM). The American study paralleled the work being undertaken by the High Level Group and, it can be presumed, provided the major technical input into it. For all the strains caused by President Carter's decision in April not to go ahead with the production and deployment of enhanced radiation weapons, it did have the effect of 'clearing the air' as far as allied discussions on LRTNF modernisation were concerned. By the Brussels meeting of the NPG in October, work was well advanced in the High Level Group on studies of various forms of LRTNF modernisation within the framework of the general requirements of theatre nuclear force modernisation.[36]

Apart from their consideration of the ongoing work of the High Level Group, the allied ministers received briefings from the American Secretary of Defense on the current state of the SALT negotiations and on President Carter's decision to produce enhanced radiation components for the 8″ Howitzer and Lance warheads.[37] The need to confront the implications of SALT for the theatre nuclear balance, and the linking of American decisions on enhanced radiation weapons to restraint on the part of the Soviet Union concerning its own theatre nuclear forces, reflected a pattern that had emerged in the work of the NPG in which arms control considerations impinged more directly than had been the case in the past. It was not so much that in formulating and examining proposals about theatre nuclear weapons the NPG gave particular attention as to how they might fit in with possible arms control arrangements, as that many of the issues with which the NPG was concerned were increasingly defined by arms control considerations. Thus, the emergence of LRTNF modernisation as an alliance issue arose from European awareness that SALT had manifold consequences for their own security, and from a desire to ensure that European interests were safeguarded. Accordingly, the Nuclear Planning Group became a more significant forum for consultation on SALT. Although the Council remained the main organ in which the United States formally told its allies about what was going on in the SALT negotiations, as these negotiations impinged on the Nuclear Planning Group's interest in theatre nuclear forces, so in turn the NPG concerned itself with them.

There was, however, another dimension to the linking of modernisation and arms control: one that linked any positive decision on modernisation with the perceived political necessity to seek an arms control agreement covering longer-range theatre nuclear forces. By the time that the High Level Group was ready to report its recommendations to the NPG the following spring, the question of grey-area arms control had become a major item on the alliance agenda. Again, it was the Germans who mirrored most clearly the domestic political sensitivity of the modernisation issue for many of the European allies. As the alliance moved towards a decision on LRTNF modernisation, Helmut Schmidt encountered considerable opposition to the prospect of new weapons deployments from within the ranks of his own party. Objections that previously had been raised against the deployment of enhanced radiation weapons were now transferred to the plan to deploy new long-range weapons; in particular, a number of prominent members of the SPD pointed out the likely adverse consequences for détente and for Germany's *Ostpolitik*. Both the Chancellor and the Defence Minister, Hans Apel, took the position that an adequate defence posture was an essential component of any détente policy and that some alliance response to the growth of Soviet Eurostrategic capabilities was necessary. Nonetheless, the German government proceeded very cautiously and was insistent that any decision on modernisation must be accompanied by an effort to secure an arms control agreement covering intermediate-range weapons. As in the case of the German response to the possibility of deploying enhanced radiation weapons, the German government was unwilling to commit itself without general support for modernisation from the other allies. An overriding concern of German policy with respect to the whole question of theatre nuclear force modernisation was to avoid the appearance of any special position respecting it. A major problem with such a policy, however, was that the strategic and political importance of the Federal Republic made it impossible for the Germans to escape from the fact that Germany was of central importance to any programme of NATO theatre nuclear force modernisation.

At the Homestead meeting of the Nuclear Planning Group

in April 1979, the High Level Group presented its report on modernisation. The report contained a set of suggested guidelines for any deployment of new long-range theatre nuclear forces. First, it was suggested that LRTNF modernisation should not result in any increase in the importance of nuclear weapons to NATO defence planning, nor should it lead to any change in the alliance's strategic concept of flexible response. Secondly, reinforcing the 'evolutionary' approach that had emerged early in the High Level Group's work, it was also suggested that modernisation should not lead to any change in the overall total of nuclear weapons in the European theatre. In other words, for every new weapon deployed, an existing delivery system should be removed. In addition, it was not felt necessary that the alliance should attempt to match Soviet deployment of the SS-20 missile on a one-for-one basis, but should simply develop the capacity for a credible response. This would involve the deployment by NATO of weapons with sufficient range to strike targets in the Soviet Union from bases in Western Europe. In order to reinforce the credibility of the proposed deployments and to reinforce public perceptions that the new forces would be 'coupled' to the American strategic deterrent, it was decided that land-based systems would be preferred. There had been some discussion of the possibility of deploying cruise missiles at sea, but this had been ruled out on the grounds that they would lack the necessary 'visibility' and, more important from the American point of view, on the grounds of cost and technical feasibility. Though it was recognised that the deployment of land-based systems would make them more vulnerable than if they were to be based at sea on either submarines or surface ships, the guidelines did lay down that any new LRTNF should have greater survivability, penetrability and accuracy than did existing systems. Finally, in achieving the goals established by the guidelines, it was felt that a mix of systems would have a maximum mutually reinforcing effect.[38]

By the time of the Homestead meeting, consideration of what weapons would be included in any long-range force had concentrated on the GLCM and Pershing II. At one time, the possibility of the United States developing a mobile medium-range ballistic missile for deployment in Europe had been discussed, but the Americans had abandoned this programme on the grounds of cost and the long lead-time that would be involved before such a missile could be operationally deployed. Agreement in principle was reached at the Homestead meeting that any deployments should take place in the early 1980s in order to cover as soon as possible the 'gap' in the spectrum of deterrence that some saw as having been opened up by the increased capabilities of the Soviet Union's own theatre nuclear forces. With respect to the size of the proposed NATO force, there was also agreement in principle to a lower limit of 200 warheads and an upper one of 600.[39] Apart from recommending that the alliance not attempt to match Soviet SS-20 deployments numerically, the High Level Group report also ruled out during its preliminary discussions the targeting of modernised LRTNF against SS-20 sites. Quite apart from the technical difficulties of deploying LRTNF in this role, given the mobility of the SS-20, apparently it was also felt necessary to avoid giving the Soviet Union the impression that the alliance was seeking a first-strike capability against Russian Eurostrategic forces from European soil.[40]

At the conclusion of the meeting Harold Brown, the American Secretary of Defense, stated in his press conference that the allies should reach a final decision on the deployment of LRTNF by the end of the year.[41] Not all the allies were as ready to meet this deadline as the Secretary of Defense implied, but Britain and Germany, as well as the United States, were anxious to keep the momentum towards a decision going and, to this end, the High Level Group was instructed to produce a further report before the end of the year containing specific proposals as to the character and composition of a modernised force of long-range theatre nuclear weapons for NATO.

It was agreed at this time to establish a 'Special Group' to examine the arms control implications of LRTNF modernisation and to develop proposals in this area. This was the result of a German initiative and reflected the view that an attempt to control theatre nuclear forces was not only necessary for the sake of domestic support for the decision, but also in order to signal the alliance's continued interest in détente and in the avoidance of an unrestrained arms race.[42] The Special Group was set up outside the framework of the NPG and, unlike the High Level Group, was a direct result of a decision at the Council level. Like the High Level Group, the Special Group was to be composed of senior officials, but unlike the High Level Group, which being part of the NPG system was drawn primarily from defence ministries, was in this case staffed mainly from foreign ministry personnel, and reflected the fact that questions of arms control and disarmament in most allied jurisdictions were mainly the responsibility of foreign policy rather than defence agencies. Notwithstanding this, the new group was to work in parallel with the High Level Group and was to produce a report on arms control that would complement that on LRTNF deployment.

The High Level and Special Groups met together in September in order to ensure that their reports were mutually consistent and complementary, and the two reports were considered at the Hague meeting of the Nuclear Planning Group in November. The United States, Britain and Germany, the major allies involved in the development of the modernisation proposal, had reached substantial agreement on the technicalities and modalities of LRTNF modernisation, but there was still no overall alliance consensus on the terms under which modernisation should go forward. Thus, at the Hague meeting the Dutch informally proposed that the new missiles be produced but that their deployment be delayed until after arms control negotiations had been tried.[43] In similar vein, shortly after the NPG meeting, the Danish Foreign Minister suggested at a news conference that a decision be postponed by six months in order to give the Soviet Union an opportunity to freeze the production and deployment of its own long-range theatre systems.[44] The Dutch and Danish suggestions indicated that some of the allies at least were prepared to respond to the Soviet overtures on the issue. In a speech in Berlin on 6 October, Brezhnev announced the unilateral withdrawal from East Germany over the next twelve months of up to 20,000 Russian troops and 1,000 tanks. The Soviet leader also indicated his readiness to discuss long-range nuclear weapons that fell outside the accepted definitions of what constituted a strategic system and, while warning the European members of NATO of the possibly dire consequences that might flow from the deployment on its part of new LRTNF, indicated that in the event that the allies did not go ahead with their deployment plans, the Soviet Union would be prepared to reduce the number of medium-range systems deployed in the western part of its territory.

The response of the United States and the other major allies was to reject any suggestion that a decision be postponed pending the exploration of Brezhnev's offer. Harold Brown argued that there was no way that the Congress would authorise the spending of large sums on weapons systems that someone might later agree should be deployed. The alliance needed to agree on numbers and then build towards them; if arms control negotiations turned out to be favourable, then subsequent adjustments in the numbers to be deployed could be made.[45] There was the feeling that if the end-of-the-year deadline was not kept, there would be a loss of momentum towards a positive decision and the alliance would find its options being determined for it by the actions of the Soviet Union. Thus, following the Hague meeting, the chairmen of the High Level and Special Groups were instructed to draft an 'Integrated Decision Document' based on the reports of their respective groups. This, together with the reports themselves, were reviewed by the permanent representatives on 28 November in preparation for a Special Meeting of Foreign and Defence Ministers planned for Brussels on 12 December 1979.[46]

Although the reports on modernisation were the main items discussed at the Hague meeting of the NPG, there was a subsidiary topic that was to have great bearing on the subsequent politics of the LRTNF decision. This was the question of the approval by the Senate of the SALT II agreements that had been signed by Presidents Carter and Brezhnev in Vienna in June. In reiterating their support in the communiqué for the early ratification of the strategic arms limitation agreements, the allied ministers were indicating the importance that they attached to the continuation of the arms control process and to the link that many Europeans had established between SALT II and the deployment of modernised LRTNF.[47] By November it was clear that SALT II was in trouble in the US Senate, and some European spokesmen were suggesting that concrete action on SALT would be necessary before agreement on deployment would be possible.[48] On the other hand, as Helmut Schmidt among others pointed out, SALT, concerned as it was with strategic systems, and the decision on long-range theatre nuclear forces were part of two different processes. In this view, one should not be dependent on the other. Anyway, given the political situation of the Carter presidency, the administration, even had it been willing to do so, was in no position to guarantee ratification, and would and could not allow the alliance decision to be tied to it. However, without a SALT treaty in place, it was clear that it would be much more difficult to sustain political support for modernisation.

The Nuclear Planning Group accepted the High Level and Special Group reports as the basis for discussion and decision in December, but took no decisions themselves. In other words, a proposal for deployment had been developed and the shape of an associated arms control initiative had been determined, but there was still no firm political agreement on implementation. This was to be the product of a further phase of intensive alliance discussion that went on right through to the Special Meeting in December; a meeting that has some claim to be among the more significant ministerial meetings in the history of the alliance.

From the time of their establishment all eleven allies who participated in the work of the NPG chose to be represented on the High Level and Special Groups, and although some, obviously, were much more involved than others the fact of full representation reflected the salience of the issue and the unwillingness of any ally to be excluded from the process of decision. Accordingly, the Hague meeting of the NPG saw the ending of the system of rotation which had been such a novel feature of the Nuclear Planning Group when first it had been established. The ending of rotation had been urged for some time by a number of the smaller allies who felt that the limitation of representation at ministerial meetings had outlived its usefulness. If for no other reason, the political need to secure as widespread support as possible for a positive decision on LRTNF modernisation encouraged full representation.

On 12 December the defence and foreign ministers of all the allied countries with the exception of France and Iceland met in Brussels to reach a decision on the question of the introduction of new intermediate-range weapons into the alliance's nuclear arsenal. All the participants realised that what was decided could have potentially far-reaching consequences for the alliance's strategic posture, for East–West relations and for inter-allied relations as well. Right up until the opening of the meeting it was unclear whether all the allies present would endorse modernisation, and it seems that some adopted their final positions only during the course of the meeting itself. In the end, unanimous acceptance was secured, but only after a number of the allies had expressed reservations about the decision reached. The Dutch, while not witholding their support for the proposed modernisation package, nonetheless postponed for two years their own decision on whether or not to accept deployment on their own territory in order, ostensibly, to see what progress had been made in arms control. In similar vein, the Belgians also delayed for six months their final decision on whether or not to accept deployments on Belgian soil. Subsequently, the Belgian government procrastinated further, and in September 1980 issued a declaration stating that a final decision would depend on the outcome of Soviet–American contacts on arms control in the area of intermediate-range nuclear forces. In the meantime, Belgium would review its position every six months.[49] In securing this measure of agreement, the linking of the new deployments to a parallel arms control initiative was crucially important. Without the commitment to arms control, unanimity would have been impossible.

Unanimity on this issue had taken on particular importance in the light of the position adopted by the German government. As in the case of enhanced radiation weapons, the Germans had stated that they would not act as the sole host for these weapons. Repeatedly the Germans had insisted that the risks of deployment be shared by the alliance as a whole and that they could not allow themselves to be diplomatically and strategically exposed by any decision to deploy new LRTNF. German spokesmen drew attention to the geo-political vulnerability of the Federal Republic and to the problems stemming from the division of Germany and Berlin. These, it was argued, gave to the Federal Republic a particularly high stake in détente and, at the same time, made it especially vulnerable to any deterioration in East–West relations. Germany's reluctance to play too prominent a role in connection with nuclear weapons led to the position that it would be damaging to the cohesion of the alliance if such an important decision were to be made by just a few allied countries with others not participating.[50] This led, in turn, to German insistence that the alliance should decide on the deployment of new systems on the basis of the unanimous assent of the members of the Defence Planning Committee. Moreover, the Germans, asserting the principle of 'non-singularity', let it be understood that at least one continental ally in addition to West Germany should accept deployment of the new weapons on its territory. One effect of this, of course, was to reinforce the importance of the positions taken by the Dutch and Belgians, giving to them a weight in the politics of the decision that they would normally not have been expected to possess.

The Special Meeting accepted the recommendation that 572 new long-range theatre nuclear warheads be deployed in Western Europe in support of the alliance. These would consist of 108 Pershing II missiles in Germany and 464 ground-launched cruise missiles to be deployed in the Federal Republic, Britain, Italy and, subject to their various reservations, in the Netherlands and Belgium. In accordance with the HLG's report, existing warheads would be withdrawn as the new systems began to be deployed in, it was anticipated, 1983–4. The communiqué also announced that in addition a further 1,000 warheads from the existing arsenal would be withdrawn and that the new warheads would be accommodated within these reduced totals.[51] The decision to reduce the NATO stockpile by 1,000 warheads may be seen as the final outcome of the Option III proposal that had been made in Vienna as part of the NATO position on MBFR. More immediately, it was thought to be a politically necessary response to Brezhnev's Berlin speech in October. The reduction was completed by the end of 1980 and saw the elimination of many redundant and obsolete warheads from the NATO arsenal. The Nuclear Planning Group, through the continuing work of the High Level Group, monitored the withdrawal of these warheads and, more importantly, began a study of the implications for the alliance of the likely consequences of LRTNF deployment on the balance of roles and weapons systems in the alliance's total theatre nuclear armoury.

The decision to deploy 572 new warheads was at the high end of the range of 200–600 warheads suggested by the HLG in its report to the Homestead meeting of the Nuclear Planning Group. These numbers had been arrived at only after considerable debate, and represented a compromise between those who argued that in order to be credible as a deterrent, a modernised force should serve clear military needs and those who, for political reasons and with different views of the conditions necessary for deterrence in Europe, argued that far fewer warheads needed to be deployed. Although some critics have suggested that 572 warheads are insufficient for strategically relevant purposes, nonetheless the number chosen was greater than would be considered necessary by those who see LRTNF as serving primarily as a link with the US strategic deterrent. In choosing the higher number, it is possible to infer that the ministers involved were conscious of the need to have a substantial 'bargaining chip' available in any future LRTNF arms control negotiations.

Strictly speaking, the arms control proposal that accompanied the LRTNF deployment decision was the product of a separate consultative process from that which had produced the deployment recommendations. The Special Group, which had been the means for developing the arms control proposal, was not part of the NPG structure, but the commitment of the alliance to a 'parallel and complementary' approach involving both modernisation and arms control meant that the work of the NPG in this area was affected by what was going on in the Special Group. The two groups had met to coordinate their

reports prior to the Special Meeting of Foreign and Defence
Ministers and the 'Integrated Decision Document' had been
produced for the December meeting.[52] There had been no
difficulty in reconciling the two reports, though it had been
much easier to secure allied agreement on the outlines of the
arms control proposal than it had been on the details of
deployment, but the subsequent history of the modernisation
issue was to see the work of the NPG being increasingly
affected by the broader political necessity to show some
progress on arms control if an allied consensus was to be
sustained.

The Special Group, in formulating its proposals for theatre
nuclear force arms control, drew up a number of guidelines
and principles to govern the Western negotiating position. A
step-by-step approach to negotiations was recommended in
which priority would be given to the securing of limitations on
the long-range missiles that were seen as constituting the
major theatre threat to NATO security. Given also that under
existing circumstances British and French forces were not
negotiable, it followed that any talks would have to take place
in a bilateral Soviet–American framework. In this respect, the
guidelines underlined the point that any limitations on the
deployment of American systems would have to be matched
by equivalent restrictions on comparable Soviet systems.
Moreover, although the proposed Pershing II and ground-
launched cruise missile deployments had not been represented
by the alliance as a direct counter to the SS-20, it was agreed
that any arms control arrangement should not endorse NATO
inferiority in land-based, medium-range missiles. In order to
reinforce this point, at German insistence the guidelines
contained the provision that any agreements on theatre
nuclear weapons should recognise *de jure* equality in both
ceilings and rights, even if the alliance did not in fact choose to
match particular categories of Soviet weapons. This provision
was yet another example of European concerns that any
overall Soviet–American arms control agreement not be made
at the expense of the possible requirements of a satisfactory
theatre balance. Nonetheless, it was recognised that any
agreement could not in the end be treated in isolation from the
larger strategic balance, and so the guidelines also indicated

that any negotiations should take place within the context of SALT. Finally, the Special Group report insisted that any limitations agreed to would have to be adequately verifiable.[53]

In pursuing a parallel approach to modernisation and arms control, alliance spokesmen sought to make clear that arms control should be complementary to modernisation and not a substitute for it. In other words, the implementation of the modernisation decision should not be dependent on progress in arms control although, as the communiqué acknowledged, ultimately the alliance's theatre nuclear force requirements would be examined in the light of concrete results achieved through arms control negotiations. This reflected the views of the main proponents of modernisation against those who favoured postponing a decision until after arms control negotiations had been attempted. Despite this, opposition to the deployment of modernised intermediate-range weapons was widespread in Europe and, indeed, this opposition grew following the December decision. The subsequent history of the LRTNF decision clearly indicated that the doubts and differences of view among the allies on the issue had not been resolved by the Special Meeting, and that many sectors of European opinion continued to hope that arms control negotiations might obviate the need actually to deploy the new systems.

As already indicated, an important and complicating factor in securing allied agreement was the political vulnerability of the SALT II agreements in the United States. The fact that these had not been ratified by the time that the LRTNF decision came to be made added to the difficulties faced by many allied governments in accepting it. Certainly, the Special Group guidelines had been drafted on the assumption that the SALT process would continue and that any arms control negotiations on theatre nuclear forces would take place within its framework. Following the Soviet Union's intervention in Afghanistan, the withdrawal of SALT II from Senate consideration and the subsequent change in the American administration, the uncertain future of SALT inevitably obscured further the relationship between new intermediate-range weapons and strategic arms control. As it happened, the United States and Soviet Union began initial discussions on the limitation of theatre nuclear forces in October 1980 outside any formal SALT framework, but it was widely recognised that, in the final analysis, any eventual agreement would be linked to the resolution of Soviet and American differences over the future of SALT.

In order to ensure continued and formalised consultation on the subject, it was agreed that the Special Group should take on more permanent form, and in January 1980 it was announced that a 'Special Consultative Group' (SCG) had been set-up in accordance with decisions taken at the Special Meeting of Foreign and Defence Ministers. The task of the SCG would be to examine and develop further the guidelines on arms control produced by its predecessor but, more generally, it was understood as being the means by which the allies would monitor and seek to influence future Soviet–American exchanges on arms control. After all, European concerns with the increasingly direct impact of SALT on their strategic and security interests had been an important catalyst for LRTNF modernisation in the first place, and the 'dual track' nature of the December decisions had simply reinforced the link between allied interests and how the two superpowers managed their bilateral strategic relationship. The role of the Nuclear Planning Group in this continuing process of consultation was to examine 'the precise nature, scope and basis of the adjustments resulting from the LRTNF deployment and their possible implications for the balance of roles and systems in NATO's nuclear armoury as a whole'.[54] This task was delegated to the High Level Group, which thus continued in existence after the modernisation decision had been made. With the decision to withdraw 1,000 existing warheads and to accommodate the new deployments within this reduced arsenal, the need to examine the impact of these changes was clear. Initially, however, the idea of what came to be termed the 'shift study' arose in order to persuade the Netherlands to support modernisation by suggesting that the acceptance of long-range systems could mean the reduction of nuclear responsibilities in other areas.[55]

The decision on LRTNF had the effect of further directing alliance attention in the area of nuclear policy away from concerns with the military and strategic implications of the theatre nuclear arsenal which characterised the work of the NPG. Now, attention was directed towards the implications of changes in the nuclear stockpile for arms control and towards the role of the alliance in arms control negotiations. The establishment of the Special Consultative Group reflected this shift in focus and was a manifestation of the general desire of America's allies to find institutional means of protecting their interests in future Soviet–American negotiations. It was clear that from December 1979 onwards the allies would attempt to extend the boundaries of consultation. Just as they had earlier dealt with problems of 'nuclear sharing' by means of consultation within the framework of the Nuclear Planning Group, so now an additional consultative body had been created in order to provide another allied point of entry into American policy-making. However, at the beginning of 1980, it was not entirely clear what the relationship between the High Level and Special Consultative Groups would be, as it was also unclear whether consultation in fact would be adequate to dealing with the political stresses that modernisation was generating.

The decision to deploy modernised LRTNF and to pursue arms control in this area thus brought about changes in the institutions and procedures by which allied consultation on nuclear policy was practised. Two previously *ad hoc* groups had been given more permanent status, and the setting up of the High Level and Special Consultative Groups may be regarded as one means by which the alliance adjusted to political and strategic change, and to which the plan to modernise the alliance's theatre nuclear forces was itself a response. How effective these institutional adaptations would be remained to be seen and, it could be predicted, would be determined not only by the quality of the consultation practised but also, and in the final analysis more importantly, by the broader political context within which European security was perceived. Within this broader political context, consultation could help sustain the alliance consensus on nuclear policy that had enabled the modernisation decision to be taken in the first place, but it should be noted that it could also serve to modify that consensus or, in the worst case, simply register its breakdown.

6. CONSULTATION AND THE NUCLEAR PLANNING GROUP

Consultation as practised in the Nuclear Planning Group has taken a number of different forms, been concerned with a wide variety of subject-matter, served a range of objectives, and resulted in different kinds of outcome. In short, the patterns and purposes of consultation in the NPG have been as various as elsewhere in the alliance. Indeed, it can be argued that such multifaceted dimensions to the consultative process are characteristic of multilateral alliances like NATO. Thus it is to be expected that the varieties of consultation will reflect the variety of purposes sought by the governments practising it. Even within a specialised institution, restricted in the subject-matter of concern to it, a wide range of purposes may be sought, and different types of consultation practised. This can occur because the issues discussed are linked to broader political concerns, or are symbolic of other policy differences. The appropriate test of a consultative mechanism then may have to include, in addition to a consideration of consultative outcomes, an estimation of the value of a particular consultative arrangement to the larger political system of which it is a part. In the case of the Nuclear Planning Group, the effectiveness of the consultation practised there has been a function not only of the success with which the Group has dealt with items on its agenda, but of the relevance or salience of that agenda to the alliance political system as a whole.

Harlan Cleveland, on the basis of his experience as United States ambassador to NATO, has described consultation in the alliance as taking the following forms. First, information may be imparted unilaterally or, in other cases, information may be exchanged on a bilateral or multilateral basis. The alliance may be notified of national decisions already taken, but without any expectation of reaction on the part of the allies. Alternatively, others may be notified of decisions in such a way as to build allied support for them. In the case of national actions that may affect the interests of others, allies may be consulted in advance, sometimes to the extent of seeking to ascertain allied reaction to possible decisions not yet made. In the latter situation, the reaction of those consulted becomes an element in the national decision itself. Finally, consultation may be used to concert action, to secure separate but parallel national actions by others, or to secure agreement for actions that by their very nature must be carried into effect collectively.[1]

Perhaps the commonest form of consultation practised within NATO, as elsewhere, involves the exchange of information. Such exchange may be the result of a unilateral initiative on the part of one of the allies, or may occur within the framework of some formal or informal understanding. At this level of consultation, the information provided often amounts to no more than the announcement by one or more of the parties to a consultative arrangement of decisions already taken. Nevertheless, at least two major purposes may be served by such announcements. In the first place, the endorsement of those consulted is sought for the changed policy and, secondly, the announcement of decisions in this fashion can be presented as a form of policy clearing with those consulted. In NATO, given the many commitments undertaken by the allies to consult on matters of common concern, the use of alliance consultative mechanisms at least involves the recognition that allied interests are affected. For genuine policy clearing to occur, however, those consulted should have the opportunity to influence the final decision in advance or subsequently to modify it. It is this opening up of national decisions to the possibility of influence by allies whose interests may be affected that has been held up by various NATO authorities as the desirable norm of inter-allied conduct.

The point was made in 1956 by the 'Committee of Three' and has been reiterated frequently.

Consultation within an alliance means more than exchange of information, though that is necessary. It means more than letting the NATO Council know about national decisions that have already been taken; or trying to enlist support for those decisions. It means that discussion of problems collectively, in the early stages of policy formation, and before national positions become fixed. At best, this will result in collective decisions on matters of common interest affecting the alliance. At the least it will ensure that no action is taken by one member without a knowledge of the views of others.[2]

In effect, consultation as recommended by the 'Committee of Three' serves as a surrogate in the absence of a strong ideological base to the alliance. By providing a rationale for cooperation as well as a technique, consultation can help define common interests and attempts to construct common policies on the basis of those interests.

Naturally, in many cases the appearance rather than the substance of consultation is all that can be achieved. Nevertheless, the very routine of consultation, even if it does not lead to collective action, may serve other alliance and national goals. Member states will pay lip-service to the obligation to consult in an attempt to mitigate stress on the alliance caused by their unilateal actions. Alternatively, the consultative mechanism may be used as a means of justifying and explaining policy so as to avoid adverse criticism. Like other forms of diplomacy, the ritual of consultation can have the effect of glossing over differences, providing the illusion of agreement and of presenting as voluntary acceptance what in fact is concession to pressure. In these circumstances a dominant power may seek to use consultation as a means of gaining the support and involvement of allies without at the same time accepting their right to influence policy formation. Many aspects of the debate on 'nuclear sharing' for example, reflected a suspicion on the part of allies of the United States that in practice American offers of consultation amounted to little more than an invitation to endorse policies already decided upon.

However, token consultation, unbalanced by more positive achievements in the area of policy coordination, can lead only to increased alliance stress in the policy arena concerned.[3] Although the preferred solution may be that every ally involved in the consultative process should feel that its interests are secured, a more realistic aspiration would be to effect a situation in which the allies feel that their interests are more likely to be protected through participation in a consultative arrangement than by standing aloof from it. One way in which this might be brought about is by reinforcing the status of those who do participate. Thus one effect of nuclear consultation in NATO, and of the institutional arrangements set up to foster it, has been to mitigate the tension between the principle of sovereign equality and the fact of major disparities in allied responsibilities and power. The development of the Nuclear Planning Group can be viewed in part as an alliance response to the difficulties created by the overwhelming dependence of NATO on the American nuclear commitment. At least the processes of consultation conducted by the NPG establish a formal basis by which the non-nuclear allies in particular can participate in the determination of alliance nuclear policy. Membership in the NPG established a 'right' to be consulted even if in practice that right has not always been observed.

This is not to suggest that membership in the Nuclear Planning Group has provided all with an equal voice, or indeed that it necessarily provides a voice at all in the making of policy. What, at minimum, the NPG does do is provide an alliance component in nuclear decision-making. This ensures that, at least from time to time, the views of the smaller allies are listened to. An ally which by itself can have little or no effect on the centres of nuclear influence in the alliance (this means predominately Washington) may find its views shared by others, and so collective influence can be exerted. The NPG provides a forum in which support for views on nuclear policy can be solicited, though the use to which that forum has been put by the various allies has varied considerably. In so far as it appears that the United States pays careful attention to what goes on in the NPG, more attention is likely to be given to the views of the smaller powers expressed within that particular framework than if they had been expressed elsewhere, or even as a result of bilateral representations.[4] Certainly the structure of the NPG has provided opportunities for individual ministers and particular national delegations to have an impact on the nuclear policy of the alliance greater than might otherwise be considered commensurate with the power and the status of the nation concerned. In other words, the successful exploitation of opportunities to consult in effect confers prestige.

In subtle ways the process of consultation transforms the diplomatic environment in which it occurs, modifying the impact of power relationships and determining influence. In a consultative situation some of the parties concerned are going to be more interested in concerting action than others. Inevitably, therefore, those more interested in being consulted find themselves dependent on the goodwill of those with greater freedom of action to act (or not act) on the matter at hand. Both the strong and the weak have an interest in being consulted on certain occasions and with respect to certain matters, and though consultation cannot overturn the facts of inequalities of power in NATO it can, nevertheless, affect the political leverage that these inequalities might otherwise confer. Consultation, then, is capable of modifying the process by which power is converted into political influence and, as such, can be a powerful diplomatic tool. One of the factors encouraging the 'institutionalisation' of consultation in an alliance like NATO is that by establishing a formal commitment to consult the dependence of one ally on the goodwill of others is reduced. Of course, the allies will attempt to interpret the commitment to consult to their advantage and indeed, on occasions, not live up to their commitments. Still, the obligation to consult can act as a significant constraint on state behaviour.

Apart from the circumstances of each particular case, a number of general inhibitions operate on alliance consultation. Foremost is the fact that governments tend to seek the greatest freedom of action possible. The obligation to consult may be seen as entailing the obligation to take into account the views of those consulted, and thus restricting the options available. Where the political and other costs of consultation seem to be greater than the advantages of retaining the option to act independently, any obligation to consult is going to be interpreted in the most restrictive way possible. In any circumstances of general concern to the alliance, the larger powers, and in particular the United States, are likely to be in a better position to undertake independent action. Thus, by and large, the smaller powers will have a greater interest in consultation than the stronger. With respect to nuclear weapons, all the allies have little choice other than to seek to commit the United States to consult with them in circumstances in which American decisions would affect their interests. The exploration of the limits of such a commitment to consult has been a fundamental task of the NPG, particularly as it would operate in a crisis.

Of course, there are circumstances in which the various allies have no desire to be consulted because they have no wish to be associated with the subject at issue. To be consulted may involve the acceptance of a responsibility to act in areas, and with respect to interests, peripheral to one's major concerns.[5] The NATO allies of the United States are all to a greater or lesser extent regional powers with national interests of far more limited scope than those of the United States. Consequently, they have been reluctant to see alliance institutions used by the United States for consultation on issues which the allies perceive to lie outside the NATO policy arena. As in the case of American discussion of Vietnam in the NPG, the allies have interpreted such consultation as an attempt to secure positive support for interests to which they are at best indifferent, and at worst unsympathetic.

Throughout the NATO system its continued functioning as a diplomatic and political instrument depends on there being a general understanding that the extent and type of consultation practised will depend on the salience of the issue, and on the capabilities and scope of the national interests of the allies involved. That is, that there be some general consensus as to what it is relevant to consult about. Also, that it is appreciated that not every ally has the same interest in all aspects of the consultative process. Nevertheless, all the allies, large and small, have some interest in consulting and being consulted in one form or another. Liska has made the point in the following manner.

Most lesser allies take a realistic view of their proper share in consultations. Their main concern is a formal one. They wish to be consulted in a way which would give a decent semblance of reality to their standing as partners and to the representative character of the major ally's diplomacy. Only when they are directly involved do lesser allies demand the right to veto as well as remonstrance. On the other hand, the major ally wishes to be consulted chiefly in order to have the opportunity to authorize or veto action, or to be able to dissociate himself from the lesser ally's conduct. The formal aspect is less important to him unless his permanent status within the alliance is in jeopardy.[6]

A point missing in Liska's formulation is the more positive interest a major ally can have in consultation. It is the alliance leaders that set the 'tone' of consultation, and by their actions largely determine the effectiveness of the consultation practised. A major task of alliance leadership is to ensure sufficient cohesion for cooperative action to be undertaken by the allies in relevant areas of concern. To the extent that the allies perceive that the dominant partner seeks genuine and appropriate forms of consultation, a sense of community is sustained and alliance cohesion reinforced.

The degree of cohesion and the extent of community can serve to encourage alliance 'integration' at any particular time. Both major and minor allies can have an interest in developing alliance integration, although these interests are not always identical, nor always compatible. For alliance leaders, integration may serve to increase their control over the alliance and over the actions of the other allies. On the other hand, for a smaller, more dependent power, integration may be seen as a way of binding major powers to their commitments. Thus, all allies may well agree to institutionalise consultation in order to further those various interests better served by greater alliance cohesion and integration.

In a nuclear environment the risks incurred by alliance with others are considerable and, indeed, it has been argued that in the nuclear age the risks are so great that the military alliance is becoming obsolete. Nevertheless, the institution of alliance persists in international relations, and consultation is one of the techniques available to make the risks of alliance acceptable.

For a nuclear power like the United States, consultation in NATO is valuable not only as a means of dissuading allies from actions that are felt to carry risks unacceptable to the guarantor power, or as enabling it to dissociate itself completely from an ally's actions, but also as a means of crisis management. Consultation may assist in this latter task by helping coordinate alliance responses to potentially dangerous situations. Thus, among the functions of the NPG has been the development of a better understanding of the kinds of consultation that would be possible in a crisis and, with respect to the possible employment of nuclear weapons, a better appreciation of the circumstances and likely consequences of their use. Of course, in a crisis the initiative for action will lie primarily with the United States. Given that the essence of crisis is time, the ability of the Americans to consult with their allies is likely to be seriously constrained by the amount of time available. So, inevitably, there is a tension between the interest of the United States in ensuring freedom to act quickly and flexibly in a crisis, and the desire of her allies to ensure that they be adequately consulted in possible emergencies. An instructive and salutary example of the difficulty of reconciling these two requirements was provided by the divisive impact on the alliance of the war in the Middle East in October 1973.

A coordinated alliance response to the questions posed by the presence of nuclear weapons in its armoury has been sought through the elaboration of an agreed strategic doctrine concerning them. The creation of such a doctrine has significance not only for military planning, but also for the likely political responses of the various allies to the prospect of crisis. Alliance agreement on nuclear strategy has thus been a crucial means by which a reconciliation of the differing allied responses to the problem of security has been attempted. As the dominant nuclear ally, the United States has been largely responsible for the formulation of the doctrine governing the alliance's nuclear posture. The extent to which there is an allied input into the determination of NATO strategy, and the means by which this is to be achieved, have of course been continuing preoccupations of alliance politics. In practice, and despite the lengthy debate on nuclear sharing, it has been shown that the role of the allies in determing alliance nuclear strategy has been essentially consultative.

In order to reduce and make more manageable the risks of its nuclear commitment to European security, the United States has always sought ultimate control over alliance strategy. Prior to 1957, when the United States deployed its nuclear weapons solely for the use of American forces, and when alliance military planning was predicated on the threat of 'massive retaliation', the alliance as such was not really concerned with nuclear strategy. The United States was free to determine unilaterally its nuclear doctrine, subject only to such influence as individual allies were able to bring to bear. In so far as there was an alliance component, this was largely restricted to the Standing Group in Washington. However, once NATO defence planning became predicated on the deployment of tactical nuclear weapons, and once 'massive retaliation' was questioned, then issues concerning nuclear strategy became contentious ones. The decisions taken in 1954 and 1957 to base alliance military planning on the availability of tactical nuclear weapons and for the allies to create nuclear-capable forces to take advantage of these weapons, completed the nuclear transformation of the alliance. This, together with the Russian diplomatic offensive that followed the launching of Sputnik, was sufficient to ensure that the question of nuclear control became a dominant alliance issue.

In many ways, by the early sixties, the debate over nuclear control and the various hardware proposals that flowed from it, obscured the fact that alliance influence on the determination of nuclear policy was negligible. Admittedly, the concern with questions of nuclear sharing and nuclear control was one form taken by opposition to American attempts at revising the strategic posture of the alliance, but such opposition in effect amounted to no more than an attempt to veto unilateral changes in alliance strategy. There were few means available by which the allies through the alliance could influence the actual content and implementation of American strategic policy. The 1962 Athens guidelines concerning nuclear consultation had been one attempt to provide such means, but these had been largely stillborn. The major allies of the United States – Britain, France and Germany – had each sought to establish their own relationship with the United States concerning strategic matters; Britain by means of the 'special relationship', France by means of the 'force de frappe', and Germany through the increasing weight of her conventional contribution and crucial political importance to East–West relations. These basically national responses did nothing, of course, to enhance alliance cohesion in the area of nuclear policy. Nor, with something of an exception for the British, did these national responses do much to ensure that there would be adequate consultation with them on matters concerning nuclear weapons. Prior to the establishment of the McNamara Committee, the situation was described by one eminent commentator as being one in which the consultative role of the allies was restricted to the technical implementation of unilaterally determined American strategic conceptions.[7] This was a situation which resulted in the Europeans trying, where possible, to resist the actual application of those American strategic innovations about which they had doubts. Since there existed no specifically European strategic view, this response served to fragment the alliance even more on issues of nuclear policy.

The Nuclear Planning Group was designed to expand the consultative role of the alliance in matters of nuclear policy and, in so far as it would encourage acceptance of a common alliance strategic doctrine, strengthen alliance cohesion. Also, it was hoped that the actual process of consultation itself would strengthen further the cooperative basis of the alliance. Implicit in this approach was the idea that the allies by practising consultation in a particular policy area would experience some kind of 'learning process' that would encourage them to develop higher levels of mutual consultation. It has been suggested, for example, that the establishment of patterns of reciprocal consultation as a routine aspect of alliance diplomacy would enable the allies to consult more effectively in a crisis.[8] The NPG might contribute to this by providing a mechanism by which the allies could help to avoid the unexpected by sounding out the views of others before committing themselves to particular policies. By this means consultation could help bring about the convergence of previously divergent positions, and strengthen the expectation that policy differences would be resolved in a way that would be politically acceptable to all the allies.

The difficulty with this, however, is that in the NPG, as throughout the alliance generally, the consultative process is very much conditioned by the fact that national delegations are under instructions from their governments and work closely to their briefs. This does not leave much scope for the easy modification of national positions. Thus, one observer has reported:

Members of national delegations stated privately that 'convergence' of originally disparate national positions was extremely difficult to achieve; rather, NATO structures produced less satisfactory outcomes of 'specialization' and 'redundancy'. Issues were assigned to groups with specialized areas of competence; but when they were elevated from low to higher groups the issues tended to be no closer to a joint solution than before.[9]

The development of the NPG structure, in particular the *ad hoc* development of the Staff Group and the High Level Group, provides a good example of 'specialization' at work. The experience of the NPG has demonstrated that consultative processes which are effective at lower levels of representation are not necessarily translated into substantive policy outcomes at higher levels of political authority. What has happened in the case of the NPG is that ministers have tended to avoid problems at the political level by referring them to technical committees made up of officials. Technical consultation by officials has thus served to avoid direct political conflict, but at the cost of failing to secure authoritative political decisions.

Not that the Nuclear Planning Group can be considered a decision-making body as such. Its function rather has been to help secure agreement with respect to declaratory alliance strategic doctrine, and support for plans and guidelines covering the possible use of nuclear weapons in defence of the NATO area. Actual decision-making power lies elsewhere: in the Council, in national capitals, and particularly in the capitals of the nuclear-weapon states. The resources available to the NPG enabling it to carry out its task lie not in the ability to reach decisions on nuclear policy, but in the encouragement of allied consultation on the subject.

By its nature, consultation tends to be far less determinate in its outcomes than other techniques for securing joint action such as formal negotiation, or subordination to delegated authority. In matters concerning nuclear strategy, the advantage that consultation has over negotiation is that it is better adapted to dealing with a constantly changing strategic and political environment. Negotiation is more appropriate to the resolution of specific issues which, once settled, can be put aside. The extent to which the allies in peacetime will delegate authority to make decisions on their behalf is of course extremely limited. Although the integrated command structure of NATO is predicated on the assumption that in the event of war authority to exercise command over NATO forces would be delegated to it, with few expectations, this authority is not available to NATO commanders in time of peace. Above all with respect to nuclear weapons, no allied government has agreed to any pre-delegation of authority over them.[10] Consultation, then, is the only means available for the development of a common allied view on nuclear policy.

The extent to which the allies have reached a common view on alliance strategy has differed with respect to various aspects of the strategic posture of the alliance. On matters directly concerning the central strategic balance, and on strategic weapons decisions taken in connection with it, the alliance has recognised that policy-making here is overwhelmingly the prerogative of the United States. Only the Americans possess the capacity to make and implement strategic decisions in this area, and the ability of the allies to influence them is limited. The role of the allies has been restricted largely to that of auditing an essentially American domestic debate, and the course of this debate has been a significant factor determining the kind and extent of the consultation that the United States has undertaken with her allies in the NPG. In the past, consultation on strategic weapons has primarily taken the form of briefings by the United States on the administration's current thinking, and the ability of the allies to modify

American conceptions has been restricted by lack of information, and by the inherent difficulties of intervening effectively in the complex operations of strategic policy determination in Washington. As far as influencing American strategic policy is concerned, the allies have usually been forced to respond *ex post facto* to American initiatives. Being in most cases unable to affect the process by which revisions in strategic doctrine and military posture are determined, the allies seek to protect their interests at the stage when policy changes affecting them are implemented. Thus, despite the creation of the Nuclear Planning Group, the situation with respect to the determination of the strategic policy of the alliance remained fundamentally unchanged in that the role of the allies has been restricted, and reciprocal consultation has occurred mainly at the level of implementation. However, in recent years, as a result of changes in the alliance's political and strategic environment, American strategic policy has been seen by allied governments as having an increasingly direct impact on their interests. One alliance response has been the further elaboration of consultative institutions in the form of the High Level and Special Consultative Groups, which represent an attempt to ensure allied input into American policy-making before it is finally determined.

Today, changes in policy at the strategic level are likely to be significant for their arms control implications, and for their political impact on détente, as they are for any direct effect they might have on the military security of the alliance. Consequently, the allied interest in influencing American strategic policy has become part of a more general interest in consulting on the development of East–West relations. On the part of the allies of the United States there is a special concern that they be kept informed of the course of the bilateral American relationship with the Soviet Union, and that they be reassured that no agreement affecting their interests will be struck 'above their heads'. In connection with subjects of more specifically strategic interest, the allies wish to monitor Russian–American arms control negotiations and to consult with the United States on them. They wish to impress on the United States that the diplomatic consequences of any adjustment in the central strategic balance brought about by arms control agreements or by unilateral American action are of concern to others. Thus, in the 1970s the issue of nuclear sharing became transformed largely into one concerning the role of the alliance in the management of détente, and the part played by the Nuclear Planning Group has necessarily been a limited one.

By and large, it is with respect to the nuclear weapons actually deployed in the European theatre that the NPG has had a real opportunity to affect the implementation of strategic policy. Unlike the strategic weapons which lie outside any system of alliance control, the theatre nuclear weapons are subject to some physical allied constraints as well as political and military ones, and there is some genuine allied input into the military planning that would govern their use.[11] It is mainly for these reasons that the allied role in the Nuclear Planning Group has been so much greater with respect to theatre nuclear weapons than with strategic forces. As a result there has been a mutual clarification of the rationale underlying the deployment of theatre nuclear weapons in Europe, even if there remain substantial differences concerning the circumstances and manner in which they might be used; differences which have been strengthened and highlighted by the modernisation issue. Still, agreement has been possible on various concepts and guidelines, and the work on these involved significant contributions from the allies. The continuing review of the issues raised, together with the continuing discussion of outstanding problems in connection with the modernisation of theatre nuclear weapons, have provided opportunities for genuine collective discussion among the United States and her allies on the nuclear posture of the alliance.

Although by the beginning of 1980 the prospect of new intermediate-range nuclear weapons being deployed in Europe on behalf of NATO was raising serious questions as to the continued credibility of the alliance's consensus on nuclear matters, nonetheless consultation in the Nuclear Planning Group had helped to sustain successfully a sufficient alliance consensus to enable continued planning in connection with the deployment and possible use of nuclear weapons in defence of the alliance to take place. After all, the basic objective had been to ensure sufficient cohesion to support a deterrent posture which was politically acceptable to the allies and, within its terms of reference, the NPG had helped support the deterrent effectiveness of the alliance by helping reduce the stress on the alliance generated by allied differences over nuclear policy. In particular, four functions performed by the NPG served to extend the area of allied agreement on nuclear policy and limit the adverse impact of any differences.

First, on the whole, the United States successfully used the Nuclear Planning Group to explain her nuclear policies and to gain support and acceptance for them. By keeping her allies 'in the know', the United States had obtained support for what were in many cases essentially unilateral policy decisions, and when the United States failed to inform there have tended to be strongly adverse reactions from her allies. In many cases, what the United States has been able to secure through consultation has not been so much positive allied action, or an alliance declaration of support, but a passive acceptance which does not lead to outright dissent. Frequently, such a response has been sufficient for alliance purposes; however, if a coordinated allied response is necessary for a policy to be effective, then consultation must attempt to build a consensus that is appropriate to the objectives sought. Thus, despite the many doubts and ambiguities which remain concerning the official alliance strategic concept of flexible response, the exploration by the NPG of its meaning, implications and ramifications has provided a means whereby the allies together have been able to analyse American strategic decisions in terms of their consequences for European security. In other words, opportunities for an allied contribution to the under-standing of the consequences of strategic changes have been provided, as have opportunities for them to influence the application of those changes to the European theatre.

Secondly, the Nuclear Planning Group has helped to isolate issues of nuclear planning and nuclear sharing from other alliance questions. By creating a rather specialised political institution to deal with problems concerning the implementation of alliance nuclear strategy, it has become easier to avoid linking allied differences over nuclear policy with other contentious issues. In this case 'specialization' helps alleviate stress by defining a narrower range of issues on which allied agreement is sought. Thus the NPG has tended to have the effect of insulating questions of nuclear planning not only from non-nuclear issues, but also from other questions involving nuclear weapons such as those concerning arms control. One symptom of the divisiveness and political sensitivity of theatre nuclear force modernisation has been the limited ability of the NPG to isolate the issue from broader strategic and political considerations including those involving arms control. Despite further institutional specialisation in the form of the High Level and Special Groups, modernisation became a matter of serious domestic and inter-allied contention.

A third function of the Nuclear Planning Group which has served to strengthen allied cohesion has been the fostering of 'entente'. Here, rather than insulating nuclear issues from other alliance concerns, the object is to encourage cooperation in this area in order to benefit from the 'spill-over' effects of this cooperation on other matters. Successful cooperation in such a sensitive and difficult area as nuclear policy can strengthen diplomatic alignments and symbolise a determination to consult generally on matters of common interest. For example, the value to their wider European and Atlantic policies of their cooperation in 1968 and 1969 in drafting guidelines covering the possible use of nuclear weapons was not lost on the British and Germans.

Finally, the Nuclear Planning Group, by means of joint studies of contentious issues, has encouraged the reconciliation of differences on aspects of nuclear policy. A standard method of dealing with issues arising in the NPG has been to submit them to the Staff Group for detailed study. In turn, *ad hoc* study groups made up of representatives from interested countries are established whose task is to prepare the initial drafts of reports which finally will be presented to the ministers for their approval. (The High Level Group may be seen as a formalised example of such study groups, albeit at a senior level.) Much of the work is then undertaken directly in national capitals and within the national delegations, and the coordination of this activity has become one of the Staff Group's major functions.[12] The intimate discussion at the official level which is generated by this procedure, together with the requirement that a report be produced for the consideration of all the members of the NPG, creates strong organisational pressures to reach agreement.

As has already been pointed out, however, a problem with procedures of this kind is that it is frequently difficult to translate the work on detail performed at the Staff level into more general political agreements at ministerial meetings and in the Defence Planning Committee. Nevertheless, common understandings developed among allied specialists can serve to limit the consequences of the failure to reach joint agreements at the highest political levels. And, of course, from time to time the work of the NPG has resulted in substantive recommendations that have become part of the nuclear policy of the alliance. Anyway, even though agreed statements of alliance doctrine may be difficult to achieve, provided there are no major expressions of dissent from the member governments, alliance nuclear planning can go forward. Although it may be politically impossible to achieve explicit endorsement of particular aspects of the nuclear posture of the alliance by the allies in the Defence Planning Committee, nevertheless, nuclear planning can take place in an environment in which the technical implications have been appreciated and analysed together by the allies at the expert level.

With the quasi-permanent status given to the High Level Group at the December 1979 Special Meeting, the Nuclear Planning Group structure can be seen as having four parts, each of which functions differently in the overall process of nuclear consultation. At the level of national delegations, the Staff Group, which usually meets weekly, provides an opportunity for the detailed discussion of items currently on the agenda of the NPG. All the members of the NPG participate as interested, together with representatives from the International Military Staff, SACEUR, SACLANT and the Secretariat. Since the discussions are generally of a technical character, and are not subject to the same political and 'representative' constraints as operate at the high levels of the NPG, there tends to be full participation by those present in advisory capacity. The Staff Group is chaired by a member of the Secretariate, the Director of the NATO Nuclear Planning Directorate, which is a position always held by an American.

When the High Level Group was established in October 1977, it was an *ad hoc* group directly subordinate to the NPG. The decision to continue the High Level Group following the decision to deploy new intermediate-range nuclear weapons in Europe has not altered its status. Participation in the work of the HLG is on an 'open-ended' basis and thus is open to all the allies who participate in the work of the NPG. Initially, eleven allies were represented; the United States, United Kingdom, Italy, the Federal Republic of Germany, the Netherlands, Norway, Canada, Turkey, Belgium, Denmark and Greece. However, since 1980, both Portugal and Luxembourg have begun to participate in the NPG on a regular basis and have subsequently participated in the work of the High Level Group. The HLG differs from other parts of the Nuclear Planning Group structure in that its agenda is restricted to the implications of the modernisation of long-range theatre nuclear forces.

Representation on the High Level Group is at the level of senior officials and, like the Staff Group, the chairmanship is undertaken by an American, the Assistant Secretary of Defense for National Security Affairs. In the work of the High Level Group, leadership of the individual delegations and the responsibility for the necessary staff work is predominantly that of the allied defence ministries. In this, the HLG reflects the fact that at the plenary level the NPG is made up of allied defence ministers and that members of the national delegations concerned with the NPG at the staff level are directed by the various allied defence ministries. However, the HLG has departed somewhat from previous practice in that foreign service personnel are frequently represented on national delegations and involved with the associated staff work.

The third manifestation of the Nuclear Planning Group is at the level of the permanent representatives to the NATO Council. The main task of these meetings is to prepare and review the agenda of the ministerial meetings and, as in the case of the Staff Group, all members participate as interested according to the principle of open-endedness.[13] The number and frequency of these meetings varies, but ranges between four and ten meetings a year.[14] Like the full ministerial meetings, the chairmanship is undertaken by the Secretary-General. Representatives of the senior NATO military authorities also attend.

At the ministerial level, since its first meeting in Washington in April 1967, the Nuclear Planning Group has met twice a year, usually in the spring and autumn. From its origins in the McNamara Committee, the basic function of the NPG has been to further the processes of nuclear consultation within the alliance by means of the direct personal involvement of defence ministers. The object of such direct ministerial participation has been to ensure that any proposals emerging from the consultative processes have the strong support of member governments, and that those who are politically responsible for national defence planning are fully informed as to the complexities of the issues associated with nuclear weapons. In effect, at the ministerial level, a key function of the NPG has been educational. To this end the attempt is made to ensure that reports and other documents are circulated well in advance in the hope that ministers will have the time to study them personally and arrive at sessions of the NPG well briefed. The extent to which the ministers do their homework is important to the quality of the discussion in the NPG and to the overall nuclear consultation process. Clearly, the manner of preparation and the quality of reports and other documents is very important in determining the course and value of the work of the NPG. Much of this work is undertaken by the national delegations in accordance with the regular policy-making procedures of their respective governments and the alliance. The value of this work, however, is greatly dependent on the quality of participation at the ministerial level. In this respect, the performance of the NPG seems to have been uneven.

A number of factors account for this state of affairs. The political salience of nuclear issues at any particular time is obviously of importance. When questions concerning nuclear policy are politically sensitive, either to individual ministers, or to the alliance as a whole, then the level of individual ministerial participation, and the general quality of ministerial contributions, tend to increase. Of course, regardless of the salience of nuclear policy, the degree of expertise and interest in nuclear matters possessed by the various ministers who are members of the Nuclear Planning Group varies considerably. Unfortunately, it has been the case that some holders of the defence portfolios of their respective countries have lacked the interest, experience, or intellectual resources to make the best use of the information and staff work available to the NPG. The key individual responsible for setting the tone of all ministerial meetings of the NPG has been the American Secretary of Defense who has been the source of most of the information available to the NPG, and who has been, directly or indirectly, the sponsor of most of the agenda items. Thus, in large part the work of the NPG has consisted of allied responses to American information and initiatives. Independent initiatives and challenges to the American position from the allied defence ministers tend to be related to their own political and security concerns, particularly when these are related to the personal expertise and political commitments of the minister involved.

By and large, the Americans keep tight control over the quantity and quality of information available. Below the Secretary of Defense, US delegations operate on strict instructions from Washington and according to a close interpretation of the United States Atomic Energy Act. Partly as a result of this, the allies have frequently been unable to challenge effectively positions taken by the Americans, or to undertake initiatives concerning alliance nuclear policy independently of the Americans. In fact there is a considerable degree of circularity in the flow of information relevant to the work of the NPG. At the staff level, in addition to the American delegation, there is great reliance on the nuclear sections of the NATO commands for technical information about nuclear weapons. However, nuclear planning within the NATO command structure is very much dominated by American personnel who, in terms of the nuclear information available to them, are subject to stringent controls from Washington. Again, in so far as the planning of the NATO commands is affected by the work of the NPG, particularly as it results in various agreed concepts and guidelines, it is these same commands which have been a major source of technical information concerning the deployment and characteristics of the nuclear weapons available to the alliance. In other words, the nature of the consultation practised by the United States and her allies is very much conditioned by the information available, information for which the United States is the primary source.

In addition, the allied contribution to the formulation of alliance nuclear policy is made much more difficult by the fragmented nature of the information available. The Americans have always been sensitive to the security implications of allied nuclear consultation and have placed great stress on the 'need to know' principle with respect to the distribution of nuclear information. The various NATO bodies dealing with nuclear questions do not all have access to the same information, or use the same channels to obtain it. Access is determined by the nature of the relevant body's tasks and the willingness of the allies possessing the information, primarily the United States, to release it. Thus, for example, the Nuclear Planning Group being concerned in the broadest sense with the political implications of nuclear weapons for the alliance as affected by such issues as the strategy, deployment and systems of command and control governing them, is not considered to require access to the sorts of detailed technical and targeting information available to the SHAPE planners.

Despite the constraints imposed on consultation in the Nuclear Planning Group by the nature of the information available, and by the varying degrees of competence and interest shown by the various ministers, the allies of the United States have nevertheless made significant contributions to the work of the NPG. Without such contributions the notion of allied consultation on nuclear policy by means of the NPG would have little substance. Not least of the allied contributions has been the improvement in national decision-making brought about by insights and information generated in the NPG. All the participants in the consultative process, including the United States, have been affected. For example, it has been suggested that the work of the NPG has produced a much better understanding and analysis of the presence and possibilities of potential use of nuclear weapons in the European theatre than had been achieved unilaterally in Washington.[15] The practice of engaging in joint studies links the work of the national delegations (and the ministers) with their respective national bureaucracies and, apart from facilitating common decisions among the allies, helps ensure that consultation at the ministerial level does not take place in a vacuum.

It should be noted that the Nuclear Planning Group is not the only alliance institution within which questions of nuclear policy are discussed. Apart from the Special Consultative Group, the International Military Staff, the major allied commands and, within the Secretariat, the Nuclear Planning Directorate, all play a part in the process by which the nuclear policy of the alliance is determined, as do the Military Committee and the Defence Planning Committee. Apart from the established pattern of representation on the Staff Group and the HLG, there are no formal lines of communication between the Nuclear Planning Group and these other bodies, but at the official level constant informal interchange takes place. However, the NPG is the only alliance organisation at the ministerial level exclusively concerned with alliance nuclear policy.

In connection with the last point, a comment on the Nuclear Defence Affairs Committee is in order. The NDAC never served any real consultative purpose but, meeting once a year in connection with a ministerial meeting of the Defence Planning Committee, the Committee served simply as a 'rubber stamp' and as a device formally identifying those allies eligible to participate in the work of the NPG. Originally, as successor to the full Special Committee of Defence Ministers, a major function of the NDAC was to accommodate those allies wishing to participate in the process of nuclear consultation, but who were unwilling to participate in the work of the NPG or, alternatively, were not currently serving on the NPG. With the full participation of Norway in the NPG and with the development of the right of continuous representation on the Staff Group, the NDAC was no longer needed to perform this function. Only Portugal, of all the members of the NDAC, did not participate in the work of the NPG. This changed with the participation of Portugal in the Staff Group in 1974, and until the fall of the Caetano government it had been assumed that Portugal would become fully involved in the NPG. In fact, it was not until the Bodö meeting of the Nuclear Planning Group in the summer of 1980 that Portugal finally took part in a ministerial meeting. With the subsequent participation of Luxembourg, all of the members of the Defence Planning Committee are now members of the NPG, and with the ending of rotation there remains no purpose for the Nuclear Defence Affairs Committee. Although no formal announcement has been made, to all intents and purposes the NDAC has ceased to function.

One function of the NPG has been to help foster an environment in which collective decisions about nuclear weapons are possible, but it should be understood that the Nuclear Planning Group is not concerned with operational planning for the possible use of nuclear weapons, which is the responsibility of national and alliance military authorities. Still, it is not entirely clear what effect recommendations emanating from the NPG have on the relevant military authorities. For example, it has been stated that the General Strike Plan (GSP) was drawn up in SHAPE in accordance with nuclear policy guidance worked out in the NPG.[16] This raises questions as to the nature of the guidance offered by the NPG and the weight it exerts on military planning. It is clear that military planning with respect to nuclear weapons should conform to the policies of the NATO political authorities, but in practice, given the different kinds and sources of nuclear information available to the military authorities, together with their different responsibilities, there must be doubt as to the ability of the military to conform in any detailed way to guidance from the NPG. Undoubtedly, one of the tasks of the military personnel involved in the work of the NPG is to ensure a degree of compatibility between political decisions and military planning by supplying information and pointing out military considerations. In turn, those whose responsibilities are primarily political must seek to ensure that the military planners are sensitive to the political context in which nuclear consultation takes place. Again, the Nuclear Planning Group is likely to function most effectively when a common 'universe of discourse' exists between all the participants in its activities. Thus the production of 'concepts' and 'guidelines' for the instruction of the military authorities of the alliance is not necessarily the most important activity of the NPG; rather it is the creation of an environment which facilitates a common approach and understanding of the nuclear problems of the alliance.

There are two very different sets of circumstances in which nuclear consultation in NATO is called for. The Nuclear Planning Group is the main vehicle by which nuclear consultation takes place as a routine and ongoing alliance function. Through this consultative process a reconciliation of allied differences with respect to nuclear policy is sought, and the building of a consensus attempted. However, the NPG is not designed to operate in circumstances in which the possible use of nuclear weapons is contemplated. In a crisis of this magnitude, how and to what extent the nuclear powers would consult with their non-nuclear allies is not clear. A crucial limitation on the consultative process in these circumstances would be the problem of combining adequate consultation with the effective operation of the command and control system in time of war. Although provision has been made for allied consultation concerning the release and use of nuclear weapons in defence of NATO, there must be considerable doubt as to how extensive such consultation could be. There must also be doubt as to whether consultation in these circumstances would bring about allied agreement on whether and how to use nuclear weapons, even following the consultation guidelines originally developed by the NPG in 1969. Thus, the nuclear powers have continued to reserve the right to take unilateral action, both to protect their own interests and as an essential component of deterrent credibility.

Consultation in the NPG has served to help elucidate for all the allies the kinds of consideration that would enter into a decision to use nuclear weapons. Thus the NPG has been used in the development of concepts and guidelines governing the possible use of various categories of nuclear weapons, and in undertaking studies and establishing guidelines in connection with allied consultation prior to any decision to use nuclear weapons. More generally, the Nuclear Planning Group has been used to build confidence among the allies that a credible nuclear posture does exist, and to attempt to reconcile the the non-nuclear allies to the fact that at best they can influence the actions of the United States (and Britain) in support of their nuclear commitment to NATO, but that ultimately they cannot determine how that commitment might be implemented.

Consultation is not an appropriate or effective way of securing *executive* decisions, least of all about the possible use of nuclear weapons. The situation in NATO, which follows inevitably from the role that they play in the military posture of the alliance, is that only the nuclear powers have the authority to decide on the use of nuclear weapons 'on behalf' of the alliance, and this authority is in no sense delegated to them by the alliance. In certain circumstances, the allies of the United States have the power to 'veto' the use of those weapons stockpiled for their use, but this is an essentially negative power which by itself cannot be said to give the allies a share of the decision. Consultation, both in the Nuclear Planning Group and elsewhere in the alliance, may serve to prepare the ground for collective agreement to the use of nuclear weapons but, in the final analysis, each individual government will have to decide for itself how it will respond to the possible use by the alliance of nuclear weapons. This will be so whatever the nuclear status of its forces. To the extent that the NPG has clarified understanding of the fact, and yet has helped generate support for contingency planning on the assumption that nuclear weapons might very possibly be used in defence of NATO Europe, the NPG has helped the alliance to survive the dilemmas which the deployment of nuclear weapons creates for it.

Still, the allies remain committed to consult before nuclear weapons are used if time and circumstances permit and according to the guidelines and procedures largely developed in the Nuclear Planning Group. The actual role that consultation might play in any decision to use nuclear weapons can be clarified by examining the procedures by which nuclear weapons would be released to military commanders for use in defence of the alliance, and by distinguishing the various components of the system by which command and control over the weapons would be exercised.

The bulk of the strategic forces of the United States which form the core component of the overall deterrent posture of NATO are of course not part of the integrated command structure of the alliance. Apart from the varying number of SSBNs committed by the United States, and the British Polaris submarines assigned to SACEUR for targeting purposes following the December 1962 Anglo-American summit meeting in Nassau, the nuclear forces covered by SHAPE planning are comprised of the warheads actually deployed in the European theatre. The potential use of these forces is governed by the General Strike Plan drawn up in SHAPE by the Nuclear Activities Branch on the basis of American and NATO guidance. The Nuclear Activities Branch of SHAPE has the responsibility of target planning for the nuclear forces assigned to NATO. It is largely manned by American personnel and coordination with the United States Joint Strategic Target Planning Staff is maintained by SHAPE liaison officers based in Omaha.[17]

Under the accepted strategic concept of flexible response, two general categories of nuclear warfare are provided for: selective use and general nuclear response. Under selective use, plans have been prepared for limited nuclear options that would permit the selective destruction of particular sets of fixed enemy military or industrial targets; and for regional nuclear options that, for example, would be designed to destroy the leading edge of an attacking force. Together, the object is to provide the Supreme Commander with a wide range of deterrent and tactical options. Theatre nuclear warfare would be the ultimate level of warfare that SACEUR would be authorised to conduct. In the event of a general nuclear response being decided upon, this would be undertaken only in conjunction with the Single Integrated Operations Plan (SIOP) of the American Joint Chiefs of Staff which provides for the synchronised use of nuclear weapons in the event of general nuclear war. Thus, the responsibility for the conduct of a general nuclear response would fall on nuclear forces based outside the European theatre and not subject to the NATO command structure.[18]

The GSP specifies a 'Scheduled Programme' of targets that would be attacked as part of a general nuclear response. A 'Priority Strike Programme' includes targets of highest priority to SACEUR and includes targets on Allied Command Europe's 'Critical Installation List'. Some of these targets are assigned to theatre nuclear forces. In addition there is a 'Tactical Strike Programme' which also would be the responsibility of theatre nuclear forces. All targets under both the Priority and Tactical Strike Programmes have been coordinated with the target list drawn up in accordance with the SIOP and maintained by the Joint Strategic Targeting Centre at Omaha.[19] Clearly, the whole process of NATO nuclear planning is inextricably bound up with the national nuclear planning processes of the United States and, whatever the strategic doctrine agreed by the alliance, will be crucially affected by changes in American strategic policy.

The authority of SACEUR to plan for the use of nuclear weapons in defence of the alliance is constrained then by a number of factors. Among these may be included the nature of the forces available; alliance strategic doctrine; guidance as to the interpretation of that doctrine offered by the nuclear allies and by other NATO authorities; guidelines and discussion on how nuclear weapons might be used that have been developed and undertaken within various NATO institutions (notably the NPG), and by the content of the SIOP. However, this circumscribed authority to plan does not entail any authority to order the release of nuclear weapons to operational units nor, necessarily, once release has been made, to order their use. Such authority can be delegated to SACEUR only by the responsible authorities in the nuclear powers. This means the President in the case of the United States, and the Prime Minister in the case of the United Kingdom. Both the

President and Prime Minister are under a general, but conditional, obligation to consult with their allies before authorising SACEUR to release and employ nuclear weapons. Such consultation would involve direct communications between national capitals as well as consultation in the North Atlantic Council and Defence Planning Committee. Nevertheless, the responsibility for deciding whether or not nuclear weapons will be used remains with the nuclear powers. The decision, once made, would then be transmitted to the major NATO commanders and to the allied governments and to their representatives at the North Atlantic Council.[20]

It appears that a number of NATO commanders are authorised to request the release and employment of nuclear weapons. The United States conducts courses in Europe to acquaint senior commanders and selected members of their staffs with the release process. In addition to the courses, there is a periodic review of the procedures and the conduct of simulation exercises to ensure that those responsible for the employment of nuclear weapons are familiar with the process by which a decision whether or not to use nuclear weapons would be reached.[21] A request for the use of nuclear weapons in defence of NATO could come either from an allied government or from an authorised NATO commander. Such a request would be communicated immediately to all allied governments and to the Defence Planning Committee. Consultation would then take the form of an expression of views as to the political and military objectives sought by the use of nuclear weapons, which in turn would be communicated to the nuclear power concerned for decision.[22] Naturally, in the great majority of cases this would be the United States.

Once the release of nuclear weapons had been authorised, it would be possible for the President of the United States to delegate the authority to employ nuclear weapons to SACEUR or SACLANT or, through them, to subordinate NATO commanders.[23] But, in principle, at all times the President can determine the scope of any delegation of authority, or revoke any delegation previously made. This power flows from the President's constitutional position as Commander-in-Chief, and it can be applied to all American nuclear weapons. In the case of those weapons assigned to NATO however, any delegation of authority or, for that matter, any revocation of authority previously given, involves an obligation to consult with the NATO allies. According to one account, SACEUR would not be authorised to use nuclear weapons unless such consultations had taken place (with the all-important caveat that time and circumstances permit). In a sense, the President can act only to release nuclear weapons unilaterally to SACEUR as a NATO Commander; any decision to order the use of nuclear weapons by the Supreme Commander would technically be taken on behalf of NATO. Of course, SACEUR is also the Commander of United States Forces in Europe, and in this capacity could be ordered by the President to employ the nuclear forces under his command. There is the implication in this same account that the NATO guidelines allow SACEUR discretion as to whether or not to fire a weapon that has been released to him: the release of the weapons to him being understood as a valid reflection of the collective interest and will of the alliance.[24]

Other sources, however, have stressed that separate Presidential authorisations are needed for release and for firing.[25] Nevertheless, the two positions can be reconciled by recognising that in certain contingencies a quick reaction is necessary, either because of the technical character of the weapons involved, or because of the political and military circumstances obtaining. In such cases the release of nuclear weapons to SACEUR would include, it seems, the authority to fire them if in his judgement it was necessary to do so.[26] But, as the continuing debate in the Nuclear Planning Group over the role of theatre nuclear weapons has shown, it is doubtful whether there is any extensive allied agreement on the circumstances in which such delegation of authority should occur. It might be expected that the extent of the Supreme Commander's authority would be subject to the consultation among the allies most immediately affected by any decision to employ nuclear weapons that is called for in the NATO guidelines. Anyway, military planning must proceed on the assumption that a decision to release nuclear weapons to operational units would be accompanied by the authority to use them. It must be understood also that once nuclear warheads are released to the nuclear-capable forces of the allies, the degree of control that the United States as the donor power can exercise over them becomes more difficult. This would be the case especially for the relatively small-yield battlefield weapons deployed forward. If such weapons are to be used in any kind of militarily effective way, then time considerations alone would seem to indicate that along with the decision to release these weapons should go the authority to use them in certain defined circumstances and in prescribed ways. Much of the discussion in the NPG on the possible follow-up use of theatre nuclear weapons once initial use had been made has been concerned with the description of these circumstances and the consideration of appropriate responses to them.

In the European theatre, the established procedure leading to a decision concerning nuclear weapons seems to be that a request for the release of nuclear weapons would pass up the chain of command from a properly authorised subordinate to SACEUR (or, where appropriate, SACLANT) who would then, if he felt the request to be justified, pass it on to the American President for final decision.[27] Apart from any political consultation among the allies that might take place at the level of the NATO Council, it appears that the Military Committee would be involved also.[28] Of course, it would be quite possible for an allied government or an allied commander taking action through his national government to step outside the procedure. Such an action could be of enormous significance in the event of warheads being released to allied nuclear-capable forces, for it is conceivable in these circumstances that these weapons might be employed (or not employed) in accordance with national commands and not according to alliance purposes as expressed through the integrated command structure.

Concern has been expressed as to the amount of time this procedure would take. It has been suggested, for example, that the constraints and impediments to the release and use of nuclear weapons are so numerous that the speed of reaction in time of stress might prove to be unacceptably slow.[29] US Army

Field Manual 100-5, issued in the summer of 1976, indicated that the request to fire a tactical nuclear weapon might take about 24 hours to pass up and down the chain of command. Apparently, a decision on use could take up to 14 hours to reach corps level and an additional 10 hours to reach an individual artillery unit. In order to dampen the escalatory effects of any use of nuclear weapons, the manual states that permission to use battlefield weapons could normally be given in the form of an authorisation to employ pre-planned packages of weapons within a specified time and in a specific geographic area according to the constraints established by the releasing authority.[30] Reports such as these point up some of the difficulties resulting from the deployment of battlefield nuclear weapons in a posture of forward defence, and the critical importance of rapid and reliable communications.

The whole problem of securing a properly authorised decision to use nuclear weapons, subsequently ensuring that the decision is implemented in a manner consistent with the terms and objectives of the original decision, and maintaining reliable and effective contact between the various political and military authorities involved, has come to be covered by the summary description 'command, control and communication' (C^3). There are both technical and political dimensions to the problem, and within NATO consultation has been a primary means by which the political problems of command and control have come to be dealt with. The technical dimension to the problem, in addition to ultimately determining the extent to which political objectives can be met, has also served to set limits to the form, content and very possibility of allied consultation on the use of nuclear weapons. It does this by setting the technical and physical parameters to the time and means available to consult and come to a decision. It determines the amount and flow of relevant information, and helps define the possible alternative actions in what is likely to be the very limited time available. This compression of decision time is a crucial factor limiting the contribution that allied consultation can make to a decision on the use of nuclear weapons.

Discussion of the detailed mechanisms by which physical

control over nuclear weapons is maintained and command over them is ensured is beyond the scope of this study (and anyway, few details are in the public realm). Nevertheless, some attention to the command and control procedures operating with respect to the nuclear weapons available to NATO can illustrate the connection between the scope of possible consultation and the limitations imposed by the nature of C^3. The warheads for the theatre nuclear weapon systems deployed in Europe are stored in about 100 sites, about two-thirds of which contain weapons earmarked for the use of allied forces. The nuclear storage arrangements are under the supervision of special warhead custodial groups which in peacetime function within the chain of command under the Commander-in-Chief of US Forces in Europe who, of course, is also SACEUR. The custodial units are deployed in close proximity to the American and allied nuclear-capable units designated to receive the various earmarked weapons and cooperate actively with them. Were authority to release these weapons for operational use to be given, then control of the custodial arrangements would pass to the relevant NATO commanders in order to facilitate the unified conduct of military operations.[31]

Depending on the deployment and type of weapon, various procedures and mechanisms exist which are designed to prevent unauthorised use and to ensure their security and safety. A basic procedural principle that seems to govern all American nuclear weapons, strategic as well as tactical, is that no one person is allowed near a nuclear weapon without a similarly qualified companion, and that the cooperation of at least two people is required before a weapon can be fired. In the case of American strategic weapons, authority to fire a weapon would come in the form of an *authenticating* code which would indicate to the officers concerned that proper authority had been received. In the case of theatre nuclear weapons various forms of permissive action link (PAL) are employed. The PAL programme consists of a variety of codes and a range of devices which are either integral to a nuclear weapon or attached to it. The object again is to ensure that no unauthorised use can take place. Unlike the strategic weapons, however, in the case of weapons equipped with PALs the codes involved are *enabling* ones; that is, without the code it is not possible to fire the weapon.[32] Considerable attention has been given in recent years by the American administration to refining and making more secure the various PAL arrangements on the different types of theatre nuclear weapon so that there is greater assurance that the United States would be able to maintain positive control over her nuclear weapons in both peace and war.

American warheads in Europe are governed by a series of bilateral agreements with the host countries. These agreements are basically of three kinds. First, an 'Atomic Energy: Cooperation for Mutual Defence Purposes' agreement sets out the general conditions governing the exchange of classified information pertaining to the weapons systems involved and to any transfer of non-nuclear parts of these weapons systems to the host country. Implementation requires two further agreements: a 'Program of Cooperation' agreement covering the specific weapons systems involved and the number and type of warheads which the United States agrees to earmark for those of its ally's forces which are specified as 'nuclear capable' by American authorities; and a stockpile agreement which covers the location of nuclear weapon storage sites, their funding and their security. All the existing stockpile agreements date from the 1950s and refer to broad categories of weapons without specifying individual systems. However, in 1967 the United States agreed to inform the countries concerned of details of the nuclear weapons stored on their territory by means of an annual report from the American Secretary of Defense to the allied Defence Minister listing their type, quantity, yield, location and the weapons with which the warheads could be used. Where appropriate, warheads stockpiled elsewhere for the use of an ally are listed also. In the event that 'significant changes' occur in the stockpile, a briefer report is made, but there is no requirement that consultation with the host country should take place.[33] The stockpile agreements presumably cover nuclear weapons earmarked for both American and allied forces. 'Atomic Energy: Cooperation for Mutual Defence Purposes' agreements have been signed with Belgium, Canada, France, West Germany, Greece, Italy, Turkey, the Netherlands, and the United Kingdom.[34] The agreement with France, which covered weapons earmarked for French forces in Germany, lapsed when France withdrew from the integrated command structure in 1966.

It can be seen from these arrangements that in time of crisis the opportunities for consultation would be limited, and that through their control of nuclear weapons the nuclear powers retain very considerable freedom of action to decide whether or not, or how, to use nuclear weapons. The obligation to consult before making a decision, if such consultations were judged to be both possible and politically and militarily desirable, can at best only serve to influence the American President's decision (or that of the British Prime Minister), it cannot ensure that the ultimate decision will be satisfactory to the parties consulted.[35] This situation emphasises yet again the importance of securing an allied consensus on alliance nuclear doctrine. For not only is it on the basis of this consensus that a politically credible posture of nuclear deterrence must be maintained, but it can be assumed that the prevailing doctrine will crucially influence any decision taken. The greatest scope for allied consultation on nuclear weapons exists at the level of the concepts and doctrines that are developed to explain and determine the nuclear posture of the alliance and, in particular, to the concepts relating to theatre nuclear weapons. This in turn raises the question, which has been a matter of continuing concern to the Nuclear Planning Group, of what are the possible roles of theatre nuclear weapons under the official alliance strategic concept of flexible response.

7. THE STRATEGIC IMPLICATIONS OF THEATRE NUCLEAR WEAPONS

As a consequence of the various decisions made in the 1950s to base allied military planning on the availability in Europe of tactical nuclear weapons, and as a result of the cooperative and stockpile agreements made between the United States and her allies following the December 1957 Council meeting, stockpiles of nuclear warheads for possible use by American and allied forces were built up in Western Europe until a total stockpile of about 7,000 warheads was established; subject to some fluctuation, the stockpile remained at this size until the decision in December 1979 to reduce it by 1,000 warheads.[1] The term 'theatre nuclear force' (TNF) has come to be applied to these weapons deployed in Western Europe in support of NATO. This has tended to replace an earlier umbrella term 'theatre nuclear weapon' (TNW), a typical American application of which was to those nuclear weapons that would be used in theatre nuclear conflict involving 'the use of nuclear weapons against or by the US or allied forces overseas, but not against the United States itself'.[2] From the point of view of the United States, theatre nuclear weapons in the European context have included not only weapon systems physically located there, but also seaborne systems, including the SLBMs carried on the submarines assigned to SACEUR for targeting purposes.[3]

What in fact constitutes a theatre nuclear weapon is not without ambiguity, and a number of points can be made in connection with a definition of theatre nuclear forces that rests on the assumption that their use would be restricted to theatre nuclear warfare. Given anticipated and existing technology, many of the tasks presently assigned to theatre nuclear weapons deployed in Western Europe could be assigned to weapon systems based outside the European theatre.[4] If such

214

systems are included, then this would affect all aspects of the alliance's nuclear posture, including current military planning under the concept of flexible response, arms control possibilities and, most importantly for intra-alliance politics, the nature and credibility of the American nuclear guarantee. On the other hand, if theatre nuclear forces are regarded as consisting only of these weapons physically located in the planned theatre of operations, then the range of strategic alternatives is narrowed, again affecting any political debate within NATO on the nuclear policy of the alliance. In this respect, two significant points to note about the NATO plan to deploy new long-range theatre nuclear forces is that they will increase the targeting options available to SACEUR and, in their undoubted ability to strike at targets in the Soviet Union, will blur even more the distinction between nuclear weapons actually deployed in Europe and the strategic forces deployed elsewhere. It is for this latter reason, among others, that the new LRTNF have been referred to as 'Eurostrategic' and 'grey-area' weapons. Indeed, what is to be considered as the theatre of operations is itself unclear, for the question arises as to whether parts of the Soviet Union fall within the European theatre. At one level this is a question of targeting policy, but the consequences of any contemplated use must be considered also. What would be the likely reaction of the Soviet Union to the use of theatre nuclear weapons on her territory? If the Soviet Union chose to regard any nuclear attack on her homeland as 'strategic' and to retaliate accordingly, then clearly this affects the strategic and political significance of those theatre nuclear weapons capable of reaching the Soviet Union.

From the perspective of military operations there is little value in conceiving of theatre nuclear forces as constituting a single class or category of nuclear weapon; rather, planning proceeds on the assumption that different types of weapon will serve a variety of different military purposes. Thus the military rationale, as distinct from political and deterrence considerations, behind the attempts to modernise the nuclear weapons deployed in Western Europe has been to provide the military planners with greater tactical flexibility.[5] The adoption by the alliance of flexible response as its strategic concept implied a much greater emphasis on planning for tactical flexibility in the possible use of theatre nuclear weapons than at the time of their original deployment in Europe when a largely undifferentiated and 'massive' use was envisaged. Now, the emergence of strategic parity and changes in the European theatre balance have combined to provide further impetus to the search for flexible options in regard to the alliance's theatre nuclear forces.

Two crucial questions raised by critics of the NATO deployment have been whether the command and control arrangements necessary for a flexible, tactical use of nuclear weapons could survive the crossing of the nuclear threshold and, once the initial nuclear threshold had been crossed, whether further thresholds could be maintained as the use of theatre weapons was extended. Indeed, a major argument for classifying all theatre nuclear weapons in a single class is related to these two questions, for it is widely assumed that the crossing of the nuclear threshold would represent a quantum change politically and strategically in the nature of any conflict. From the point of view of arms control and crisis management, many have stressed the importance of maintaining the threshold between conventional and nuclear warfare and have resisted any development which might be interpreted as lowering that threshold, fearing that any use of nuclear weapons could lead to uncontrollable escalation. Thus, the significance of drawing distinctions between categories of nuclear weapon is questioned; instead, the important distinction stressed is that between the character of conventional and nuclear weapons. A further consequence of this line of reasoning is that the value of distinguishing between theatre and strategic weapons is questioned also. The notion of theatre nuclear warfare implies that a clear distinction can be drawn between the tactical and strategic use of nuclear weapons and that there is tacit agreement at least by all concerned, including the enemy, on what constitutes such tactical and strategic use; however, it can be argued that it is impossible to label a weapon 'tactical' in such a way as to make it unambiguously clear that its use is not a prelude to the raising of the level of nuclear exchange to 'strategic' proportions with all the uncertainties as to anticipated retaliation that this would involve.[6]

The ambiguities surrounding the terminology applied to the nuclear weapons available to NATO reflect, in part, the uncertainties and dilemmas raised by their existence as part of the arsenal available to the alliance. Almost from the very beginning of their deployment in the NATO area, theatre nuclear weapons have been subject to controversy and debate. Agreement on a consistent and adequate doctrine governing their possible use has been difficult to achieve, and many would argue that it in fact has not been secured.

The framework within which a doctrine governing the use of TNF can be formulated has been that established by the strategic concept of flexible response, which was adopted by the NATO Council in December 1967, and is contained in NATO Document MC 14/3 which replaced the earlier 'Overall Strategic Concept for the NATO Area', Document MC 14/2.[7] Flexible response emphasises the escalatory use of theatre nuclear weapons and, in contrast to the automatic strike programmes that prevailed before 1967, tends to downplay the threat of a general nuclear response in the event of a major attack. Instead, emphasis is placed on the ability to meet any attack by adequate means with the possibility of nuclear weapons being used tactically should conventional means prove to be inadequate. There is the clear implication that under certain circumstances NATO would be prepared to undertake first use of nuclear weapons. Naturally, given the sensitive and far-reaching character of the issues involved, there have been major divisions between the allies as to how and under what circumstances resort to nuclear weapons would occur. A major political function of the nuclear consultation processes of the alliance has been to ensure that sufficient agreement on alliance strategy exists for the diplomatic and deterrent posture of the alliance to be credible in the strategic and political circumstances facing it.

Flexible response implies a very close connection and interaction between the three concepts of deterrence, defence and controlled, deliberate escalation. Flexible response requires a force structure able to combine a credible 'war-fighting' capability with the capacity to inflict punishment at levels increasingly unacceptable to the enemy. The extent to which NATO forces are perceived as able to deny an enemy his military objectives is a measure of their defensive capability which, in turn, provides a measure of their capacity for 'deterrence by denial'. To the extent that NATO possesses a capacity for escalation, which is both credible and controlled at levels of force which would inflict unacceptable costs on an attacker with respect to the objectives that he pursued, even though they may be militarily obtainable, this is a measure of the ability of the alliance to exercise 'deterrence by punishment'. Theatre nuclear weapons are part of the triad of forces available for the implementation of flexible response (conventional forces, theatre nuclear weapons and strategic forces) and, consequently, the question arises as to how and to what extent they contribute to the total deterrent effect of the alliance and thus give credibility to the concept of flexible response.

Perhaps, of all the questions surrounding theatre nuclear weapons in NATO, their ability to contribute to the effective military defence of the alliance has been subject to the greatest controversy. When nuclear weapons for tactical purposes were first deployed in the 1950s, the assumption was made that they would enhance the war-fighting capability of the general-purpose forces available to the alliance by compensating for the inferiority in manpower available to NATO *vis-à-vis* the Soviet Union and its allies, and that they would favour the defence over an attacking force. Coincident with the decision to deploy these weapons, however, studies and exercises undertaken both in the United States and Europe, of which the SHAPE war game 'Carte Blanche' held in 1955 was the most publicised, called these optimistic assumptions into question. In the 1950s, under the strategic doctrine then obtaining ('massive retaliation'), theatre-wide use of nuclear weapons was envisaged, but the dreadful and unacceptable collateral effects on central Europe of such use called into question the credibility of such a defensive posture.[8] For the battlefield areas the level of destruction would be on a level associated with an all-out strategic exchange and, indeed, it was only the linking of the theatre nuclear weapons with the strategic forces of the United States by means of integrated strike plans that gave them any strategic purpose; that is, they augmented the capacity of the strategic deterrent of the United States to deter by threat of punishment rather than offering a credible means of denying an enemy his objectives, particularly in a situation in which the enemy also possessed theatre nuclear capabilities. As the Soviet Union developed an increasingly convincing capacity to inflict an unacceptable level of retaliatory destruction on the United States directly, the credibility of this strategic posture declined. It was partly in response to this that Secretary of Defence McNamara introduced from 1962 onwards the series of doctrinal and postural changes which became designated as the strategy of flexible response. Although a link between theatre and strategic nuclear forces was still postulated, under the strategy the theatre nuclear weapons were given a more autonomous role which included their being used to reinforce the conventional defence of the alliance.[9]

Flexible response has sought to make theatre nuclear weapons more credible by emphasising among other things the possibilities for limited and selective employment on the battlefield; nevertheless, doubts as to the ability of the tactical use of nuclear weapons to reinforce credibly the defence of the NATO area persist.[10] First, the ability of NATO to defend itself effectively by the tactical use of nuclear weapons against an all-out attack in the European theatre, which itself had recourse to nuclear weapons, can be questioned. An attacker determined to use nuclear weapons tactically from the beginning of his campaign would be under great temptation to attempt a pre-emptive attack on the TNWs deployed on behalf of NATO, particularly since in the view of some observers NATO theatre nuclear forces are highly vulnerable to pre-emption.[11] In these circumstances, after absorbing a pre-emptive strike, there are doubts as to whether the reciprocal use of nuclear weapons would effectively deny an enemy his objectives let alone confer on the alliance any clear military advantage. In any case it is unlikely that an effective military response would be provided by a limited and selective battlefield use of nuclear weapons;

rather, the ability to defeat the enemy in the sense of halting and destroying his forces would rest on the use of nuclear weapons on a scale comparable to that used by the attacker. Like the strike programmes envisaged under massive retaliation, the devastation of the battlefield areas would be enormous and widespread.

The costs of conducting a successful defence have to be considered, and for the European allies in general and the Germans especially the costs of any defensive use of nuclear weapons would be high. In many conceivable cases, including the conduct of a tactical nuclear defence against a nuclear 'blitzkrieg', it is difficult to postulate circumstances in which European governments directly involved would find the costs politically acceptable. The great problem, of course, in any defensive use by NATO of theatre nuclear weapons is the collateral damage that would occur quite apart from any actions that the enemy might undertake. The deployment of enhanced radiation weapons advocated by some as an answer to this problem does not necessarily improve the chances of a successful defence at acceptable cost. In order to defeat and turn back an attacking enemy it is likely that the use of considerable numbers of these weapons would be required, particularly in the event of a fluid armoured battle in which both sides dispersed as a tactical result of fighting in a nuclear environment. However selective in use and limited in yield each warhead would be, severe civilian casualities accompanied by massive physical destruction could be expected over an extended nuclear battlefield.[12] Given that nuclear weapons would be used by both sides in the conflict and that the Soviet Union has given no indication that it would exercise similar 'restraint', it does not seem that the deployment of enhanced radiation weapons would alter the pessimistic conclusions reached regarding the usability of battlefield nuclear weapons in defence of NATO in the European theatre against an opponent committed to a tactical nuclear campaign.[13]

The argument developed so far should not be interpreted, of itself, as ruling out any possible use of theatre nuclear weapons in an effective and politically acceptable war-fighting capacity. Within the strategy of flexible response, it has been suggested, for example, that theatre nuclear weapons can help provide a defence against an all-out conventional attack. In effect, the argument is revived that theatre nuclear weapons can compensate for the perceived conventional force inferiority of NATO as compared with the Warsaw Pact. Current alliance strategy allows for the possible first use of theatre nuclear weapons in the event of a large-scale conventional attack which threatened to break through NATO defences. Not the least of the problems associated with this posture is the political question of alliance consultation prior to any decision to use nuclear weapons, and one to which the Nuclear Planning Group has given considerable attention. Nevertheless, the hope is that the selective use of nuclear weapons against military targets would assist the conventional forces of the alliance in halting the attack and would confront the enemy with the choice of abandoning unsecured objectives or similarly escalating to the nuclear level. In resorting to the first use of nuclear weapons in an attempt to halt a conventional attack, the intention would be to gain time for political bargaining and for reconsideration on the part of the attacker. The criterion for the successful defensive use of nuclear weapons in these circumstances would be to secure a temporary military advantage as a precondition for the restoration of deterrence and the successful practice of 'crisis management'. Clearly, the scope of a 'war-fighting' function for theatre nuclear weapons in this scenario is restricted as compared to the functions it is hoped that they would perform with respect to deterrence and controlled escalation.

The point at which the alliance would resort to first use of nuclear weapons and the scale on which they would be used has been the subject of considerable debate and disagreement among the allies, a debate by no means resolved by the various 'guidelines' and 'concepts' developed by the NPG. The problem is compounded by the commitment of the alliance to forward defence on which the Germans understandably have placed a great deal of emphasis. Given the manner in which the forces assigned to NATO are deployed on the Central Front, together with their lack of depth, it has been assumed that, in the event of a conventional breakthrough by the attacker, early recourse to nuclear weapons would be required if the objectives of forward defence were to be secured. Although it has been suggested frequently that NATO could with reasonable effort acquire a conventional defence that would not require initial use of nuclear weapons, there has never been allied agreement on what in fact would be necessary to acquire such a defence, or a willingness substantially to increase conventional capabilities.[14] Indeed, the steady improvement in Warsaw Pact conventional forces has challenged the alliance's ability to offer the 'stalwart' defence required by current military plans, and was a major factor in the 1977 decision to undertake a long-term defence programme. The conventional aspects of this programme were directed as much to maintaining the relative position of the alliance in the conventional military balance in Europe as they were in increasing the likelihood of the alliance being able to offer a successful defence against an all-out conventional assault.

In order to reduce the risk of uncontrollable mutual escalation following first use, the suggestion has been advanced from time to time that initial use should be restricted to 'demonstration' shots. The value of the demonstration use of theatre nuclear weapons was much discussed within the framework of the NPG in 1968 and 1969 when the political guidelines for the initial defensive tactical use of nuclear weapons were being drawn up, and differences of view appeared between some of the European allies on one side and the Americans on the other. Basically, it seems that the US was far more sceptical as to the value of a demonstration option than were, for example, the authors of the Anglo-German working paper from which the political guidelines on initial use of TNWs were developed; they, it was reported, favoured an earlier and more limited use of nuclear weapons than did the Americans.[15] It is by no means clear to what extent these differences have been resolved and, although the NPG has addressed itself to the problem on a number of occasions since 1968 and presumably has had an impact on the General Strike Plan developed by SHAPE, considerable ambiguity remains concerning the status of possible demonstration use in NATO planning.[16]

The demonstration use of TNWs would be designed to evidence alliance determination to resist an attack and to warn the enemy that his actions inexorably increase the likelihood of a more general nuclear response. A problem that arises with the use of demonstration shots in this way as the first step in a controlled ladder of nuclear escalation is the difficulty of identifying appropriate and unambiguous firebreaks; that is, identifying differences in the character of nuclear weapons or in the manner of their use which would designate and define thresholds appropriate to the threat of subsequent escalation.[17] Of course, this is a problem general to the whole theory of nuclear escalation, and it exists quite apart from another general problem: that of maintaining adequate political and military command and control. However limited the demonstration use, suggested examples have included airbursts, use against clearly military targets with little risk of collateral damage, and the limiting of attacks to a prescribed territory; nevertheless, there remains the difficulty of ensuring that the enemy does not interpret this as merely the first shot in a larger-scale use of nuclear weapons and does not retaliate accordingly. If the demonstration shot is designed to minimise this risk by causing minimal civilian or military damage, then the question arises as to the value of crossing the nuclear threshold in a way which has no military value in terms of the conventional fighting taking place. As General Beaufre pointed out, warning shots would give the enemy the initiative with respect to a more general use of nuclear weapons and, in his view, theatre nuclear weapons should be used only in such a way as to draw the maximum dividends from them.[18] Rather than demonstrating resolve, the militarily ineffective use of theatre nuclear weapons might well be interpreted as indicating an unwillingness to increase the stakes and costs involved in the fighting. Thus, instead of strengthening the defenders' bargaining position, the use of nuclear weapons in this way might weaken it. It was for reasons such as these that the Americans favoured delaying the initial use of nuclear weapons as long as possible and then resorting to them on a scale sufficient to ensure at least a temporary military advantage. In effect, the argument was being made that the demonstration effect of theatre nuclear weapons could not be separated from their war-fighting capacity. A Secretary-General of NATO, seemingly in support of the American position, thus argued that: 'A demonstrative use of such (tactical) nuclear weapons may be effective only if we are prepared to use them on a larger defensive scale, if the enemy refuses to accept our warning. We should be prepared to do it and the enemy should know we are.'[19]

A strong counter-consideration to these arguments, however, is that the attempt to use theatre nuclear weapons in a demonstration role may well be preferable to the initiation of a nuclear battle by even the most selective and limited use of them. The consequences of any escalation would be momentous and, in the circumstances likely to be prevailing in which the initial use of nuclear weapons would be contemplated, demonstration use might well seem to be plausible as a last desperate attempt to avoid the risks and costs of nuclear war. Even a demonstration shot would be launched in a mood of pessimism in the hope that the enemy would respond in an appropriate fashion which would enable the crisis to be contained. Given the risks and costs of any use of nuclear weapons under the strategy of flexible response, it is to be hoped that their use would be designed primarily to attempt to restore a situation of deterrence which had broken down. The firing of a demonstration shot would signal that the political and military command structure of the alliance had survived the shock of the outbreak of war, and this in itself would be of major significance, providing the attacker with a strong incentive to revise his decision to go to war. The demonstration use of theatre nuclear weapons might not of themselves be enough to force an attacker to relinquish any gains, but the restoration of a situation in which political bargaining could take place might well be preferable, for both sides, to the continuation of a war that would be likely to go fully nuclear.

The political and military plausibility of a posture that provides for the demonstration use of theatre nuclear weapons will be affected by the likely circumstances in which a conventional assault might occur. Basically, a different situation obtains whether a full-fledged, premeditated conventional attack or the conventional escalation of some local crisis is considered. In the event of a premeditated conventional attack, presumably the enemy has considered the risks involved in his actions and discounted them accordingly, and in these circumstances the arguments sceptical of the value of demonstration use have considerable weight. On the other hand an enemy who has allowed a local crisis to escalate to a level of conventional conflict which threatens the whole defensive position of the alliance may well respond to a demonstration use of nuclear weapons rather than run the risk of further nuclear escalation. In other words, demonstration use would be designed to stop fighting which had escalated to a level incommensurate with the issues and interests which had caused the conflict in the first place. Without stretching the concept of 'rationality' too far in considering the hypothetical circumstances in which war in Europe might occur, and recognising that the members of NATO themselves might face a major difficulty in determining the enemy's intentions, there is surely some value in anticipating that an enemy is likely to respond differently to a nuclear demonstration in circumstances in which an essentially inadvertent conventional conflict had got out of hand and one in which the enemy had launched a conventional attack in the expectation of achieving military victory.

Finally, with respect to this aspect of theatre nuclear weapons, the credibility of using TNWs in a demonstration role against a conventional assault is in part dependent on the likelihood of a conventional attack. At the time that Secretary of Defense McNamara and his aides were urging the strategy of flexible response on the allies, a major concern of American policy was to get the Europeans to build up their conventional capabilities to a level which would enable the alliance to meet a full scale conventional attack by the Warsaw Pact without recourse to nuclear weapons. Although NATO formally adopted the doctrine of flexible response in 1967, a decision made possible by the withdrawal of France from the integrated military structures of the alliance, the European allies of the United States never accepted the need, or indeed the political possibility, of building up their conventional forces to match those of the Warsaw Pact. In effect, the Europeans found the idea that the Warsaw Pact might be so aggressive as to plan a full-scale attack on Western Europe and at the same time to attack a nuclear armed opponent with conventional forces alone to constitute an extremely unlikely contingency, against which it would be absurd to guard.[20] In the European view a conventional build-up would simply serve notice of a major reduction in the degree of the American commitment of both strategic and theatre nuclear forces to the defence of the alliance.

If then a purely conventional assault is considered to be a remote possibility, a strategic posture which includes the option of a demonstration use of nuclear weapons may well have utility, not least because such a posture may have the great political benefit of commanding wide inter-allied acceptance. Certain conditions, however, would have to be met. It should be clear that the alliance does not entertain the expectation of fighting a full-scale conventional campaign. To do so would be to 'decouple' effectively the defence of NATO not only from the strategic forces of the United States but from the theatre nuclear forces as well. The threshold between the demonstration use of theatre nuclear weapons and the next step in the escalatory process must not be too great. In this respect the introduction of modernised weapons into the armoury of the alliance could be valuable. The intention and effect is not so much to lower the nuclear threshold, as many critics of the reliance on theatre nuclear weapons and of the introduction of the new systems maintain, as to indicate to a potential enemy, in a situation in which the chances of a conventional attack either deliberate or indeed through miscalculation are considered low, that the risks are high that the nuclear threshold would be crossed in the event of war. Nor does such a posture downgrade conventional forces to a purely tripwire function, for they are crucially important to the possibility of an effective local defence which would either succeed in itself or open up the possibility of escalation. The possibility of demonstration use of theatre nuclear weapons, backed up by a range of targeting options made available by weapons which offer greater flexibility than the older nuclear arsenal of NATO, might well increase the military reasonable-ness of the alliance adopting a posture of nuclear escalation. The deterrent effect of a posture of escalation is enhanced to the extent to which in any given situation the resort to escalation by a defender confers on him a significant, if only temporary, differential advantage, for there is a connection between the credibility of escalation and the achievement of military superiority.[21]

The source of many of the differences between the Euro-peans and the Americans with respect to the possible first use of theatre nuclear weapons lies in different attitudes towards the role and deterrent function of nuclear weapons in the alliance. At its simplest level the difference consists of many Europeans wishing to downplay any 'war-fighting' posture, including the use of nuclear weapons in this role, in favour of one which stresses the ability of nuclear weapons to deter any war at all. On the other hand the American position has stressed the desirability of possessing a wide range of conventional and nuclear war-fighting options in order both to reinforce the total deterrent posture of the alliance and to strengthen the bargaining position of the allies *vis-à-vis* the Warsaw Pact. Underlying this position, of course, is the American concern with reducing the risks of what, in an era of nuclear parity, has become the essentially 'irrational' com-mitment to suffer the possibility of nuclear destruction on behalf of interests in Western Europe. These differences raise the question of what deterrent functions, in the sense of 'deterrence by punishment', are served by the theatre nuclear weapons deployed in Europe.

It can be argued that the nuclear weapons available in the European theatre by themselves are not suitable for and cannot offer credible direct deterrence of an attack on Western Europe through the threat of punishment. It has been pointed out that these weapons by their range, yield and penetration capabilities are not fitted for and are not intended to perform punishment roles. Although the threat of the use of these weapons is a fearful one for the countries of Central Europe, owing to the collateral damage that would occur, the threat that they pose to the Soviet Union cannot be compared to that posed by the central strategic forces of the United States. Thus the conclusion can be drawn that the destructive power of theatre nuclear weapons can add nothing to direct strategic deterrence.[22]

With respect to this argument a number of points of qualification can be made. At the time of the December 1979 decision to deploy 572 new long-range theatre nuclear warheads in Europe, the United States and her allies deployed over 300 aircraft capable of undertaking two-way nuclear missions against targets in the Soviet Union.[23] These aircraft fall within the category of what the Soviet Union prefers to call the 'forward based systems' (FBS), although in fact the Russians have always claimed that the number of such systems in the NATO armoury is much greater, including, for example, British and French SLBMs. The NATO long-range aircraft, together with the longer-range missiles such as the Pershing Ia are designed primarily to perform interdiction tasks and, it can be assumed, in many cases are assigned targets outside of Soviet territory. The use of these weapons in a punishment role as part of strategic deterrence would seem to be not 'cost-effective' and of doubtful credibility. Nonetheless, such use apparently is provided for in the General Strike Plan of SACEUR in conjunction with the Single Integrated Operations Plan of the US Joint Chiefs of Staff. One argument for the deployment of the new long-range warheads is that they will be able to perform tasks more effectively than the long-range systems that they will replace. The targeting of NATO's longer-range theatre nuclear weapons within the context of a strategy of flexible response implicitly involves assumptions about how the Soviet Union would view nuclear warfare in Europe that involved the territory of her allies, but did not affect her own territory directly. It is clear, however, that, for the allies of the Soviet Union in the Warsaw Pact, the deterrent threat of NATO's theatre nuclear weapons in terms of the potential destruction that they could cause is comparable to that posed to each of the two superpowers by their respective strategic arsenals. The allies of the Soviet Union, like the European allies of the United States, face the possibility of becoming a nuclear battlefield while the territory of the major protagonists remains unscathed.

The theatre nuclear strike forces available to NATO and, in particular, the intermediate-range systems can be seen also as some form of counterweight to the IRBMs, MRBMs and bombers that the Soviet Union has targeted against Western Europe. That is, the theatre nuclear strike forces of the alliance can contribute to a posture of 'minimum deterrence' for Western Europe by posing a retaliatory threat to any pre-emptive use by the Soviet Union of its own strike forces. Of course, in so far as a retaliatory threat exists, the component contributed by theatre nuclear forces is small, but they do have the important political characteristic of being within the command and control procedures of the alliance. The whole debate within the alliance on nuclear sharing attested to the importance placed by a number of European allies on having a sense of significant participation in the strategic policies associated with nuclear strike forces. In part, because the requirement formulated by General Norstad in 1957 for weapons under his command as SACEUR that were capable of directly countering the European strike forces of the Soviet Union was never met, the presence in the alliance area of nuclear strike systems in which the European allies can participate has assumed great symbolic political importance. In this respect the long-range systems are more significant than the Polaris and Poseidon submarines nominally assigned by the British and the Americans to SACEUR for targeting purposes.

Throughout the history of their deployment in defence of the alliance, the policies associated with theatre nuclear weapons have had an important impact on alliance cohesion, not least because, regardless of any credibility they may have as a minimum deterrent, these weapons have come to be seen as an essential link between the alliance forces in Europe and the central strategic forces of the United States. In this way theatre nuclear weapons may be said to have an indirect deterrent effect on any attack on Western Europe. In turn the credibility of theatre nuclear weapons as an indirect deterrent is crucially affected by the degree of confidence that friend and foe alike have in the coupling of the strategic forces of the United States with the security of Europe. It has been argued that theatre nuclear weapons help achieve this.

The presence of theatre nuclear weapons in Europe creates a risk that their use would 'trigger' the subsequent use of strategic weapons and, thus, general nuclear war. After all, these are weapons deployed in an area of high political interest and commitment, and it is not necessary to postulate an inexorable ladder of escalation from the initial use of tactical weapons to general nuclear war in order to appreciate that any resort to theatre nuclear weapons would create a situation in which the possibility of general nuclear war had increased. Theatre nuclear weapons, by their presence, contribute to the element of uncertainty of response that the French in particular have stressed as an important element in deterrence. This element of uncertainty contributed by theatre nuclear weapons can be seen as reinforcing the deterrent posture of the alliance in two somewhat paradoxical ways. Just as the Soviet Union cannot be certain that any regional conflict in Europe would not escalate to a general nuclear exchange, so there remains a doubt, on the other hand, as to whether the United States would escalate to the strategic level in the event of conflict in Europe. This element of ambiguity is politically essential to the United States in order that her commitment to European security is not found to be unacceptably binding and so, reinforcing the element of paradox, it strengthens the credibility of her nuclear commitment.[24]

For the alliance there exists a tension between the 'virtues' of uncertainty and the desirability for political and planning purposes of clearly defined criteria of use. Thus, it can be argued that it is not in the interests of Western security for open pronouncements to be made concerning the exact stage at which the alliance would resort to nuclear weapons; the argument being that a degree of uncertainty concerning the exact situation in which these weapons would be used is an essential part of the deterrent, particularly with respect to the threat of escalation. The alliance should concentrate, in this view, on trying to ensure that a potential aggressor realises that it is certain that nuclear weapons will be used if he persists with an attack in the face of warnings, but that it should be left uncertain as to when the alliance would go nuclear and in what ways. In the words of Manlio Brosio: 'The prospective enemy should have no doubts about our determination, but must have no certainty about our ways of reacting. To my mind it is this combination of certainty and uncertainty which represents the most effective deterrent.'[25] Actually, it is inherent in the nature of NATO as an alliance that there should be uncertainty of response. In a nuclear context it is politically impossible, as well as dangerous, to legislate a response to crisis in advance. Nevertheless, for those countries likely to be most immediately affected by any use of theatre nuclear weapons, there are clear interests in the working out of acceptable guidelines for use and for trying to ensure that any use of theatre nuclear weapons would occur in a fashion and at a time which best accorded with their own view of their national interests. With respect to the latter point, this helps explain the continuing German concern with the question of a 'host country veto' over the use of theatre nuclear weapons.

In a situation in which the use of nuclear weapons is considered at all, it is more credible to contemplate the possible use of theatre nuclear weapons initially rather than to escalate immediately to the strategic level. Once a strategy of massive retaliation was ruled out as a credible or appropriate way of manifesting the American nuclear commitment to the security of Europe, and once the implications of mutual assured destruction and nuclear parity became public currency, there was no alternative to considering the selective use of theatre nuclear weapons as a means by which the United States could provide a nuclear guarantee. The presence of theatre nuclear weapons ensures that the US President has a nuclear alternative to strategic retaliation, and successive posture statements by American Secretaries of Defense have argued just this: that a major rationale for TNWs within a strategy of flexible response has been that they help to make the overall American deterrent more realistic by providing an alternative to a strategic nuclear response in the event of a localised theatre attack. The link that theatre nuclear weapons provide with American strategic forces, however, is not simply one of providing an intermediate step in a ladder of escalation but rather one which alters the whole calculus of risks faced by the instigator of an attack on Western Europe. Wolfgang Heisenberg has argued that the attacker must wish to take into account all possible developments and that the defender must wish to retain the flexibility to meet a specific danger as it arises. Accordingly, since the existence of theatre nuclear weapons reduces the danger of automatic strategic escalation for the defender, he is more likely to use them against major aggression than strategic weapons. Since the aggressor must take into account the possibility of escalation to the strategic level, the possession of theatre nuclear weapons by the defender increases the credibility of overall nuclear deterrence.[26] Theatre nuclear weapons then, are an essential component in the spectrum of deterrence.

Qualifying this argument, however, is the fact that increasingly in recent years the credibility of theatre nuclear weapons being able to link the strategic forces of the United States with the conventional defences of the alliance has been questioned. At the level of the central strategic balance it has been argued that nuclear parity, and the explicit recognition of that parity by the United States in the Moscow Agreements of May 1972, means that the United States will not commit her strategic forces against the Soviet Union except in response to a direct threat to her own survival. This being the case, there is no way that the United States can allow theatre nuclear weapons to couple her strategic forces to the defence of Europe.

Fundamentally, of course, it has been possible to argue this ever since the Soviet Union achieved a substantial second-strike capability, but the Americans, until the mid-sixties at least, retained a real strategic superiority which the 'McNamara strategy' (as originally formulated) sought to exploit. It was within the framework of this perceived strategic superiority that the strategy of flexible response was developed and within which a role for theatre nuclear weapons in NATO was articulated. Strategic parity has now undermined the original assumptions underlying the strategy of the alliance, calling into question for some the validity of flexible response and for others the value of theatre nuclear weapons. If theatre nuclear weapons no longer form a clearly perceived link with the strategic forces of the United States, then the value of such weapons as an indirect deterrent is lowered. Consequently, if the American nuclear commitment to Europe is seen as resting primarily on the nuclear forces deployed in the European theatre, a great deal of political stress will be generated by any doubts as to their value as a direct deterrent. In other words the political salience of the strategy governing nuclear weapons in the alliance has increased because what had once been thought a secondary function of theatre nuclear weapons (direct deterrence) has become far more central to European security. An additional consequence which is of concern to Europeans is that they have always wanted a NATO strategy that did not leave Europe as the only potential nuclear battlefield. Despite the continuing flourishes of alliance rhetoric on this point, many now doubt that they have such a strategy.[27]

From their point of view, the European allies cannot be anything other than sensitive to any development that can be construed as 'decoupling' the American strategic deterrent from European security. Among the developments in recent years that have affected European sensitivities in this respect has been the general pattern of bilateral Soviet–American diplomacy on security and strategic matters; this pattern, partly formalised within the framework of SALT, inevitably raises fears that agreements vitally affecting their security might be negotiated over their heads. Fears of this kind played a part in the emergence of theatre nuclear force modernisation in the alliance, and the reassurance of the allies in this respect is likely to be a major function of the Special Consultative Group. The SCG is likely to have a role also in reassuring the allies that, in pursuit of further arms control agreements with the Soviet Union, the United States will not respond to Soviet pressure with respect to the transfer of nuclear information so as to limit in undesired ways any future options with respect to nuclear arrangements within the alliance. A further relevant development has been the widespread perception that adverse changes have occurred in the alliance's strategic environment. Quite apart from the impact of parity at the strategic level, the increase in the number and technical capability of Soviet battlefield nuclear weapons, when coupled with the deployment of new long-range systems, has eliminated the basis for any alliance claim to superiority at the theatre nuclear level. As a result, there is concern that the Soviet Union is close to neutralising NATO's theatre nuclear options within the framework of flexible response.[28]

The cumulative effect on the European members of the alliance has been to weaken the psychological credibility of the American nuclear commitment and to revive questions of nuclear sharing and nuclear control as alliance issues. However, the political and diplomatic context in which these issues arise today has been transformed from that which existed in the fifties and sixties. Nevertheless, as before, the response of NATO in terms of intra-alliance politics and diplomacy has been to emphasise the importance of adequate consultation and to give urgency to debates about alternative alliance structures and alignments that might operate more effectively in a changing political and strategic environment. In terms of NATO conceived as a political system, these environmental changes can be considered a source of stress to which the individual member-states have responded in a variety of ways with differing political and diplomatic consequences.

These responses have threatened the cohesion of the alliance and have challenged the ability of the United States to exercise effectively centralised control over the implementation of alliance strategy and over East–West relations. The doctrine of limited nuclear options publicised by Secretary of Defense Schlesinger in 1974 and the 'countervailing strategy' announced by the Carter administration in 1980 can be understood, in part, as an attempt to deal with these challenges by reinforcing the credibility of the American strategic deterrent. Explicit justification for the targeting and doctrinal changes associated with these reviews of American strategic policy was made on the grounds that they were necessary for the continued linkage of American strategic forces to the security of Western Europe.[29] An important means by which the link has been reaffirmed is for American military planners to take more direct account of theatre nuclear forces in planning for limited options. The distinction between strategic and theatre nuclear weapons is, in effect, obscured in an attempt to provide an integrated nuclear posture that will provide deterrence across a wide range of possibilities.[30] In so far as the new targeting doctrines are implemented, one important effect will be to draw the declaratory policy of the alliance concerning flexible response into greater harmony with the SIOP. In presenting his proposals, Schlesinger revealed that, despite the long-standing abandonment of massive retaliation, the SIOP provided only for relatively massive strikes; the thrust of his proposals and their implementation in the 'countervailing strategy' was to provide the United States with a greater capacity to provide a limited and controlled strategic component to the alliance strategy of flexible response.[31]

The final deterrent role that is ascribed to theatre nuclear weapons is that of deterring the use of equivalent weapons by the forces of the Warsaw Pact. It is argued that their presence as part of NATO forces in the European theatre helps deter a limited first use of nuclear weapons by an opponent and helps create a general deterrent against either conventional or nuclear aggression. The argument is that they have a direct deterrent effect at the theatre or tactical level by denying an opponent the opportunity to disarm the conventional defences of the alliance by means of resorting to his own theatre nuclear weapons. It becomes necessary, then, for NATO to possess theatre nuclear weapons because the putative enemy possesses them. Even the strongest advocates of the view that the alliance is able to provide a full conventional defence accept this. Even if the possibility of a complete conventional defensive capability is accepted, it nevertheless remains necessary to retain a theatre nuclear capacity. Indeed, it can be argued that the more credible a conventional defence appears, the more likely a conflict in Europe, particularly on the Central Front, would go nuclear from the beginning. To assume that a major conventional assault on Western Europe is credible, it is necessary to assume also that an attacker, in the event that his forces were being defeated, would not be likely to resort to nuclear weapons. And the more effective the conventional defences facing an attacker, the greater the temptation for him to use nuclear weapons pre-emptively against his opponent's theatre nuclear weapons and conventional forces. This in turn creates a requirement that the theatre nuclear weapons available to NATO possess a second-strike capability sufficient to retaliate against the enemy's conventional and theatre nuclear forces and against interdiction targets.

With respect to deterrence at the theatre level two critical points have been made about the nuclear forces at the disposal of the alliance. First, it has been suggested that the theatre nuclear weapons currently deployed are extremely vulnerable to a pre-emptive strike and do not represent a second-strike capability in which it is possible to place a high degree of confidence. Secondly, it has been argued that the present arsenal, deployment and posture of theatre nuclear weapons are not the best designed to achieve theatre nuclear deterrence since they are largely the product of haphazard growth stemming from the outdated strategic assumptions of the fifties. It is noteworthy that both proponents and critics of a theatre nuclear weapon strategy for NATO have made these criticisms and in many cases share a scepticism as to the credibility of the whole strategic posture of flexible response.

Without entering into a discussion of the merits of these arguments, it is clear that the American government has shown itself sensitive to these issues by undertaking measures to improve the command and control arrangements governing theatre nuclear weapons, to reduce their vulnerability, and to modernise their warheads and means of delivery. What has not changed is the basic strategic posture laid down in MC 14/3. Even here, however, within the framework of flexible response, nuclear doctrine and force posture have been subject to evolution.[32] Nevertheless, until the decisions to deploy the new intermediate-range weapons and to reduce the total stockpile by 1,000 warheads were made, there had been surprisingly few major changes in the types and deployment of nuclear weapons in the European theatre. Changes in the character and composition of the nuclear arsenal have tended to be incremental and cumulative in their effects and, again until the December 1979 decisions, there had been a tendency towards a reduction in the average yield of the nuclear warheads deployed in Western Europe.[33] Along with this evolution in the composition of the nuclear stockpile, changes have occurred in the area of military planning as it affects the possible use of nuclear weapons in Europe and in the related concepts and guidelines worked out in the Nuclear Planning Group and other alliance institutions.

Presumably these military plans take into account both the defensive and deterrent roles of the weapons available for theatre use. Indeed, one justification that can be offered for the large number and relatively wide variety of warheads and delivery systems available to NATO in the European theatre is the need to meet the different demands of defence and deterrence within the framework of flexible response. The arsenal of theatre nuclear weapons required for a defensive, war-fighting posture is different, it can be argued, from that which is needed to maintain a purely deterrent-by-punishment role. For the possible defensive use of theatre nuclear weapons emphasis is placed on such criteria as flexibility, accuracy, rapid target acquisition and effective command, control and communications. A wide variety of weapons in terms of yield and range is required to cover various military contingencies. Given that it is very likely that the defensive use of theatre nuclear weapons would involve their use on the defenders' own territory, it is desirable that warheads be designed to minimise collateral damage by such means as high accuracy, minimum yields and fallout. A further consideration is that the stockpile of weapons should be large enough and various enough to enable a war involving the tactical use of nuclear weapons to be fought to the end.[34]

An obvious consideration with respect to the last point is the serious doubt as to whether it would be possible to conduct military operations in an area devastated by the large-scale tactical use of nuclear weapons. In addition it is doubtful whether the countries most likely to be immediately involved would be willing to countenance such a defensive strategy. Long before the stage of large-scale (and perhaps relatively prolonged) nuclear defence is reached, pressure for the deterrent use of nuclear weapons is likely. Most European governments would agree with General Beaufre that it is not a question of fighting a tactical nuclear battle but of making this impossible by the creation of an effective deterrent posture at the tactical level.[35]

The question arising here is the extent to which theatre

nuclear weapons, in order to have a deterrent effect, should have a usable war-fighting capability. Although a number of commentators have questioned whether in fact the nuclear weapons deployed in Europe have a usable role in any conceivable conflict, the official stance of the alliance is clear:

There is no such thing as a deterrent... if there is no serious plan and will to use these weapons appropriately and effectively. There are ways of choosing the appropriate nuclear weapons according to yields, accuracy and effects, in order to limit destruction and to ensure a positive military effect. The possession of a large number of different kinds of nuclear weapons gives us a range of options which in turn makes their deterrent effect more credible.[36]

For purposes of the various kinds of deterrence – 'minimum', 'indirect', 'tactical' – and for use in an attempt to restore deterrence once fighting had broken out that could not be contained by conventional means, the requirements of the nuclear arsenal are somewhat different from those required for defence. Basically, it would seem that fewer weapons and a smaller variety of weapons are required for deterrence than for a wholehearted war-fighting posture.[37] The deterrent effect of theatre nuclear weapons is a consequence of the risks involved in conflict which might cross the threshold between the use of conventional and nuclear forces. Consequently the theatre nuclear arsenal should be of a size and type to ensure that the threshold could be crossed and that it would be in the interests of the defenders in certain circumstances to do so.

At the minimum level the arsenal should be large enough to hold out the possibility of usage on other than a demonstration basis. The small number of weapons necessary for purely demonstration purposes would be too vulnerable to a pre-emptive strike and, anyway, the point about demonstration use is that the prospect of further escalation must be present. Again, the deterrent effect of the arsenal is enhanced to the extent that it has the capacity to inflict punishment either to indicate seriousness of intention or to retaliate against the first use of nuclear weapons by an opponent. A final consideration in connection with the character of the nuclear arsenal required for deterrence is that it should enable military purposes on the battlefield to be served either by direct battlefield use or by interdiction. After all, the desperate hope in using nuclear weapons in this context would be to restore a deterrent situation which had broken down. And the means of doing this should include not only the threat of further escalation, but also, by halting or delaying an attack, the assistance in creating conditions in which political action to restore deterrence could occur.[38]

As at the strategic level, the question of vulnerability is crucial. In recent years the alliance has given more attention to this aspect of its theatre nuclear posture, but the more extreme critics of this posture appear to have exaggerated the vulnerability of the theatre nuclear arsenal and the extent to which the current deployment invites pre-emption. The very presence of theatre nuclear weapons in Europe generates risks that they may be used. This is basic to their deterrent effect, but the nature of their vulnerability and the degree of provocation that they offer is inseparably bound up with the circumstances in which it is envisaged that warfare in Europe might break out. There have been differences among the allies as to the likelihood and significance of various possibilities but no great sense among allied governments that the current alliance deployment is unnecessarily provocative or too vulnerable. The impact on the theatre nuclear arsenal of NATO of a pre-emptive, counter-force attack is susceptible to technical analysis, though one suspects hardly of definitive technical conclusions; however, the important point politically is that, given the size and variety of the arsenal currently available, an attacker would have to possess a remarkable degree of confidence in the effectiveness of his forces in order to feel confident that a pre-emptive attack would shield him from an unacceptable level of retaliation.

Above all, for a credible deterrent posture to be maintained and for any hope of the restoration of deterrence in the event of conflict, it is necessary that an effective system of political command and control exists which stands a reasonable chance of surviving the outbreak of hostilities. Such a system of command and control would have to be effective in terms of inter-allied consultation, ability to communicate with the enemy and ability to ensure that the military forces available continue to serve the political purposes of the alliance. Cogent arguments have been put forward as to the extreme difficulty of maintaining political and military control on a nuclear battlefield, but here again any tentative conclusions as to the possibilities of maintaining an effective system of command and control will depend on the circumstances in which it is envisaged that nuclear weapons might be used. As in the case of the degree of vulnerability of theatre nuclear forces to surprise attack, in recent years the alliance has been giving increased attention to problems of command, control and communications.

The ability to solve these problems must rest on an analysis which in essence fortunately remains hypothetical, but there is perhaps greater chance of using nuclear weapons tactically in order to restore deterrence in circumstances which allow for their selective use at a level well below that of 'general nuclear response'. That is, the decision-making mechanisms of the alliance are likely to be better able to withstand the restrained use of nuclear weapons than the conditions of all-out theatre nuclear war. Ultimately the alliance survives on the assumption that it would be completely irrational for the Soviet Union to initiate a full-scale attack on Western Europe. Therefore, any onset of war must be seen, in the first instance at least, as a result of miscalculation and thus subject to reconsideration on the part of the attacker. In these circumstances, the ability to stop an enemy attack is wanted even if it should require the use of nuclear weapons. This, in turn, can be taken as a strategic argument for the introduction of a new generation of battlefield nuclear weapons into the NATO arsenal which might be able to have a demonstrative and military effect, but with much less collateral damage than most of the weapons currently available.[39]

Given the character of the nuclear weapons that are presently deployed in the European theatre, the deterrent roles seem better served than do those required for defence. And, given the ambiguities and divergencies of the allies' positions with respect to flexible response, this probably best serves the objective of alliance cohesion. However, to argue this is not to accept the view of Doctor Pangloss, for many difficulties and doubts exist with respect to the contribution made by theatre nuclear weapons to the security of the alliance and, hence, to the security of Western Europe.

These difficulties arise in part from doubts about the technical character and the nature of the deployment of the weapons. For example, there is continuing concern about the vulnerability of the nuclear-capable aircraft. One can consider also that the political control problems posed by the deployment of nuclear artillery close to the frontier and the possibility of emplacing atomic demolition munitions (ADMs) are by no means fully resolved. The difficulty here is that, in accordance with the commitment to forward defence, these weapons are deployed forward and risk being over-run in the early stages of an assault, conventional or otherwise. Thus the politically very difficult choice would have to be faced in what is likely to be a very short time period of either losing them or crossing the nuclear threshold. Such problems point up the incompatibilities between the requirements of weapons suitable for battlefield use and theatre nuclear weapons suitable for longer-range interdiction and retaliatory purposes. Battlefield use emphasises the need for rapid target acquisition, accuracy, dispersion, relatively short range and low yield. In contrast, the longer-range weapons are easier to subject to stringent command and control procedures, and, if in the form of missiles, are capable of exhibiting a high degree of invulnerability.

It can be inferred from the current force posture of NATO, both conventional and nuclear, that the actual implementation of the strategy of flexible response could involve only a limited phase of defensive war-fighting. This would be so whether or not battlefield nuclear weapons were used by either side. Soon, if deterrence restoration had not occurred, the alliance would be faced with the prospect of either surrender or theatre nuclear war. The force posture itself generates powerful escalatory pressures which would be difficult to control and considerable doubt must remain as to whether the discriminate use of nuclear weapons is possible. In some ways the present doctrine of flexible response when coupled with the forces available to the alliance seems to make the possibility of distinguishing in operation between the 'demonstration', 'war-fighting' and 'controlled escalation' use of theatre nuclear weapons more difficult. As one commentator has pointed out, the allies seem to have reached agreement on the stages of nuclear response that are possible under the accepted doctrine but there is considerable disagreement as to the likely time scale that would and should operate.[40] Disagreements such as these have raised doubts as to the operational feasibility of a strategy of flexible response.

A full analysis of the doctrine of flexible response has not been attempted here, but it can be noted that the circumstances under which it was originally formulated have changed. Also, it should be noted in addition that the whole 'McNamara strategy' out of which the doctrine of flexible response grew was essentially of an interim character.[41] The thrust of the McNamara policy was to develop a posture based on American strategic 'superiority' and with an appropriate targeting doctrine by which the United States could exercise centralised control over a nuclear war. The theatre nuclear weapon programme that was inherited from the previous administration could be incorporated as part of an escalatory ladder that was capable of being controlled. Nevertheless, a future was envisaged in which the Soviet Union would catch up and achieve parity. In these circumstances the American ability to control a nuclear war centrally would be lost and the credibility of her nuclear commitment would be greatly reduced. Hence there was the emphasis on the alliance developing a full conventional option in order to strengthen the 'irrational' strategic commitment of the United States to the security of Western Europe.

What happened of course is that a full conventional option was never really attempted; instead, there have been measures to sustain the existing military balance through such measures as the programmes developed in the AD 70 study and in the long-term defence programme. Inevitably, the possibility of the early use of nuclear weapons remains an important element in the deterrent threat to an all-out attack on Western Europe. Unfortunately, from the perspective of the alliance, the achievement of strategic parity by the Soviet Union has been accompanied by developments in the theatre balance that have undermined many of the assumptions on which the strategic posture of the alliance is based. One important response of the alliance to the changing strategic environment was the political commitment to détente; another, the attempt by the United States to exercise control over the diplomatic management of détente as a condition of her strategic commitment. This had led to stress on the political processes of the alliance as they have been concerned with East–West relations, and the transatlantic tensions that have developed have become linked with the issue of theatre nuclear force modernisation.

The continuing political debate within the alliance on nuclear strategy and nuclear issues remains ambiguous and unsettled. As many critics of the nuclear posture of the alliance have pointed out, the alliance has no clear operational doctrine that settles these ambiguities; yet in the past these critics have tended to overlook the extent to which the strategic concept of flexible response has 'held things together'.[42] In such a crucial and sensitive area as national security in a nuclear environment, a degree of ambiguity in the alliance's strategic posture is essential. In effect, strategic doctrine serves as an ideology: on the one hand it has to be coherent enough to allow for interpretations acceptable to the differing national interests of the various allies; but on the other hand it has to be coherent enough to enable policies to be coordinated and planning to take place. With respect to the latter point, it can be said that the strategic doctrine must serve alliance purposes by serving the interests of its members. Manipulation of the doctrine thus becomes a very important lever by which the reconciliation of the individual national interests of the allies can be attempted.

A major question raised for the alliance by the modernisation issue has been whether flexible response can continue to sustain a consensus sufficient for the political credibility of its strategic posture. An alliance strategy can be judged successful to the extent that it helps reconcile the allies' national interests and the alliance interest in cohesion in an equilibrium sufficient for its major proclaimed purposes: that is, in the case of NATO, the security of its members from military coercion.

Whatever the strategic inadequacies of flexible response, it does currently provide a rationale for the theatre nuclear weapons deployed in Western Europe which all European governments have accepted as an essential component of their security. Seen from this perspective, the political dimension, operating in conjunction with military and strategic considerations, is all important in determining the credibility and usefulness of theatre nuclear weapons. In this respect, a crucial task of the Nuclear Planning Group has been to provide an effective institutional means by which political, strategic and military considerations can be reconciled. Until December 1979 when the decision on the deployment of new intermediate-range missiles was taken, the Nuclear Planning Group had proved its effectiveness; however, whether it will be able to perform as well in the changed strategic and political conditions of the 1980s remains to be seen.

NOTES

Preface

1 The major studies relevant to the period covered by this study are cited in the text, and will be found in the bibliography.

2 Among studies on NATO which have emphasised the importance of alliance mechanisms as a significant component of the alliance political process are included: E. Vandervanter, Jr, 'Studies on NATO: An analysis of integration', RAND Memorandum RM-5006-PR, Santa Monica, Calif., August 1966; A. Buchan, *NATO in the 1960s*, rev. edn, Praeger, New York, 1963; W.T.R. Fox & A.B. Fox, *NATO and the Range of American Choice*, Columbia UP, New York, 1967; E.H. Fedder, *NATO: The Dynamics of Alliance in the Postwar World*, Dodd, Mead & Co., New York, 1973.

3 Apart from casual reference to the Nuclear Planning Group in the general literature on NATO, the main published accounts of the work and structure of the NPG are: Thomas G. Wiegele, 'Nuclear Consultation Processes in NATO', *Oribs*, XVI, 2, Summer 1972, pp. 462–87; Harvey B. Seim, 'Nuclear Policy-Making in NATO', *NATO Review*, 21, 6, 1973, pp. 11–13; Robert M. Krone, 'NATO Nuclear Policy Making' in J.P. Lovell and P.S. Kronenberg (eds.), *New Civil–Military Relations*, Transaction Books, New Brunswick, New Jersey, 1974, pp. 193–227. In addition, a good 'insider' account of the genesis of the NPG can be found in Harlan Cleveland, *NATO: The Transatlantic Bargain*, Harper & Row, New York, 1970, pp. 53–64 and passim.

1 The impact of nuclear weapons on NATO

1 A good general account of these developments can be found in R.E. Osgood, *NATO: The Entangling Alliance*, The University of Chicago Press, Chicago, 1962, chs. 4–5, pp. 64–146.

2 *Ibid.*, pp. 105–25.

3 Some British forces, earmarked for a tactical nuclear role, are equipped with British-owned warheads, and thus, at least in theory, could be employed independently of the Americans.

4 For further discussion of C³ as it affects nuclear weapons in NATO, see Chapter 6.

5 Harland B. Moulton, *From Superiority to Parity: the US and the Strategic Arms Race, 1961–1971*, Greenwood Press, Westport, Connecticut, 1973, p. 84. Robert S. McNamara, Address at the Commencement Exercises, University of Michigan, Ann Arbor, 16 June 1961, as quoted in W.W. Kaufmann, *The McNamara Strategy*, Harper & Row, New York, 1964, p. 117.

6 Good discussions of the development of German policy in this period can be found in J.L. Richardson, *Germany and the Atlantic Alliance*, Harvard UP, Cambridge, Mass., 1966; R. Morgan, *The United States and West Germany 1945–73*, Oxford UP for the RIIA, London, 1974; C.M. Kelleher, *Germany and the Politics of Nuclear Weapons*, Columbia UP, New York, 1975.

7 See Chapter 3, and the references cited there.

8 A commentator sympathetic to the McNamara policies, Alastair Buchan, suggested that the debate over nuclear sharing in NATO reflected a confusion between the English concept of 'control', meaning the physical capacity to influence operations and decisions, and the French concept of 'controle', meaning access to planning and policy decisions. In his view, Britain and France became nuclear powers in order to acquire the benefits of 'controle' rather than 'control'. In other words, given the development of appropriate means of consultation, their national nuclear forces would be redundant. The main desire of the European allies, in Buchan's assessment, was to gain influence over the formulation of American strategic policy, and the Athens proposals were to be seen as a positive move towards accommodating these desires. The subsequent policies of the British and French towards nuclear sharing in the alliance, however, clearly demonstrated that both France and Britain sought the benefits of 'control' as well as 'controle'. As this study attempts to show, allied differences over nuclear sharing rested on more substantial grounds than semantic confusion. Alastair Buchan, *NATO in the 1960s*, rev. edn, Praeger, New York, 1963, pp. 96–100; 'The Reform of NATO', *Foreign Affairs*, 40, 2, January 1962, pp. 165–82.

9 Speech by General Norstad to the NATO Parliamentarians' Conference, Paris, 21 November 1960, *Documents on International Affairs 1960*, Oxford UP for RIIA, London 1964, pp. 124–30.

10 For accounts of British and French policy, see Andrew J. Pierre, *Nuclear Politics*, Oxford UP, London 1972; A.J.R. Groom, *British Thinking About Nuclear Weapons*, Francis Pinter, London, 1974; W.L. Kohl, *French Nuclear Diplomacy*, Princeton UP, Princeton, New Jersey, 1971; W. Mendl, *Deterrence and Persuasion*, Faber and Faber,

London, 1970.

11 McNamara Press Conference, Washington, 3 April 1967, USIS Transcript, Supplementary release, 6 April 1967.

12 John D. Steinbruner, *The Cybernetic Theory of Decision*, Princeton UP, Princeton, New Jersey, 1974, pp. 183–5. Also, Kelleher, *op.cit.*, pp. 136–7.

13 Kelleher, *op.cit.*, p. 131.

14 Norstad, *op.cit.*, p. 129.

15 Kohl, *op.cit.*, pp. 134–5.

16 Kelleher, *op.cit.*, p. 142. Also Steinbruner, *op.cit.*, provides a comprehensive account of nuclear sharing proposals in this period. See also: T.C. Wiegele, 'The Origins of the MLF Concept 1957–60', *Orbis*, XII, 2, Summer 1968, pp. 465–89; A. Buchan, 'The Multilateral Force: An Historical Perspective', *Adelphi Papers*, 13, October 1964.

17 Steinbruner, *op.cit.*, p. 188.

18 *Ibid.*, p. 190.

19 *Ibid.*, p. 188. Also, Robert R. Bowie, 'Strategy and the Atlantic Alliance', *International Organization*, XVII, 3, Summer 1963, pp. 709–32.

20 Bowie, *op.cit.*, p. 720.

21 Steinbruner, *op.cit.*, pp. 201–3.

22 Speech by President Kennedy to the Parliament of Canada, Ottawa, 17 May 1961, *Documents on International Affairs 1961*, Oxford UP for RIIA, London, 1965, p. 66.

23 Steinbruner, *op.cit.*, pp. 185–6.

24 *Ibid.*, pp. 211–12.

25 Joint Statement by President Kennedy and Mr Macmillan, Nassau, 21 December 1962, *Documents on International Affairs 1962*, Oxford UP for RIIA, London, 1971, p. 484. The Skybolt crisis is fully discussed in Richard E. Neustadt, *Alliance Politics*, Columbia UP, New York, 1970, pp. 30–55.

26 Steinbruner, *op.cit.*, p. 233. Steinbruner provides a very complete account of the course of American policy concerning the MLF. In addition to the references cited in n.16 above, useful accounts of the MLF can be found in J. Boulton, 'NATO and the MLF', *Journal of Contemporary History*, 7, 3 & 4, July/October 1972, pp. 275–94; H.A. Kissinger (ed.), *The Troubled Partnership*, McGraw-Hill, New York, 1965, ch. 5, pp. 127–60; D. Truchet, *Le Projet de force de frappe multilatérale*, Presses Universitaires de France, Paris, 1972.

27 Joint Statement of President Kennedy and Mr Macmillan, *loc.cit.*

28 D.C. Watt, *Survey of International Affairs 1962*, Oxford UP for RIIA, London, 1970, pp. 167–8.

29 Steinbruner, *op.cit.*, p. 273.

30 Bowie, *op.cit.*, p. 278.
31 Communiqué, Ministerial Meeting of the NATO Council, Ottawa, 22–4 May 1963.
32 *Ibid.* For an account of the Nuclear Deputy see J.S. Hodder, 'SACEUR's First Nuclear Deputy', *NATO Letter*, June 1964, pp. 9–12.
33 Boulton, *op.cit.,* p. 285.
34 Truchet, *op.cit.*, p. 63.
35 Steinbruner, p. 271.
36 Pierre, *op.cit.*, p. 248.
37 *Ibid.*, pp. 293–4.
38 For a description of the command and custodial arrangements governing the warheads stockpiled in the European theatre, see Chapter 6.
39 *Ibid.*, pp. 248–9.

2 The origins of the Nuclear Planning Group

1 Communiqué, Defence Ministers Meeting, Paris, 31 May–1 June 1965. *New York Times*, 1 June 1965.
2 USIS Press Release, Paris, 2 June 1965. *Observer*, London, 6 June 1965. Harlan Cleveland, *NATO: The Transatlantic Bargain*, Harper & Row, New York, 1970, p. 53.
3 *New York Times*, 1 June 1965. *Guardian*, London, 18 June 1965.
4 Cleveland, *op.cit.*, p. 49. Thomas C. Wiegele, 'Nuclear Consultation Processes in NATO', *Orbis,* XVI, 2, Summer 1972, p. 471.
5 Henry A. Kissinger, 'For an Atlantic Confederacy', *Reporter* XXIV, 2 February 1961, p. 20, cited in R.E. Osgood, *NATO: The Entangling Alliance*, University of Chicago Press, Chicago, 1962, p. 300.
6 Robert S. McNamara, testimony delivered to the Sub-Committee on National Security and International Operations of the Committee on Government Operations, US Senate, 21 June 1966, reprinted in Senator Henry M. Jackson (ed.), *The Atlantic Alliance*, Praeger, New York, 1967, p. 271.
7 A succinct account of the ANF proposal and the political uses to which it was put by the government of Harold Wilson can be found in Andrew J. Pierre, *Nuclear Politics: The British Experience with an Independent Strategic Force, 1939–70*, Oxford UP, London, 1972, pp. 276–83.
8 Personal Communication.
9 Cleveland, *op.cit.*, p. 53.
10 Henry L. Trewhitt, *McNamara*, Harper & Row, New York, 1971, p. 184.

11 *New York Times*, 1 June 1965.
12 The development of French strategic doctrine and the political background to French opposition to American strategic policy are dealt with in Wilfred L. Kohl, *French Nuclear Diplomacy*, Princeton UP, Princeton, New Jersey, 1971; and Wolf Mendl, *Deterrence and Persuasion*, Faber and Faber, London, 1970.
13 *New York Herald Tribune*, 9 June 1965.
14 *Washington Post*, 9 November 1965. *New York Herald Tribune*, 10 November 1965.
15 Official announcement of meeting of Special Committee of Defence Ministers, 27 November 1965. Paris, 23 November 1965.
16 NATO Press Release (65) 19, Paris, 27 November 1965.
17 USIS Press Release, Paris, 29 November 1965. McNamara testimony, Jackson, *op.cit.*, p. 251.
18 Cleveland, *op.cit.,* p. 54.
19 *New York Herald Tribune*, 29 November 1965. *Guardian*, London, 2 December 1965.
20 *Guardian*, London, 20 October 1965.
21 Cleveland, *op.cit.*, pp. 52–3.
22 Statement of Secretary of Defense Robert S. McNamara before the House Armed Services Committee on the Fiscal Year 1966–70 Defense Program and 1966 Defense Budget, 19 February 1965, pp. 27–8.
23 Cleveland, *op.cit.*, p. 55.
24 *Le Monde*, Paris, 18 December 1965. *Sunday Times*, London, 19 December 1965.
25 *Observer*, London, 12 December 1965. *Christian Science Monitor*, Boston, 20 December 1965. *Financial Times*, London, 21 December 1965.
26 *New York Times*, 22 December 1965. *The Economist*, London, 21 December 1965.
27 *The Times*, London, 30 November 1965.
28 Johnson–Erhard Joint Communiqué, Washington, 21 December 1965.
29 Cleveland, *op.cit.,* p. 55.
30 Personal Communication.
31 Dieter Mahnke, *Nukleare Mitwirkung: Die Bundesrepublik Deutschland in der Atlantischen Allianz, 1954–70*. Walter de Gruyter, Berlin, 1972, p. 229. *The Times*, London, 19 and 22 February 1966. *New York Times*, 23 February 1966.
32 USIS Press Release, Washington, 24 February 1966.
33 Jackson, *op.cit.*, pp. 240–1, p. 252.
34 Cleveland, *loc.cit.*.
35 *The Times*, London, 30 April 1966.

36 For a representative view of these doubts concerning the tactical use of nuclear weapons see F.W. Mulley, *The Politics of Western Defence*, Thames & Hudson, London, 1962, pp. 49–121, passim.

37 The British government, under domestic pressure to reduce defence costs, hoped, by redefining the role of NATO's conventional forces on the Central Front, to effect substantial savings in the cost of BAOR. The British position had been put forward at the Defence Ministers' Meeting in the spring of 1965 and was developed in successive NATO discussions on the military posture of the alliance. For a discussion of the British government's view, see the parliamentary debate of 3 March 1965, *Hansard*, Vol. 707 (1964–5), 1327–1452.

38 For an authoritative statement of the American argument concerning the ability of NATO forces to counter Soviet conventional capabilities see Alain C. Enthoven and Wayne K. Smith, *How Much Is Enough?* Harper & Row, New York, 1971. The development of American strategic doctrine in this period is discussed in W.W. Kaufmann, *The McNamara Strategy*, Harper & Row, New York, 1964, and Jerome H. Kahan, *Security in the Nuclear Age*, The Brookings Institution, Washington, 1975.

39 Trewhitt, *op.cit.,* pp. 186–7.

40 cf. A. Buchan & P. Windsor, *Arms and Stability in Europe*, Chatto & Windus, London, 1963, p. 81.

41 During the period 1961–4 there had been a 60% increase in the tactical nuclear forces deployed in Europe. See Statement of Secretary of Defense Robert S. McNamara before the House Armed Services Committee on the Fiscal Year 1965–9 Defense Program and 1965 Defense Budget, 27 January 1964, pp. 4–5.

42 *Guardian*, London, 30 April 1966. *Washington Post*, 30 April 1966.

43 *Washington Post*, 1 May 1966.

44 Kai-Uwe von Hassel, 'Organising Western Defence', *Foreign Affairs*, 43, 2, January 1965, p. 211.

45 Communiqué, Meeting of the Nuclear Planning Working Group, NATO Special Committee of Defence Ministers, London, 28–9 April 1966.

46 USIS, Backgrounder, 28 July 1966.

47 Communiqué, Meeting of the Ministerial Council, Paris, 15–16 December 1966.

48 WEU Assembly Proceedings, 12th Sitting, 2nd Part, December 1966, Document 392, *State of European Security*, Report on behalf of the Committee on Defence Questions and Armaments, p. 232.

49 Cleveland, *op.cit.*, p. 57.

50 *Ibid.*, p. 56. Personal Communication.

51 Harvey B. Seim, 'Nuclear Policy-Making in NATO', *NATO Review*, 21, 6, 1973, pp. 11–12.

52 *Ibid.*
53 *State of European Security, loc.cit.*
54 Thomas C. Schelling testimony, Jackson, *op.cit.*, pp. 163–4.
55 *New York Herald Tribune*, 16 December 1966.
56 In December, Schröder, in one of his earliest statements as Defence Minister in the new German government, had raised the question of a German veto over the use of nuclear weapons launched from German territory or directed towards targets on German soil. Mahnke, *op.cit.*, p. 230.
57 R.J. Hill, 'Political Consultation in NATO', ORAE Memorandum No. M64, Operational Research and Analysis Establishment, Department of National Defence, Ottawa, March 1975, p. 36.
58 Staff Report of the Sub-Committee on National Security and International Operations of the Senate Committee on Government Operations, 18 February 1966. Reprinted in Jackson, *op.cit.*, p. 20. See also, Dirk U. Stikker, *Men of Responsibility*, Harper & Row, New York, 1966, pp. 291–2.
59 The US SSBNs (together with the British Polaris submarines) that have been nominally assigned to SACEUR for targeting purposes provide the exceptions.
60 For a full discussion of the restrictive provisions covering the release of nuclear information, see H.L. Nieburg, *Nuclear Secrecy and Foreign Policy*, Public Affairs Press, Washington, 1964, pp. 33–57, 177–82.
61 McNamara Press Conference, Washington, 3 April 1967, USIS Transcript.

3 The early years: 1967–9

1 McNamara Press Conference, Washington, 3 April 1967, USIS Transcript.
2 Harlan Cleveland, *The Transatlantic Bargain*, Harper & Row, New York, 1970, p. 54.
3 Robert S. McNamara, testimony delivered to the Sub-Committee on National Security and International Operations of the Committee on Government Operations, US Senate, 21 June 1966, reprinted in Senator Henry M. Jackson (ed.), *The Atlantic Alliance*, Praeger, New York, 1967, p. 272.
4 Communiqué, NATO Nuclear Planning Group, 7 April 1967.
5 *New York Herald Tribune*, 10 April 1967.
6 Communiqué, NPG, 7 April 1967.
7 Kai-Uwe von Hassel, 'Organising Western Defence', *Foreign Affairs*, 43, 2, January 1965, pp. 209–16.

8 *New York Times*, 6 April 1967. Also *New York Herald Tribune*, 10 April 1967.

9 *Washington Post*, 6 April 1967.

10 WEU Assembly Proceedings, 13th Ordinary Session, 2nd Part, December 1967, Assembly Documents, Document 425, *State of European Security*, Report on behalf of the Committee on Defence Questions and Armaments, p. 106.

11 Communiqué, NPG, 7 April 1967.

12 *Sunday Times*, London, 9 April 1967. *New York Times*, 17 April 1967.

13 *New York Times*, 17 April 1967.

14 WEU Assembly Proceedings, 14th Ordinary Session, 1st Part, October 1968, Document 440, *State of European Security. The Tactical Use of Nuclear Weapons and the Defence of Western Europe*, Report of the Committee on Defence Questions and Armaments, p. 59.

15 *Ibid.*, p. 66.

16 Communiqué, NPG, 7 April 1967.

17 There are a number of ambiguities associated with the terminology applied to the non-strategic weapons deployed in support of the alliance. For a further discussion see Chapter 7.

18 McNamara Press Conference, Ankara, 27 September 1969, USIS Transcript.

19 Cleveland, *op.cit.*, p. 59.

20 A useful and succinct account of this decision can be found in Morton H. Halperin, 'The Decision to Deploy the ABM: Bureaucratic and Domestic Politics in the Johnson Administration', *World Politics*, XXV, 1, October 1972, pp. 62–95. See also, Bensen D. Adams, 'McNamara's ABM Defense Policy, 1961–7', *Orbis*, XII, 1, Spring 1968, pp. 200–25.

21 *Daily Telegraph*, London, 3 October 1967.

22 Halperin, *op.cit.*, p. 89.

23 *Ibid.*, p. 87.

24 *Ibid.*, p. 89.

25 Communiqué, NPG, 7 April 1967.

26 Cleveland, *op.cit.*, p. 60.

27 Communiqué, NPG, 7 April 1967.

28 Bruce Reed and Geoffrey Williams, *Denis Healey and the Policies of Power*, Sidgwick and Jackson, London, 1971, p. 257.

29 cf. Robert Hunter, *Security in Europe* (2nd edn), Paul Elek, London, 1972, p. 257.

30 See the testimony of Dean Rusk to the Sub-Committee on National Security and International Operations, Jackson, *op.cit.*, p. 241.

31 Fred Mulley, *Hansard*, Vol. 768, 8 July 1968, 5–10. For a fuller discussion of this point, see Bernard Burrows and Christopher

Irwin, *The Security of Western Europe*, Charles Knight & Co., London, 1972, pp. 73–4.

32 *The Times*, London, 20 April 1968.

33 *New York Times*, 28 April 1968.

34 Canada at this time occupied a rather special position in that she deployed nuclear-capable forces in the Central Front region according to SHAPE plans and for which warheads were stored in Europe, but the direct impact of theatre nuclear weapons on her security was negligible. Canada subsequently gave up a nuclear role for her forces deployed in Europe.

35 Communiqué, NATO Nuclear Planning Group, 19 April 1968.

36 Thomas C. Wiegele, 'Nuclear Consultation Processes in NATO', *Orbis*, XVI, 2, Summer 1972, p. 485. Note that these arrangements did not preclude continued bilateral US–British liaison and consultation on joint plans concerning the targeting of the British strategic deterrent.

37 Personal Communication.

38 For a discussion of this point see E. Vandervanter Jr, 'NATO's Men on Horseback', RAND, P-2841-1, Santa Monica, California, February 1964, pp. 6–8.

39 Robert M. Krone, 'NATO Nuclear Policy Making', Ph.D. dissertation, UCLA, 1972, Microfilm, p. 154. Krone was SHAPE representative to the NPG Staff Group between June 1971 and June 1972.

40 Communiqué, NATO Nuclear Planning Group, 11 October 1968.

41 *Financial Times*, London, 11 October 1968. J.C. Burney Jr, 'Nuclear Sharing in NATO', *Military Review*, XLIX, 6, June 1969, p. 65. (Burney was Assistant for Nuclear Planning in the Office of the Assistant Secretary of Defense for National Security Affairs in Washington.)

42 *New York Times*, 12 October 1968.

43 *The Economist*, London, 7 June 1969. *The Times*, London, 31 May 1969. *International Herald Tribune*, Paris, 30 May 1969.

44 W. Heisenberg, 'The Alliance and Europe: Crisis Stability in Europe and Theatre Nuclear Weapons', *Adelphi Papers*, 96, Summer 1973, p. 3. *The Times*, London, 30 May 1969.

45 Communiqué, NATO Nuclear Planning Group, 30 May 1969.

46 WEU Assembly Proceedings, 14th Ordinary Session, 1st Part, 6th Sitting, 17 October 1968, pp. 206–7; 16th Ordinary Session, 2nd Part, 5th Sitting, 17 November 1970, pp. 76–9; 17th Ordinary Session, 1st Part, 5th Sitting, June 1971, pp. 164–6.

47 Brosio, *ibid.*, 17 November 1970, p. 79.

48 *loc.cit.*

49 The possible roles of theatre nuclear weapons within a strategy of flexible response are discussed at length in Chapter 7.

50 Statement of Minister of Defence Gerhard Schröder to the Bundestag, 6 December 1967, *Bulletin* of the Press and Information Office of the German Federal Government, 12 December 1967, pp. 358–9.

51 WEU Assembly Proceedings, 14th Ordinary Session, 1st Part, 6th Sitting, 17 October 1968, pp. 196–202.

52 *Ibid.*, p. 201.

53 *Ibid.*, p. 200.

54 Reed and Williams, *op.cit.*, p. 142. Denis Healey, Address to the North Atlantic Assembly, 20 October 1969.

55 Reed and Williams, *op.cit.*, p. 258.

56 Statement of Secretary of Defense Robert S. McNamara before the House Armed Services Committee on the Fiscal Year 1966–70 Defense Program and 1966 Defense Budget, 19 February 1965, p. 74.

57 Statement of Secretary of Defense Robert S. McNamara before the Senate Armed Services Committee on the Fiscal Year 1969–73 Defense Program and the 1969 Defense Budget, 22 January 1968, p. 29.

58 Statement of Secretary of Defense Clark M. Clifford on the Fiscal Year 1970–4 Defense Program and 1970 Defense Budget, 15 January 1969, p. 31.

59 For an American view sympathetic to European criticisms, see J.I. Coffey, 'Strategy, Alliance Policy and Nuclear Proliferation', *Orbis*, XI, 4, Winter 1968, pp. 975–95.

60 *Daily Telegraph*, London, 10 November 1969.

61 Helmut Schmidt, *The Balance of Power*, William Kimber, London, 1971, pp. 76–7. The German edition had been published in 1969 as *Strategie des Gleichgewichts*.

62 Communiqué, NATO Nuclear Planning Group, 12 November 1969. The communiqué did not make clear that the political guidelines covering the possible use of nuclear weapons tactically were restricted to initial use. This was made public subsequently.

63 Personal Communication.

64 Communiqué, Ministerial Meeting of the NATO Council, Athens, May 4–6, 1962. Krone, *op.cit.*, p. 14.

65 US Senate, 93rd Congress, 1st session, 2 December 1973, *U.S. Security Issues in Europe: Burden Sharing and Offset, MBFR and Nuclear Weapons*, Staff Report prepared for the Sub-Committee on US Security Agreements and Commitments Abroad of the Committee on Foreign Relations, Washington, GPO, 1973, p. 20. Testimony of Secretary of Defense, James R. Schlesinger, *Nuclear Weapons and*

Foreign Policy, Hearings before the Sub-Committee on US Security Agreements and Commitments Abroad and the Sub-Committee on Arms Control, International Law and Organization of the Committee on Foreign Relations, US Senate, 93rd Congress, 2nd session, 7, 14 March and 4 April 1974, p. 157.

66 Dieter Mahnke, *Nukleare Mitwirkung: Die Bundesrepublik Deutschland in der Atlantischen Allianz, 1954–70*, Walter de Gruyter, Berlin, 1972, p. 245. *New York Times*, 4 December 1969.

67 Schlesinger, *loc.cit.*

68 US House of Representatives, *Authority to Order the Use of Nuclear Weapons*, Report prepared for the Sub-Committee on International Security and Scientific Affairs of the Committee on International Relations, prepared by the Congressional Research Service, Library of Congress, 94th Congress, 1st Session, Washington, GPO, 1975, pp. 5–6.

69 Cleveland, *op.cit.*, p. 63.

4 The evolution of the Nuclear Planning Group: 1970–4

1 For details of the 'gentleman's agreement' and for membership procedures in the NPG, see Chapter 2.

2 Communiqué, Nuclear Planning Group, Venice, 9 June 1970.

3 *The Times*, London, 9 June 1970.

4 USIS Press Release, London, 9 June 1970.

5 A. Hartley, 'American Foreign Policy in the Nixon Era', *Adelphi Papers*, 110, Winter 1974/5, p. 1.

6 These commitments to consult can be found in the Address by President Nixon to NATO, Brussels, 24 February 1969. (*New York Times*, 25 February 1969), and in the Address by President Nixon to the NATO Ministers Council, Washington, 10 April 1969 (*New York Times*, 11 April 1969).

7 WEU Assembly Proceedings, 15th Ordinary Session, 1st Part, June 1969, Document 481, *Political Organization of Western Defence*, Report of the Committee on Defence Questions and Armaments, p. 190.

8 See Chapter 3.

9 At least this was the case with respect to consultation in the NPG. On such matters affecting strategic weapons as SALT, for example, linked as they were to the broad spectrum of East–West relations, mere advice as to the direction of American policy was unsatisfactory to the allies. However, discussions of questions such as these took place elsewhere, rather than in the NPG.

10 Communiqué, Nuclear Planning Group, Ottawa, 30 October 1970.

11 *New York Times*, 28 October 1970.
12 US Senate, 93rd Congress, 1st session, 2 December 1973, *US Security Issues in Europe: Burden Sharing and Offset, MBFR and Nuclear Weapons*, Staff Report prepared for the Sub-Committee on US Security Agreements and Commitments Abroad of the Committee on Foreign Relations, Washington, GPO, 1973, p. 21. The communiqué issued after the Ottawa meeting made no direct reference to the 'Concepts' document, stating only that the ministers had 'refined' the political guidelines which had been adopted a year before. Communiqué, NPG, Ottawa, 30 October 1970.
13 The withdrawal of the Davy Crockett and Jupiter systems by the United States in the 1960s had aroused a number of misgivings among the European allies, not only because the previous host countries could see their security as being affected, but also because of the unilateral character of the American decision.
14 Robert Hunter, *Security in Europe*, 2nd edn, Paul Elek, London, 1972, p. 171.
15 Evidence of General Giller before the Joint Committee on Atomic Energy, US Congress, 93rd Congress, 1st session, 16 April 1973, Hearings: *Military Application of Nuclear Technology. Part 1*, p. 17.
16 US Senate, *US Security Issues in Europe*, p. 15.
17 *International Herald Tribune*, Paris, 2 November 1970. *New York Times*, 28 October 1970.
18 *New York Times*, 28 October 1970.
19 See Chapter 3.
20 It was suggested that improvements could be made to the fusing and firing mechanisms, to the design of the warheads, and that improved sensor technology could be incorporated into the system. The suggestions arose as part of a general attempt on the part of the American administration to secure appropriations for a modernised TNW arsenal. See evidence of General Giller, *op.cit.*, p. 18.
21 US Senate, *US Security Issues in Europe*, p. 15.
22 *Ibid*.
23 Report of Secretary of Defense Donald H. Rumsfeld to the Congress on the FY 1977 Budget and its Implications for the FY 1978 Authorization Request and the FY 1977–81 Defense Programs, 27 January 1976, p. 107.
24 The adoption by the alliance of a strategy of flexible response had completely ruled out any 'tripwire' strategy. Among the many critiques of a NATO strategy of flexible response, one containing a strong restatement of the value of a nuclear 'tripwire' can be found in Philip A. Karber, 'Nuclear Weapons and "Flexible

Response" ', *Orbis*, XIV, 2, Summer 1970, pp. 292–4.

25 The building of a 'nuclear tripwire' would be one instance of the 'manipulation of risk' discussed in chapter 3 of Thomas C. Schelling, *Arms and Influence*, Yale UP, New Haven, 1966, pp. 92–125. See also *The Strategy of Conflict*, Oxford UP, New York, 1963, pp. 119–31, 187–203.

26 WEU Assembly Proceedings, 19th Ordinary Session, 1st Part, June 1973, Document 607, *Nuclear Policies in Europe*, Report on behalf of the Committee on Scientific, Technological and Aerospace Questions, p. 223. The rapporteur, G. Kahn-Ackermann, was an SPD deputy in the Bundestag, and the hesitancies and ambiguities of the SPD position on theatre nuclear weapons are well revealed in this report. See pp. 222–3.

27 Communiqué, NPG, Ottawa, 30 October 1970.

28 Personal Communication. It has been suggested that at Ottawa the American Secretary of Defense, Melvin Laird, showed a lack of interest in the continuation of the NPG, and that American agreement to continue was the result of European pressure. Bruce Reed and Geoffrey Williams, *Denis Healey and the Policies of Power*, Sidgwick and Jackson, London, 1971, p. 257. Given the usefulness of the NPG to the United States in securing allied acceptance of its strategic policies I find this suggestion surprising. I have been able to find no corroboration for this supposed American lack of interest in the continuation of the NPG.

29 Communiqué, Nuclear Planning Group, Mittenwald, Germany, 25–6 May 1971.

30 Communiqué, Meeting of the Ministerial Council, Brussels, 4 December 1970.

31 R.J. Hill, *Political Consultation in NATO*, ORAE Memorandum, No. M64. Operational and Research and Analysis Establishment, Dept of National Defence, Ottawa, March 1975, pp. 13–14.

32 Communiqué, Ministerial Council, Brussels, 4 December 1970.

33 USIS Press Release, London, 28 October 1971.

34 Communiqué, Ministerial Council, Brussels, 4 December 1970.

35 Statement of Secretary of Defense Melvin R. Laird before the House Armed Services Committee on the FY 1973 Defense Budget and FY 1973–7 Program, 17 February 1972, p. 112 (Laird, *FY 1973 Posture Statement*).

36 White Paper 1971–2, *The Security of the Federal Republic of Germany and the Development of the Federal Armed Forces*, Press and Information Office of the German Federal Government, December 1971, p. 18.

37 *Ibid.*, p. 13.

38 Communiqué, Nuclear Planning Group, Copenhagen, 18–19

May 1972.

39 Communiqué, Nuclear Planning Group, London, 26–7 October 1972.

40 US Senate, *US Security Issues in Europe*, p. 21.

41 *Ibid.*, p. 22.

42 In 1969 the Canadian government announced a reduction of approximately 50% in the strength of its forces assigned to Allied Command Europe. A rationale for the new deployment can be found in the *Defence in the 1970s*, White Paper on Defence, Ottawa, August 1971.

43 Statement of Secretary of Defense Melvin R. Laird before the House Armed Services Committee on the FY 1972–6 Defense Program and the 1972 Defense Budget, 9 March 1971, p. 62. (Laird, *FY 1972 Posture Statement*)

44 Jerome H. Kahan, *Security in the Nuclear Age*, The Brookings Institution, Washington, 1975, p. 149.

45 *US Foreign Policy for the 1970s: Shaping a Durable Peace*, Report to Congress by Richard Nixon, President of the United States, 3 May 1973, p. 202.

46 Laird, *FY 1972 Posture Statement*, p. 12.

47 *Ibid.*, p. 22.

48 *US Foreign Policy for the 1970s: Building for Peace*, Report to Congress by Richard Nixon, President of the United States, 25 February 1971, p. 14.

49 William C. Cromwell, *The Eurogroup and NATO*, Research Monograph 18, Foreign Policy Research Institute, Philadelphia, Penn., Lexington Books, Lexington, Mass., 1974, p. 3.

50 Laird, *FY 1972 Posture Statement*, p. 23.

51 *Ibid.*, p. 76.

52 Kahan, *op.cit.*, p. 148.

53 Laird, *FY 1973 Posture Statement*, pp. 79–80.

54 Discussion of the technical and tactical possibilities of 'mini-nukes' and related conventional technologies can be found in Richard Burt, 'New Weapons Technologies and European Security', *Orbis*, XIX, 2, Summer 1975, pp. 514–32; John H. Morse, 'New Weapons Technologies: Implications for NATO', *Ibid.*, pp. 497–513; Richard Burt, 'New Weapons Technologies: Debates and Directions', *Adelphi Papers*, 126, Summer 1976; James Digby, 'Precision Guided Weapons', *Adelphi Papers*, 118, Summer 1975; Trevor Cliffe, 'Military Technology and the European Balance', *Adelphi Papers*, 89, August 1972; G. Kemp, R.L. Pfaltzgraff, Jr, and Uri Ra'anan (eds.), *The Other Arms Race, New Technologies: Implications for Non-Nuclear Conflict*, D.C. Heath, Lexington Books, Lexington, Mass., 1975; Steven Canby, 'The Alliance and Europe, Part IV,

Military Doctrine and Technology', *Adelphi Papers*, 109, Winter 1974–5; C.S. Gray, 'New Weapons and the Resort to Force', *International Journal*, XXX, 2, Spring 1975, pp. 238–58.

55 Favourable views of the possibilities of 'mini-nukes' can be found in Robert M. Lawrence, 'On Tactical Nuclear War', Parts 1 & 2, *Revue Generale Militaire*, January 1971, pp. 46–59, February 1971, pp. 237–61; Philip A. Karber, *op.cit.*; Colin S. Gray, 'Mini-nukes and Strategy', *International Journal*, XXIX, 2, 1974; J.H. Polk, 'The Realities of Tactical Nuclear Warfare', *Orbis*, XVII, 2, Summer 1973; W.S. Bennet, R.D. Sandoval, and R.G. Shreffler, 'A Credible Nuclear Emphasis Defense for NATO', *Orbis*, XVII, 2, Summer 1973, pp. 463–79.

56 Lawrence, *op.cit.*, p. 244.

57 Cliffe, *op.cit.*, p. 7.

58 Evidence of Morton H. Halperin, *Nuclear Weapons and Foreign Policy*, Hearings before the Sub-Committee on US Security Agreements and Commitments Abroad and the Sub-Committee on Arms Control, International Law and Organization of the Committee on Foreign Relations, US Senate, 93rd Congress, 2nd session (on US nuclear weapons in Europe and US–USSR strategic doctrines and policies), 7, 14 March and 4 April 1974, Washington, GPO, 1974, p. 20.

59 A fuller discussion of the strategic considerations affecting theatre nuclear weapons in Europe can be found in Chapter 7.

60 US Senate, *US Security Issues in Europe*, p. 22.

61 See evidence of General Giller, *op.cit.*, p. 36. Also evidence of General Goodpaster before the Joint Committee on Atomic Energy, US Congress, 93rd Congress, 1st session, 29 June 1973, Hearings: *Military Applications of Nuclear Technology, Part 2,* p. 62.

62 US Senate, *US Security Issues in Europe*, p. 22.

63 *Ibid.*

64 Evidence of Secretary of Defense James Schlesinger, US Senate, *Nuclear Weapons and Foreign Policy*, pp. 208–9.

65 Statement by Ambassador Martin to the Conference of the UN Committee on Disarmament, 23 May 1974, reprinted in *Survival*, XVI, 5, September/October 1974, pp. 248–9.

66 Reported in US Senate, *US Security Issues in Europe*, p. 23.

67 Evidence of Schlesinger, *op.cit.*, pp. 187–8.

68 A discussion of some of the limitations of the 1969 consultative arrangements and guidelines on initial use of nuclear weapons can be found in Chapter 3.

69 Communiqué, Nuclear Planning Group, Ankara, 16 May 1973.

70 *Ibid.*

71 *Ibid.*

72 Hill, *op.cit.*, p. 20.
73 The text of this agreement can be found in *Survival*, XV, 5, September/October 1973, pp. 243–4.
74 Roger Morgan, *The United States and West Germany 1945–73: A Study in Alliance Politics*, Oxford UP for RIIA, London, 1974, pp. 241–2.
75 *Ibid.*, p. 244.
76 Communiqué, Nuclear Planning Group, The Hague, 6–7 November 1973.
77 James Schlesinger, Press Conference, Washington, 30 November 1973, Official Text, US Embassy, London, 3 December 1973.
78 Final Communiqué, The Hague, 6–7 November 1973.
79 Personal Communication: Communiqué, Nuclear Planning Group, Bergen, 12 June 1974.
80 Communiqué, NPG, Bergen, 12 June 1974. Edgar Ulsamer, 'The Neutron Bomb Media Event', *Air Force Magazine*, November 1979, p. 70.
81 Personal Communication. *Guardian*, London, 31 October 1974.
82 *International Herald Tribune*, 15 November 1974.

5 New directions: 1975–80

1 *The Times*, London, 10 December 1974.
2 *Ibid. Financial Times*, London, 10 December 1974.
3 Jeffrey Record, *Force Reductions in Europe: Starting Over*, Special Report, Institute for Foreign Policy Analysis, Washington, DC, October 1980, p. 50.
4 See Jerome C. Heldring, 'Rhetoric and Reality in Dutch Foreign Policy', *World Today*, 34, 10, October 1978, pp. 409–16; Moses W.A. Weers, 'The Nuclear Debate in the Netherlands', *Strategic Review*, IX, 2, Spring 1981, pp. 67–77.
5 These doubts surfaced in much of the testimony given in *Nuclear Weapons and Foreign Policy*, Senate Hearings before the Sub-Committee on US Security Agreements and Commitments Abroad and the Sub-Committee on Arms Control, International Law and Organization of the Committee on Foreign Relations, 7, 14 March and 4 April 1974, Washington, GPO, 1974. The 1,000 warhead figure was suggested by Alain C. Enthoven, *ibid.*, p. 86.
6 James R. Schlesinger, *The Theatre Nuclear Force Posture in Europe*, Report to the United States Congress in compliance with Public Law 93-365, 1975, p.i.
7 Schlesinger Press Conferences, Brussels, 9 and 11 December 1974, USIS Texts, Brussels, 10 and 12 December 1974.

8 Communiqué, Nuclear Planning Group, Brussels, 10 December 1974.

9 Personal Communication. Communiqué, Nuclear Planning Group, Monterey, California, 16–17 June 1975.

10 *Strategic Survey 1975*, IISS, London, 1976, p. 110.

11 Schlesinger, *The Theatre Nuclear Force Posture in Europe*, p. 27.

12 For an official discussion of 'limited nuclear options' see Report of the Secretary of Defense James R. Schlesinger to the Congress on the FY 1975 Defense Budget and FY 1975–9 Defense Program, 4 March 1974, pp. 32–45; also, *Briefing on Counterforce Attacks*, Hearing before the Sub-Committee on Arms Control, International Law and Organization of the Committee on Foreign Relations, US Senate, 11 September 1974, GPO, Washington, 1975.

13 Communiqué, NPG, Monterey, 16–17 June 1975.

14 J.J. Holst, 'Flexible Options in Alliance Strategy' in J.J. Holst and Uwe Nerlich (eds.), *Beyond Nuclear Deterrence*, Crane, Russak, New York, 1977, p. 270.

15 Communiqué, Defence Planning Committee, Brussels, 23 May 1975.

16 See, for example, Edward N. Luttwak, 'Strategic Power: Military Capabilities and Political Utility', *Washington Papers*, IV, Sage, Beverly Hills, California, 1975, pp. 61–2; Paul H. Nitze, 'Deterring our Deterrent', *Foreign Policy*, 25, Winter 1976–7, pp. 195–210. Schlesinger addressed himself partly to this question in *Briefing on Counterforce Attacks*, pp. 38–43.

17 Gerhard Wettig, *East–West Security Relations on the Euro-Strategic Level*, Berichte des Bundesinstituts für ostwissenschaftliche und internationale Studien, 27–80, Cologne, 1980, p. 17.

18 The plan to assign more Poseidon re-entry vehicles to SACEUR had been mentioned in Schlesinger's report *The Theatre Nuclear Force Posture in Europe*, p. 29. The announcement that an additional 84 F-III aircraft would be based in England was made in October 1976. *Strategic Survey 1976*, IISS, London, 1977, p. 123.

19 See text of President Carter's letter to Senator Stennis, 11 July 1977 in S.T. Cohen, *The Neutron Bomb: Political, Technological and Military Issues*, Special Report, Institute for Foreign Policy Analysis, Washington DC, November 1978, pp. 94–5. The briefing was based, apparently, on a report entitled 'Improving the Effectiveness of NATO's Theatre Nuclear Forces'. See Edgar Ulsamer, 'The Neutron Bomb "Media Event" ', *Air Force Magazine*, November 1978, p. 70.

20 Communiqué, Nuclear Planning Group, Ottawa, 8–9 June 1977.

21 *Guardian*, London, 19 November 1976.
22 *Aviation Week and Space Technology*, 1 August 1977.
23 General H.F. Zeiner Gunderson, 'Military Perspective on NATO's Long-Term Defence Programme', *NATO Review*, 26, 3, June 1978, p. 9.
24 Communiqué, NPG, Ottawa, 8–9 June 1977.
25 See interview with Henry Kissinger, *The Economist*, London, 9 February 1979.
26 *Atlantic News*, 966, 12 October 1977.
27 *International Herald Tribune*, Paris, 11 March 1978.
28 *Strategic Survey 1978*, IISS, London, 1979, p. 108.
29 North Atlantic Assembly, Military Committee, *General Report on the Security of the Alliance: The Role of Nuclear Weapons* (Klaas de Vries: Rapporteur), October 1979.
30 Helmut Schmidt, 'The 1977 Alastair Buchan Memorial Lecture', reprinted in *Survival*, XX, 1, January/February 1978, pp. 2–10.
31 *The Security of the Federal Republic of Germany and the Development of the Federal Armed Forces*, White Paper 1979, Bonn (English version), p. 107.
32 *SALT and the NATO Allies*, Staff Report to the Sub-Committee on European Affairs of the Committee on Foreign Relations, US Senate, GPO, Washington 1979, p. 12.
33 Stanley R. Sloan, 'NATO Theatre Nuclear Forces: Modernization and Arms Control', *Issue Brief*, The Library of Congress Congressional Research Service, 2 November 1981, p. 3.
34 Robert Metzger and Paul Doty, 'Arms Control Enters the Grey Area', *International Security*, 3, 3, Winter 1978/9, p. 17.
35 Lawrence S. Korb, 'The Question of Deploying US TNF in Europe', US International Communications Agency, 9 August 1980.
36 Personal Communication.
37 Communiqué, Nuclear Planning Group, Brussels, 18–19 October 1978.
38 North Atlantic Assembly, Military Committee, *General Report on the Security of the Alliance*, pp. 8–10. *The Modernization of NATO's Long-Range Theatre Nuclear Forces*, Report prepared for the Sub-Committee on Europe and the Middle East of the Committee on Foreign Affairs, US House of Representatives, by the Foreign Affairs and National Defense Division, Congressional Research Service, Library of Congress, 31 December 1980, pp. 20–3.
39 *SALT and the NATO Allies*, p. 7.
40 Wettig, *op.cit.*, p. 24.
41 Brown Press Conference, 25 April 1979, Official Text, US International Communications Agency, 26 April 1979.

42 *The Modernization of NATO's Long-Range Theatre Nuclear Forces*, p. 30.
43 *Ibid.*, p. 38. Jeffrey C. Barlow, *Backgrounder 110*, The Heritage Foundation, Washington DC, 14 February 1980, p. 22.
44 *The Times*, London, 26 November 1979.
45 Press conference quoted in Assembly of Western European Union: Proceedings, 25th Ordinary Session, 2nd part, December 1979, Assembly Document 827, *New Weapons and Defence Strategy*, Report submitted on behalf of the Committee on Defence Questions and Armaments, p. 240.
46 Stephen R. Hanmer, Jr, 'NATO's Long-Range Theatre Nuclear Forces: Modernisation in Parallel with Arms Control', *NATO Review*, 28, 1, February 1980, p. 6.
47 Communiqué, Nuclear Planning Group, The Hague, 13–14 December 1979.
48 This was the gist of what Willem Schotten, the Dutch Defence Minister, was reported to have said to the Aaron mission sent to Europe in October by the United States in order to persuade reluctant allies to support modernisation. *International Herald Tribune*, 24 October 1979.
49 *The Modernization of NATO's Theatre Nuclear Forces*, p. 63.
50 See the testimony of Peter Corterier, who was then an SPD spokesman on defence matters, before a Congressional committee in September. *Western Security Issues: European Perspectives*, testimony of European representatives to the North Atlantic Assembly before the Sub-Committee on International Affairs and on Europe and the Middle East of the Committee on Foreign Affairs, House of Representatives, 12 September 1979, pp. 14–15.
51 Communiqué, Special Meeting of Foreign and Defence Ministers, Brussels, 12 December 1979.
52 Hanmer, *loc.cit.*
53 Communiqué, Special Meeting, Brussels, 12 December 1979. A fuller account of the guidelines developed by the Special Group can be found in *The Modernization of NATO's Long-Range Theatre Nuclear Forces*, pp. 30–1.
54 Communiqué, Special Meeting, Brussels, 12 December 1979.
55 *The Modernization of NATO's Long-Range Theatre Nuclear Forces*, p. 39.

6 Consultation and the Nuclear Planning Group

1 Harlan Cleveland, *The Transatlantic Bargain*, Harper & Row, New York, 1970, p. 54.
2 Report of the Committee on Non-Military Cooperation in

NATO, 1956, para. 42, *NATO: Facts and Figures*, Brussels, December 1975.

3 To the extent that there is a range of linked policy issues on which the allies can be expected to coordinate or harmonise policy, these can be considered as constituting a policy arena. c.f. Stuart A. Scheingold, 'The North Atlantic Area as a Policy Arena', *International Studies Quarterly*, 15, 1, March 1975, p. 34.

4 R.J. Hill, *Political Consultation in NATO*, ORAE Memorandum No. M64, Operational Research and Analysis Establishment, Ottawa, March 1975, p. 35.

5 Cleveland, *op.cit.*, p. 25.

6 George Liska, *Nations in Alliance*, Johns Hopkins UP, Baltimore, 1962, p. 74.

7 Henry A. Kissinger (ed.), *The Troubled Partnership*, McGraw-Hill, New York, 1965, pp. 94–5.

8 Thomas C. Wiegele, 'Nuclear Consultation Processes in NATO', *Orbis*, XVI, 2, Summer 1972, pp. 463–4.

9 Francis A. Beer, *Integration and Disintegration in NATO*, Ohio State UP, Columbus, 1969, pp. 43–4. I have confirmed the applicability of this comment to the work of the NPG in interviews conducted with officials.

10 From time to time suggestions for a limited pre-delegation of authority to use nuclear weapons in an emergency have been discussed within NATO. Reportedly, there was an Anglo-American proposal to this effect at the Athens NATO Council of 1962, and similar suggestions have been raised in connection with ADMs.

11 The Polaris and Poseidon submarines which the British and Americans have nominally assigned to SACEUR for targeting purposes may be considered something of an exception to this statement that strategic weapons are outside alliance control. Nevertheless, the role of the non-nuclear allies in determining their deployment and contingency arrangements is at best limited.

12 Robert M. Krone, 'NATO Nuclear Policy Making', in J.P. Lovell and P.S. Kronenberg (eds.), *New Civil–Military Relations*, Transaction Books, New Brunswick, New Jersey, 1974, p. 213. See also, R.J. Hill, *Political Consultation in NATO: Parliamentary and Policy Aspects*, ORAE Memorandum No. M72, Operational Research and Analysis Establishment, Department of National Defence, December 1975, p. 20.

13 The 'open-ended' principle is widely used throughout the NATO committee system by which it is not necessary for representatives of each member country to attend in order to

have a meeting. It enables national representatives to attend on a limited basis, when matters of particular concern or interest are being discussed, and so helps expedite the work of committees. An interesting precedent for the NPG arrangements was established with the creation of the Defence Planning Committee in October 1963 on the basis of open-ended representation; at the same time, subordinate to the DPC, the Defence Planning Working Group was set up on the same open-ended basis, but provided for representation from the International Staff and NATO Military authorities, Bjarne Eriksen, *The Committee System of the NATO Council*, Universitetsforlaget, Oslo, 1967, p. 29.

14 Harvey B. Seim, 'Nuclear Policy-Making in NATO', *NATO Review*, 21, 6, 1973, p. 12.

15 Cleveland, *op.cit.*, pp. 27–8.

16 US Senate, 93rd Congress, 1st session, 2 December 1973, *US Security Issues in Europe: Burden Sharing and Offset, MBFR and Nuclear Weapons*, Staff Report prepared for the Sub-Committee on US Security Agreements and Commitments Abroad of the Committee on Foreign Relations, Washington, GPO, 1973, pp. 16–17.

17 WEU Assembly Proceedings, 15th Ordinary Session, 1st Part, June 1969, Assembly Documents, Document 481, *Political Organization of Western Defence*, Report of the Committee on Defence Questions and Armaments, p. 190.

18 US Senate, *US Security Issues in Europe*, pp. 21–2. See also, Report of Secretary of Defense, Harold Brown to the Congress on the FY 1981 Budget, FY 82 Authorization Request and FY 1981–5 Defense Programs, 29 January 1980, p. 94.

19 US Senate, *US Security Issues in Europe*, p. 22.

20 See the testimony of Secretary of Defence James R. Schlesinger, *Nuclear Weapons and Foreign Policy*, Hearings before the Sub-Committee on US Security Agreements and Commitments Abroad and the Sub-Committee on Arms Control, International Law and Organization of the Committee on Foreign Relations, US Senate, 93rd Congress, 2nd session, 7, 14 March and 4 April 1974, p. 157.

21 Testimony of Vice-Admiral Gerald E. Miller, *First Use of Nuclear Weapons: Preserving Responsible Control*, Hearings before the Sub-Committee on International Security and Scientific Affairs of the Committee on International Relations, House of Representatives, 94th Congress, 2nd session, 16, 18, 23 and 25 March 1976, p. 51.

22 US Senate, *US Security Issues in Europe*, p. 20.

23 *Authority to Order the Use of Nuclear Weapons*, Report prepared for the Sub-Committee on International Security and Scientific Affairs of the Committee on International Relations, House of

Representatives, by the Congressional Research Service, Library of Congress, 94th Congress, 1st session, Washington, GPO, 1975, p. 1. Apparently, at one time the Commander of NORAD had been delegated the authority to use nuclear weapons in certain circumstances. There seems to be no public evidence that any other specific delegation of authority has taken place. *Ibid.*, p. 3. Also, see testimony of Vice-Admiral Miller, *op.cit.*, pp. 50, 75–6.

24 US Senate, *US Security Issues in Europe*, p. 20.
25 *Authority to Order the Use of Nuclear Weapons*, p. 1. Vice-Admiral Miller, *op.cit.*, p. 50.
26 James R. Schlesinger, *The Theatre Nuclear Force Posture in Europe*, Report to Congress in compliance with Public Law 93-365, 1975, p. 7.
27 Testimony of General Goodpaster (SACEUR), before the Joint Committee on Atomic Energy. US Congress, 93rd Congress, 1st session, 29 June 1973, Hearings: *Military Applications of Nuclear Technology: Part 2*, p. 66.
28 Nuclear Planning Group, Final Communiqué, Bergen, 12 June 1974.
29 Vice-Admiral Miller, *op.cit.*, p. 51.
30 US Army, *Field Manual FM 100-5*, Washington, 1 July 1975, pp. 10-8-9.
31 US Senate, *US Security Issues in Europe*, pp. 14–15. Irving Heymont, 'The NATO Nuclear Bilateral Forces', *Orbis*, 9, 4, Winter 1966, pp. 1036–8. Other sources have indicated that there has been a substantial reduction in the number of storage sites in recent years. Some estimates have suggested as few as 50 sites. See Gregory Treverton, 'Nuclear Weapons in Europe', *Adelphi Papers*, 168, IISS, London, 1981, p. 13.
32 Vice-Admiral Miller, *op.cit.*, p. 93. George Quester, 'Presidential Authority and Nuclear Weapons', *First Use of Nuclear Weapons*, pp. 215–16. Phil Stanford, 'Who Pushes the Button?', *ibid.*, pp. 227–8.
33 US Senate, *US Security Issues in Europe*, pp. 16–17.
34 Heymont, *op.cit.*, p. 1033.
35 The Bulk of British nuclear forces are assigned to NATO, which means that they are targeted in accordance with NATO plans and would be used independently only when it was decided that 'supreme national interests' were at stake. Assignment to NATO does not mean that NATO or SACEUR could use them independently of a decision by the British government which, like the American, has committed itself to consult with its allies according to the agreed NATO guidelines. It is usually accepted that effectively the final authority with respect to any decision to

use British nuclear weapons would lie with the Prime Minister. Any British decision with respect to nuclear weapons would be constrained by the fact that not only are its nuclear forces largely deployed and targeted according to alliance plans, and thus are highly integrated with American nuclear forces, but also that a significant part of its tactical nuclear capability is dependent on American warheads. These warheads are subject to the same command and control arrangements as all other American weapons earmarked for possible allied use. *Authority to Order the Use of Nuclear Weapons*, p. 10. Bernard Burrows and Christopher Irwin, *The Security of Western Europe*, Charles Knight & Co., London, 1972, pp. 61–2.

7 The strategic implications of theatre nuclear weapons

1 The figure of approximately 7,000 warheads has wide currency and was confirmed in the early seventies by Secretary of Defense Schlesinger in *Nuclear Weapons and Foreign Policy*, Hearings before the Sub-Committee on US Security Agreements and Commitments Abroad and the Sub-Committee on Arms Control, International Law and Organization of the Committee on Foreign Relations, US Senate, 7, 14 March, 4 April 1974, Washington, GPO, 1974, p. 199.

2 Statement of Secretary of Defense Elliot L. Richardson before the House Armed Services Committee on the FY 1974 Defense Budget and the FY 1974–8 Program, 10 April 1973, p. 27.

3 *The Theatre Nuclear Force Posture in Europe*, Report to the Congress by Secretary of Defense James R. Schlesinger in compliance with Public Law 93-365, 1975, p. 18.

4 Currently, the aircraft of Strategic Air Command, the ICBMs based in the United States and the SLBMs are available; however, a greater number of possibilities will be opened up with the full development and deployment of air- and sea-launched cruise missiles. For a useful discussion, see Richard Burt, 'The Cruise Missile and Arms Control', *Survival*, XVIII, 1, January–February 1976, pp. 10–17.

5 See the evidence of General Goodpaster, *To Consider NATO Matters*, Hearing before the Joint Committee on Atomic Energy, US Congress, 93rd Congress, 2nd session, 19 February 1974. Also, evidence of James Schlesinger, *Nuclear Weapons and Foreign Policy*, p. 155.

6 The implications of asymmetries between Warsaw Pact and NATO theatre nuclear weapon doctrines, deployments and operational characteristics are not considered here. It is doubtful

if there exists any substantial mutual understanding, tacit or otherwise, as to what constitutes 'tactical use', although these matters have arisen within the context of SALT and MBFR. For some discussion of these issues, see Steven C. Canby, 'Damping Nuclear Counterforce Incentives: Correcting NATO's Inferiority in Conventional Military Strength', *Orbis*, XIX, 1, Spring 1975, pp. 47–71; S.T. Cohen and W.C. Lyons, 'A Comparison of U.S. Allied and Soviet Tactical Nuclear Force Capabilities and Policies', *ibid.*, pp. 72–92; Jeffrey Record (with the assistance of T.I. Anderson), *US Nuclear Weapons in Europe; Issues and Alternatives,* The Brookings Institute, Washington, 1974, pp. 37–44.

7 US Senate, *US Security Issues in Europe: Burden Sharing and Offset, MBFR and Nuclear Weapons*, Staff Report prepared for the Sub-Committee on US Security Agreements and Commitments Abroad of the Committee on Foreign Relations, Washington, GPO, 1973, p. 19.

8 On the assumptions of 'Carte Blanche', which included the explosion of 335 weapons, casualties of 1.7 m. killed and 3.5 m. wounded were calculated. R.E. Osgood, *NATO: The Entangling Alliance*. University of Chicago, Chicago, 1962, p. 126.

9 Evidence of General Goodpaster before the Joint Committee on Atomic Energy, 29 June 1973, *Military Applications of Nuclear Technology, Part 2*, Hearings before Joint Committee on Atomic Energy (Sub-Committee on Military Applications), 27 May, 29 June 1973, p. 62. Report to Congress by the Chairman of the Joint Chiefs of Staff, Admiral Thomas H. Moorer, *United States Military Posture for the Fiscal Year 1975*, March 1974, pp. 77–9.

10 Two succinct discussions questioning the defensive credibility of theatre nuclear weapons deployed by NATO can be found in Wolfgang Heisenberg, 'The Alliance and Europe: Part I: Crisis Stability in Europe and Theatre Nuclear Weapons', *Adelphi Papers*, 96, Summer 1973; and Record, *op.cit.*, p. 52.

11 Secretary of Defense Schlesinger emphasised that measures were being taken to reduce vulnerability in his report *The Theatre Nuclear Force Posture in Europe*, p. 239. One argument in favour of the deployment in Europe of GLCMs and the Pershing II is that they would be less vulnerable to pre-emption than existing intermediate-range systems. However, even here, it has been admitted that total invulnerability is not possible. See Report of Secretary of Defense Harold Brown to the Congress on the FY 1981 Budget, FY 82 Authorization Request and FY 1981–1985 Defense Programs, 28 January 1980, p. 146.

12 Kent F. Wisner, 'Military Aspects of Enhanced Radiation Weapons', *Survival*, XXIII, 6, November–December 1981, pp. 246–51.

13 A study done on behalf of the UN Secretary-General on the effects of tactical nuclear war in Europe came to very pessimistic conclusions as to the amount of destruction and the large number of casualties that would occur. The conclusions were based on the assumption that the weapons would be in the range of 5–50 kilotons with an average yield of 30 kilotons. The study thought that the conclusions as to the casualties and destruction would not be significantly altered if the use of cleaner, lower yield weapons in the 1–10 kiloton range was assumed. *Report of the Secretary-General on the effects of the possible use of nuclear weapons and on the security and economic implications for states of the acquisition and further development of these weapons.* Admittedly, this study was undertaken before the technical possibilities of enhanced radiation weapons had been fully explored. For arguments suggesting that by careful use of low-yield, enhanced radiation weapons, collateral damage might be limited, at least at levels below what might be expected in a major conventional conflict, see S.T. Cohen and W.R. Van Cleave, 'Western European Collateral Damage from Tactical Nuclear Weapons', *Journal of the Royal United Services Institute for Defence Studies*, 121, 2, June 1976, pp. 32–8. Also, S.T. Cohen, 'On the Stringency of Dosage Criteria for Battlefield Nuclear Operations', RAND Paper P-5332, Santa Monica, California, January 1975.

14 See, for example, Alain C. Enthoven and Wayne K. Smith, *How Much is Enough?* Harper & Row, New York, 1971, ch. 4, pp. 117–64; Richard D. Lawrence and Jeffrey Record, *US Force Structure in NATO: An Alternative*, The Brookings Institution, Washington, 1974; Steven L. Canby, 'The Alliance & Europe, Part IV, Military Doctrine and Technology', *Adelphi Papers*, 109, Winter 1974–5, pp. 1–42.

15 *The Times*, London, 31 May 1969; Heisenberg, *op.cit.*, p.3.

16 This ambiguity was not clarified by the contradictory statements of Secretary of State Haig and Secretary of Defense Weinberger before Senate Committees in November 1981. President Reagan's press conference a few days later did nothing to clarify the actual status of demonstration use in NATO planning either. See *New York Times*, 5, 6, 11, November 1981.

17 Neville Brown, *European Security 1972–80*, Royal United Services Institute for Defence Studies, London, 1972, p. 70.

18 A. Beaufre, *Strategie pour demain*, Plon, Paris, 1972, p. 126.

19 Manlio Brosio, speech to the Assembly of Western European Union, WEU Assembly Proceedings, 14th Ordinary Session, 1st Part, October 1968, *Official Reports of Debates*, 6th Sitting, 17 October 1968, p. 206.

20 Bernard Brodie, *Escalation and the Nuclear Option*, Princeton UP, Princeton, 1966, p. 51. Also, *War and Politics*, Cassell, London, 1974, pp. 400–6.
21 Brodie, *Escalation and the Nuclear Option*, pp. 30–2.
22 Heisenberg, *op.cit.*, p. 5.
23 These consisted of somewhere between 150 and 170 F-111s, approximately 60 A6/A7 aircraft on US Carriers, between 48 – 56 V bombers of the RAF and, with the important caveat that they were not assigned to NATO, approximately 33 French Mirage IVa. Stephen R. Hanmer Jr, 'NATO's Long-Range Theatre Nuclear Forces', *NATO Review*, 28, 1, February 1980, p. 5. *The Military Balance 1979–80*, IISS, London, 1979, pp. 118–19.
24 Heisenberg, *op.cit.*, p. 5.
25 Manlio Brosio, *op.cit.*, p. 207.
26 Heisenberg, *loc.cit.*
27 Kenneth Hunt, 'The Alliance and Europe: Part 2: Defence with Fewer Men', *Adelphi Papers*, 98, Summer 1973, p. 18.
28 This warning was sounded in an influential Senate report: *NATO and the New Soviet Threat*, Report of Senator Sam Nunn and Senator Dewey F. Bartlett to the Committee on Armed Services, 24 January 1977, GPO, Washington, 1977.
29 For Schlesinger's 'limited nuclear options' see Report of the Secretary of Defense James R. Schlesinger to the Congress on the FY 1975 Defense Budget and FY 1975–1979 Defense Program, 4 March 1974, pp. 32–45. Also, Schlesinger's testimony in *US–USSR Strategic Policies*, Hearing before the Sub-Committee on Arms Control, International Law and Organization of the Committee on Foreign Relations, US Senate, 4 March 1974, GPO, Washington, 1974. For the 'countervailing strategy', see Report of the Secretary of Defense, Harold Brown, to the Congress on the FY 1982 Budget, FY 1983 Authorization Request and FY 1982–1986 Defense Programs, 19 January 1981, pp. 38–45. Also, Walter Slocombe, 'The Countervailing Strategy', *International Security*, 5, 4, Spring 1981, pp. 18–27.
30 Lynn Etheridge Davis, 'Limited Nuclear Options: Deterrence and the New American Doctrine', *Adelphi Papers*, 121, Winter 1975–6, p. 5.
31 Schlesinger, *FY 1975 Annual Report*, p. 82. See also, Henry S. Rowen, 'The Evolution of Strategic Nuclear Doctrine' in Laurence Martin (ed.), *Strategic Thought in the Nuclear Age*, Johns Hopkins UP, Baltimore, 1979, pp. 131–2.
32 Schlesinger, *The Theatre Nuclear Posture in Europe*, p. 235.
33 Schlesinger, *Nuclear Weapons and Foreign Policy*, p. 198.
34 Heisenberg, *op.cit.*, p. 13.

35 Beaufre, *op.cit.*, p. 127.
36 Manlio Brosio, *op.cit.*, p. 206. This point was reiterated by Schlesinger in *The Theatre Nuclear Posture in Europe*, pp. 236–7.
37 Several critics have argued that the contribution of theatre nuclear weapons to deterrence in Europe could be achieved with far fewer weapons than presently deployed and of a type that could be drawn back from the front lines. For example, see the testimony of Morton H. Halperin, Paul Warnke and Alain C. Enthoven, *Nuclear Weapons and Foreign Policy*, pp. 55–70.
38 Heisenberg, *loc.cit.*
39 For example, Colin S. Gray, 'Deterrence and Defence in Europe: Revising NATO's Theatre Nuclear Posture', *Journal of the Royal United Services Institution for Defence Studies*, December 1974, pp. 7–10.
40 *Ibid.*, p. 4.
41 I am indebted to Philip Windsor for this point.
42 R.H. Sinnreich, 'NATO's Doctrinal Dilemma', *Orbis*, XIX, 2, Summer 1975, p. 406.

BIBLIOGRAPHY

I Official Publications

Canada

Defence in the 1970s. White Paper on Defence. Ottawa, August 1971.

Federal Republic of Germany

Press and Information Office of the German Federal Government. *Bulletin.*

The Security of the Federal Republic of Germany and the Development of the Federal Armed Forces. White Paper 1971–2. Press and Information Office of the German Federal Government, Bonn, December 1971.

The Security of the Federal Republic of Germany and the Development of the Federal Armed Forces. White Paper 1979. Press and Information Office of the German Federal Government, Bonn, 1979.

North Atlantic Assembly

Military Committee. *General Report on the Security of the Alliance: The Role of Nuclear Weapons.* October 1979.

North Atlantic Treaty Organisation

NATO Facts and Figures. Brussels, December 1975.

NATO Press Releases.

NATO. Texts of Final Communiqués 1949–80. NATO Information Service, Brussels, n.d.

United Kingdom

House of Commons. Twelfth Report from the Expenditure Committee, *Nuclear Weapon Programme.* HMSO, London, 19 July, 1973.

United Nations

Report of the Secretary-General on the effects of the possible use of nuclear weapons and on the security and economic implications for states of the acquisition and further development of these weapons. UN General Assembly, 10 October 1967, A/6858.

Statement by US Ambassador Martin to the Conference of the UN Committee on Disarmament. 23 May 1974. Reprinted in *Survival*, XVI, 5, September/October 1974, pp. 248–9.

United States

Department of State. *The Department of State Bulletin*.

Statement of Secretary of Defense Robert S. McNamara before the House Armed Services Committee on the Fiscal Year 1965–9 Defense Program and 1965 Defense Budget, 27 January 1964.

Statement of Secretary of Defense Robert S. McNamara before the House Armed Services Committee on the Fiscal Year 1966–70 Defense Program and 1966 Defense Budget, 19 February 1965.

Statement of Secretary of Defense Robert S. McNamara before the Senate Armed Services Committee on the Fiscal Year 1969–73 Defense Program and the 1969 Defense Budget, 22 January 1968.

Statement of Secretary of Defense Clark M. Clifford on the Fiscal Year 1970–4 Defense Program and 1970 Defense Budget, 15 January 1969.

Statement of Secretary of Defense Melvin R. Laird before the House Armed Services Committee on the Fiscal Year 1972–6 Defense Program and the 1972 Defense Budget, 9 March 1971.

Statement of Secretary of Defense Melvin R. Laird before the House Armed Services Committee on the Fiscal Year 1973 Defense Budget and the Fiscal Year 1973–7 Defense Program, 17 February 1972.

Statement of Secretary of Defense Elliot L. Richardson before the House Armed Services Committee on the Fiscal Year 1974 Defense Budget and the Fiscal Year 1974–8 Defense Program, 10 April 1973.

Report of the Secretary of Defense James R. Schlesinger to the Congress on the Fiscal Year 1975 Defense Budget and Fiscal Year 1975–9 Defense Program, 4 March 1974.

Report of Secretary of Defense Donald H. Rumsfeld to the Congress on the Fiscal Year 1977 Budget and its implications for the Fiscal Year 1978 Authorization Request and the Fiscal Year 1977–81 Defense Programs, 27 January 1976.

Report of the Secretary of Defense Harold Brown to the Congress on the FY 81 Budget, FY 82 Authorization Request and FY 1981–5 Defense Programs, 28 January 1980.

Report of the Secretary of Defense Harold Brown to the Congress on the FY 1982 Budget, FY 1983 Authorization Request and FY 1982–6 Defense Programs, 19 January 1981.

Report to Congress by the Chairman of the Joint Chiefs of Staff, Admiral Thomas H. Moorer. *United States Military Posture for the Fiscal Year 1975*, 4 March 1974.

President, *US Foreign Policy for the 1970s: A New Strategy for Peace*. A Report by President Richard Nixon to the Congress, 18 February 1970.

US Foreign Policy for the 1970s: Building for Peace. A Report by President Richard Nixon to the Congress, 25 February 1971.

US Foreign Policy for the 1970s: The Emerging Structure of Peace. A Report by President Richard Nixon to the Congress, 9 February 1972.

US Foreign Policy for the 1970s: Shaping a Durable Peace. A Report by President Richard Nixon to the Congress, 3 May 1973.

US Senate, 93rd Congress, 1st session, 2 December 1973. *US Security Issues in Europe: Burden Sharing and Offset, MBFR and Nuclear Weapons*. Staff Report prepared for the Sub-Committee on US Security Agreements and Commitments Abroad of the Committee on Foreign Relations. GPO, Washington, 1973.

US Senate, 93rd Congress, 2nd session, 7, 14 March and 4 April 1974. *Nuclear Weapons and Foreign Policy*. Hearings before the Sub-Committee on US Security Agreements and Commitments Abroad and the Sub-Committee on Arms Control, International Law and Organization of the Committee on Foreign Relations. GPO, Washington, 1974.

US Senate. *US–USSR Strategic Policies.* Hearing before the Sub-Committee on Arms Control, International Law and Organization of the Committee on Foreign Relations, 4 March 1974. GPO, Washington, 1974.

US Senate. *Briefing on Counterforce Attacks*. Hearing before the Sub-Committee on Arms Control, International Law and Organization of the Committee on Foreign Relations, 11 September 1974. GPO, Washington, 1975.

US Senate. *NATO and the New Soviet Threat*. Report of Senator Sam Nunn and Senator Dewey F. Bartlett to the Committee on Armed Services, 24 January 1977. GPO, Washington, 1977.

US Senate. *SALT and the NATO Allies*. Staff Report to the Sub-Committee on European Affairs of the Committee on Foreign Relations. GPO, Washington, 1979.

US House of Representatives, 94th Congress, 1st session. *Authority to*

Order the Use of Nuclear Weapons. Report prepared for the Sub-Committee on International Security and Scientific Affairs of the Committee on International Relations, by the Congressional Research Service, Library of Congress. GPO Washington, 1975.

US House of Representatives, 94th Congress, 2nd session, 16, 18, 23 and 25 March 1976. *First Use of Nuclear Weapons: Preserving Responsible Control.* Hearings before the Sub-Committee on International Security and Scientific Affairs of the Committee on International Relations.

US House of Representatives. *Western Security Issues: European Perspectives.* Hearings before the Sub-Committee on International Affairs and on Europe and the Middle East of the Committee on Foreign Affairs, 12 September 1979.

US House of Representatives. *The Modernization of NATO's Long-Range Theatre Nuclear Forces.* Report prepared for the Sub-Committee on Europe and the Middle East of the Committee on Foreign Affairs and National Defense Division, Congressional Research Service, Library of Congress, 31 December 1980.

US Congress, 93rd Congress, 1st session, 16 April 1973. *Military Applications of Nuclear Technology. Part 1.* Hearings before the Joint Committee on Atomic Energy.

US Congress, 93rd Congress, 1st session, 29 June 1973. *Military Applications of Nuclear Technology. Part 2.* Hearings before the Joint Committee on Atomic Energy.

US Congress, 93rd Congress, 2nd session, 19 February 1974. *To Consider NATO Matters.* Hearings before the Joint Committee on Atomic Energy.

James R. Schlesinger. *The Theatre Nuclear Force Posture in Europe.* A report to Congress in compliance with Public Law 93-365, 1975.

US Army. *Field Manual FM 100-5*, Washington, 1 July 1976.

US Information Service. Press Release. Paris, 2 June 1965.

Press Release. Paris, 29 November 1965.

Press Release. Washington, 24 February 1966.

Backgrounder. Washington, 28 July 1966.

McNamara Press Conference. Transcript. Washington, 3 April 1967.

McNamara Press Conference. Transcript. Ankara, 27 September 1969.

Press Release. London. 9 June 1970.

Schlesinger Press Conference. Official Text. Washington, 30 November 1973.

US International Communications Agency. Brown Press Conference. Official Text. 26 April 1979.

Lawrence S. Korb. 'The Question of Deploying US TNF in Europe'. 9 August 1980.

Library of Congress Congressional Research Service. Stanley R. Sloan. 'NATO Theatre Nuclear Forces: Modernization and Arms Control', *Issue Brief*, 2 November 1981.

Western European Union

Assembly Proceedings. 12th Ordinary Session, 2nd Part, December 1966. Document 392, *State of European Security*. Report on behalf of the Committee on Defence Questions and Armaments.

13th Ordinary Session, 2nd Part, December 1967. Document 425, *State of European Security*. Report on behalf of the Committee on Defence Questions and Armaments.

14th Ordinary Session, 1st Part, October 1968. Document 440, *State of European Security. The Tactical Use of Nuclear Weapons and the Defence of Western Europe*. Report of the Committee on Defence Questions and Armaments.

14th Ordinary Session, 1st Part, 6th Sitting, 17 October 1968. *Official Report of Debates*.

15th Ordinary Session, 1st Part, June 1969. Document 481, *Political Organization of Western Defence*. Report of the Committee on Defence Questions and Armaments.

16th Ordinary Session, 2nd Part, 5th Sitting, 17 November 1970. *Official Report of Debates*.

17th Ordinary Session, 1st Part, 5th Sitting, June 1971. *Official Report of Debates*.

19th Ordinary Session, 1st Part, June 1973. Document 607, *Nuclear Policies in Europe*. Report on behalf of the Committee on Scientific, Technological and Aerospace Questions.

25th Ordinary Session, 2nd Part, December 1979. Document 827, *New Weapons and Defence Strategy*. Report submitted on behalf of the Committee on Defence Questions and Armaments.

II Document Collections and Surveys

Royal Institute for International Affairs. *Documents on International Affairs 1960*. Oxford UP for RIIA, London, 1964.

Royal Institute for International Affairs. *Documents on International Affairs 1961*. Oxford UP for RIIA, London 1965.

Royal Institute for International Affairs. *Documents on International Affairs 1962*. Oxford UP for RIIA, London, 1971.

International Institute for Strategic Studies. *The Military Balance*. London, 1966–80.

International Institute for Strategic Studies. *Strategic Survey*. London, 1966–80.

III Periodicals and Newspapers

Atlantic News
Aviation Week and Space Technology
Christian Science Monitor
Daily Telegraph
The Economist
Financial Times
Guardian
International Herald Tribune
Le Monde
New York Herald Tribune
New York Times
Observer
Sunday Times
The Times
Washington Post

IV Articles

Adams, Bensen D. 'McNamara's ABM Defense Policy, 1961–7'. *Orbis*, XII, 1, Spring 1968.
Bennet, W.S., Sandoval, R.D. and Shreffler, R.G. 'A Credible Nuclear Emphasis Defense for NATO'. *Orbis*, XVII, 2, Summer 1973.
Boulton, J. 'NATO and the MLF'. *Journal of Contemporary History*, 7, 3 & 4, July/October 1972.
Bowie, Robert R. 'Strategy and the Atlantic Alliance'. *International Organization*, XVII, 3, Summer 1963.
Brenner, Michael J. 'Tactical Nuclear Strategy and European Defence: A Critical Reappraisal'. *International Affairs*, 51, 1, January 1975.
Buchan, Alastair. 'The Reform of NATO'. *Foreign Affairs*, 40, 2, January 1962.
Burney, John C. Jr. 'Nuclear Sharing in NATO'. *Military Review*, XLIX, 6, June 1969.
Burt, Richard. 'New Weapons Technologies and European Security'. *Orbis*, XIX, 2, Summer 1975.
   'The Cruise Missile and Arms Control'. *Survival*, XVIII, 1, January–February 1976.
Canby, Steven L. 'Damping Nuclear Counterforce Incentives:

Correcting NATO's Inferiority in Conventional Military Strength'. *Orbis*, XIX, 1, Spring 1975.

Coffey, J.I. 'Strategy, Alliance Policy and Nuclear Proliferation'. *Orbis*, XI, 4, Winter 1968.

Cohen, S.T. and Lyons, W.C. 'A Comparison of US, Allied and Soviet Tactical Nuclear Force Capabilities and Policies'. *Orbis*, XIX, 1, Spring 1975.

Cohen, S.T. and Van Cleave, W.R. 'Western European Collateral Damage from Tactical Nuclear Weapons'. *Journal of the Royal United Services Institute for Defence Studies*, 121, 2, June 1976.

Eckelen, W.R. van. 'Development of NATO's Nuclear Consultation'. *NATO Letter*, XVIII, 7–8, July–August 1970.

Gray, Colin S. 'Mini-Nukes and Strategy'. *International Journal*, XXIX, 2, Spring 1974.

'Deterrence and Defence in Europe: Revising NATO's Theatre Nuclear Posture'. *Journal of the Royal United Services Institute for Defence Studies*, 119, 4, December 1974.

'New Weapons and the Resort to Force'. *International Journal*, XXX, 2, Spring 1975.

Gunderson, General H.F. Zeiner. 'Military Perspective on NATO's Long-Term Defence Programme'. *NATO Review*, 26, 3, June 1978.

Halperin, Morton H. 'The Decision to Deploy the ABM: Bureaucratic and Domestic Politics in the Johnson Administration'. *World Politics*, XXV, 1, October 1972.

Hanmer, Stephen R. Jr. 'NATO's Long-Range Theatre Nuclear Forces: Modernisation in Parallel with Arms Control'. *NATO Review*, 28, 1, February 1980.

Hassel, Kai-Uwe von, 'Organising Western Defence'. *Foreign Affairs*, 43, 2, January 1965.

Heymont, Irving. 'The NATO Nuclear Bilateral Forces'. *Orbis*, 9, 4, Winter 1966.

Heldring, Jerome C. 'Rhetoric and Reality in Dutch Foreign Policy'. *World Today*, 34, 10, October 1978.

Hodder, J.S. 'SACEUR's First Nuclear Deputy'. *NATO Letter*, XII, June 1966.

Karber, Philip A. 'Nuclear Weapons and "Flexible Response" '. *Orbis*, XIV, 2, Summer 1970.

Lawrence, Robert M. 'On Tactical Nuclear War', Parts 1 & 2. *Revue Generale Militaire*, January 1971, February 1971.

Metzger, Robert and Doty, Paul. 'Arms Control Enters the Grey Area'. *International Security*, 3, 3, Winter 1978/9.

Morse, John H. 'New Weapons Technologies: Implications for NATO'. *Orbis*, XIX, 2, Summer 1975.

Nitze, Paul H. 'Deterring our Deterrent'. *Foreign Policy*, 25, Winter 1976–7.

Polk, H.J. 'The Realities of Tactical Nuclear Warfare'. *Orbis*, XVII, 2, Summer 1973.

Scheingold, Stuart A. 'The North Atlantic Area as a Policy Arena'. *International Studies Quarterly*, 15, March 1975.

Schmidt, Helmut. 'The 1977 Alastair Buchan Memorial Lecture', reprinted in *Survival*, XX, 1, January/February 1978.

Seim, Harvey B. 'Nuclear Policy-Making in NATO'. *Nato Review*, 21, 6, 1973.

Sinnreich, R.H. 'NATO's Doctrinal Dilemma'. *Orbis*, XIX, 2, Summer 1975.

Slocombe, Walter. 'The Countervailing Strategy'. *International Security*, 5, 4, Spring 1981.

Ulsamer, Edgar. 'The Neutron Bomb "Media Event" '. *Air Force Magazine*, November 1978.

Weers, Moses W.A. 'The Nuclear Debate in the Netherlands'. *Strategic Review*, IX, 2, Spring 1981.

Wiegele, T.C. 'The Origins of the MLF Concept 1957–60'. *Orbis*, XII, 2, Summer 1968.

'Nuclear Consultation Processes in NATO'. *Orbis*, XVI, 2, Summer 1972.

Wisner, Kent F. 'Military Aspects of Enhanced Radiation Weapons'. *Survival*, XXIII, 6, November/December 1981.

V Pamphlets and Monographs

Barlow, Jeffrey C. *Backgrounder, 110*. The Heritage Foundation, Washington DC, 14 February 1980.

Buchan, Alastair. 'The Multilateral Force: An Historical Perspective'. *Adelphi Papers*, 13, October 1964.

Burt, Richard. 'New Weapons Technologies: Debates and Directions'. *Adelphi Papers*, 126, Summer 1976.

Canby, Steven L. 'The Alliance and Europe, Part IV, Military Doctrine and Technology'. *Adelphi Papers*, 109, Winter 1974/5.

Cliffe, Trevor. 'Military Technology and the European Balance'. *Adelphi Papers*, 89, August 1972.

Cohen, S.T. 'On the Stringency of Dosage Criteria for Battlefield Nuclear Operations'. RAND P-5332, Santa Monica, California, January 1975.

Cromwell, William C. *The Eurogroup and NATO*. Research Monograph 18, Foreign Policy Research Institute, Philadelphia, Penn., Lexington Books, Lexington, Mass. 1974.

Davis, Lynn Etheridge. 'Limited Nuclear Options: Deterrence and the New American Doctrine'. *Adelphi Papers*, 121, Winter 1975–6.

Digby, James. 'Precision Guided Weapons'. *Adelphi Papers*, 118, Summer 1975.

Hartley, A. 'American Foreign Policy in the Nixon Era'. *Adelphi Papers*, 110, Winter 1974/5, p. 1.

Heisenberg, Wolfgang. 'The Alliance and Europe: Part 1: Crisis Stability in Europe and Theatre Nuclear Weapons'. *Adelphi Papers*, 96, Summer 1973.

Hill, R.J. *Political Consultation in NATO: Parliamentary and Policy Aspects.* ORAE Memorandum M72, Operational and Research Analysis Establishment, Department of National Defence, Ottawa, December 1975.

Hunt, Kenneth, 'The Atlantic Alliance and Europe: Part II: Defence with Fewer Men'. *Adelphi Papers*, 98, Summer 1973.

Lawrence, Richard D. & Record, Jeffrey. *US Force Structure in NATO: An Alternative.* The Brookings Institution, Washington, 1974.

Luttwak, Edward N. 'Strategic Power: Military Capabilities and Political Utility'. *Washington Papers*, IV, Sage, Beverly Hills, California, 1975.

Nerlich, Uwe. 'The Alliance and Europe: Part V: Nuclear Weapons and East–West Negotiation'. *Adelphi Papers*, 120, Winter 1975–6.

Record, Jeffrey. *Force Reductions in Europe: Starting Over.* Special Report, Institute for Foreign Policy Analysis, Washington, DC, October 1980.

Record, Jeffrey (with the assistance of Anderson, T.I.). *US Nuclear Weapons in Europe: Issues and Alternatives.* The Brookings Institution, Washington, 1974.

Treverton, Gregory. 'Nuclear Weapons in Europe'. *Adelphi Papers*, 168, 1981.

Vandervanter, E. Jr. 'NATO's Men on Horseback'. RAND, P-2841-1, Santa Monica, California, February 1964.

'Studies on NATO: An Analysis of Integration'. RAND Memorandum, RM-5006-PR, Santa Monica, California, August 1966.

Wettig, Gerhard. *East–West Security Relations on the Euro-Strategic Level.* Berichte des Bundesinstituts für ostwissenschaftliche und internationale Studien, 27–80, Cologne, 1980.

VI Books

Beaufre, A. *Strategie pour demain.* Plon, Paris, 1972.

Beer, F.A. *Integration and Disintegration in NATO.* Ohio State UP Columbus, Ohio, 1969.

Brodie, Bernard. *Escalation and the Nuclear Option.* Princeton UP, Princeton, New Jersey, 1966.

War and Politics. Cassell, London, 1974.

Brown, Neville. *European Security 1972–80*. Royal United Services Institute for Defence Studies, London, 1972.

Buchan, Alastair. *NATO in the 1960s*. rev. ed, Praeger, New York, 1963.

Buchan, Alastair & Windsor, Philip. *Arms and Stability in Europe*. Chatto & Windus, London, 1963.

Burrows, Bernard & Irwin, Christopher. *The Security of Western Europe*. Charles Knight & Co., London, 1972.

Cleveland, Harlan. *NATO: The Transatlantic Bargain*. Harper & Row, New York, 1970.

Enthoven, Alain, & Smith, Wayne K. *How Much is Enough?* Harper & Row, New York, 1971.

Eriksen, Bjarne. *The Committee System of the NATO Council*. Universitetsforlaget, Oslo, 1967.

Fedder, E.H. *NATO: The Dynamics of Alliance in the Postwar World*. Dodd, Mead & Co., New York, 1973.

Fox, W.T.R. & Fox, A.B. *NATO and the Range of American Choice*. Columbia UP, New York, 1967.

Groom, A.J.R. *British Thinking About Nuclear Weapons*. Francis Pinter, London, 1974.

Holst, J.J. and Nerlich, Uwe (eds.). *Beyond Nuclear Deterrence*. Crane, Russak, New York, 1977.

Hunter, Robert. *Security in Europe*. 2nd edn, Paul Elek, London, 1972.

Jackson, Henry M. (ed.). *The Atlantic Alliance*. Praeger, New York, 1967.

Kahan, Jerome H. *Security in the Nuclear Age: Developing U.S. Strategic Arms Policy*. The Brookings Institution, Washington, 1975.

Kaufmann, W.W. *The McNamara Strategy*. Harper & Row, New York, 1964.

Kelleher, Catherine McArdle. *Germany and the Politics of Nuclear Weapons*. Columbia UP, New York, 1975.

Kemp, G., Pfaltzgraff, R.L. Jr, and Ra'anan, U. (eds.). *The Other Arms Race, New Technologies: Implications for Non-Nuclear Conflict*. D.C. Heath, Lexington Books, Lexington, Mass., 1975.

Kissinger, Henry A. (ed.). *Problems of National Strategy*. Praeger, New York, 1965.

——— (ed.). *The Troubled Partnership*. McGraw-Hill, New York, 1965.

Kohl, Wilfred L. *French Nuclear Diplomacy*. Princeton UP, Princeton, New Jersey, 1971.

Liska, George. *Nations in Alliance*. Johns Hopkins UP, Baltimore, 1962.

Lovell, J.P. & Kronenberg, P.S. (eds.). *New Civil–Military Relations*. Transaction Books. New Brunswick, New Jersey, 1974.

Mahnke, Dieter. *Nukleare Mitwirkung: Die Bundesrepublik Deutschland in der Atlantischen Allianz, 1954–70.* Walter de Gruyter, Berlin, 1972.

Martin, Lawrence (ed.). *Strategic Thought in the Nuclear Age.* Johns Hopkins UP, Baltimore, 1979.

Mendl, Wolf. *Deterrence and Persuasion.* Faber and Faber, London, 1970.

Morgan, Roger. *The United States and West Germany 1945–73: A Study in Alliance Politics.* Oxford UP for RIIA, London, 1974.

Moulton, Harland B. *From Superiority to Parity: The U.S. and the Strategic Arms Race 1961–1971.* Greenwood Press, Westport, Connecticut, 1973.

Mulley, F. *The Politics of Western Defence.* Thames & Hudson, London, 1962.

Neustadt, R.E. *Alliance Politics.* Columbia UP, New York, 1970.

Nieburg, Harold L. *Nuclear Secrecy and Foreign Policy.* Public Affairs Press, Washington, 1964.

Osgood, R.E. *NATO: The Entangling Alliance.* University of Chicago Press, Chicago, 1962.

Pierre, Andrew J. *Nuclear Politics: The British Experience with an Independent Strategic Force 1939–70.* Oxford UP, London, 1972.

Reed, Bruce and Williams, Geoffrey. *Dennis Healey and the Policies of Power.* Sidgwick and Jackson, London, 1971.

Richardson, J.L. *Germany and the Atlantic Alliance.* Harvard UP, Cambridge, Mass., 1966.

Schelling, Thomas C. *The Strategy of Conflict.* Oxford UP, New York, 1963.

Arms and Influence. Yale UP, New Haven, 1966.

Schmidt, Helmut. *The Balance of Power.* William Kimber, London, 1971.

Steinbruner, J.D. *The Cybernetic Theory of Decision.* Princeton UP Princeton, New Jersey, 1974.

Stikker, Dirk U. *Men of Responsibility.* Harper & Row, New York, 1966.

Trewhitt, H.L. *McNamara.* Harper & Row, New York, 1971.

Truchet, D. *Le Projet de force de frappe multilaterale.* Presses Universitaires de France, Paris, 1972.

Watt, D.C. *Survey of International Affairs 1962.* Oxford UP for RIIA, London, 1970.

Windsor, Philip. *Germany and the Management of Detente.* Chatto & Windus, London, 1971.

VII Unpublished Sources

Krone, R.M. 'NATO Nuclear Policy Making'. Ph.D. dissertation, University of California at Los Angeles (UCLA), mimeo, 1972.

Interviews and personal communications with officials and former officials connected with the work of the NPG in Brussels, London and Ottawa. These officials were of the following nationalities: British, Canadian, German, Italian and American. Some were connected with the Staff/Secretariat, others were associated with national delegations.

INDEX